Amal and the Shi^ca

Modern Middle East Series, No. 13

Sponsored by the Center for Middle Eastern Studies

THE UNIVERSITY OF TEXAS AT AUSTIN

AMAL AND THE SHIʿA
Struggle for the Soul of Lebanon

by Augustus Richard Norton
Foreword by Leonard Binder

UNIVERSITY OF TEXAS PRESS, AUSTIN

To Deanna

Copyright © 1987 by the University of Texas Press
All rights reserved
Printed in the United States of America

First Edition, 1987

Requests for permission to reproduce material from this work should be sent to Permissions, University of Texas Press, Box 7819, Austin, Texas 78713-7819.

The opinions and views presented in this book are not intended to represent and should not necessarily be construed to represent the position or the policy of the United States government or any of its institutions.

LIBRARY OF CONGRESS CATALOGING-IN-PUBLICATION DATA

Norton, Augustus R.
  Amal and the Shiʿa.

  (Modern Middle East series ; no. 13)
  Bibliography: p.
  Includes index.
  1. Shiites—Lebanon—Politics and government.
  2. Lebanon—Politics and government—1975–
  3. Islam and politics—Lebanon. 4. Amal (Movement)
  I. Title. II. Series: Modern Middle East series
  (Austin, Tex.) ; no. 13.
  DS80.5.N67 1987   956.92'044   86-24994
  ISBN 0-292-73039-X
  ISBN 0-292-73040-3 (pbk.)

Title page: A procession in Bir al-ʿAbd. (Copyright © 1984 by Tom Masland of the *Philadelphia Inquirer.*)

Contents

Foreword

Twenty-five years ago, inspired by the achievements of the Shihab government, a group of scholars, diplomats, journalists, and civil servants met to consider the prospects for development and for democracy in Lebanon. Though hopeful for the future, the general tone of the meeting was skeptical. Few expected, even if some warned of, the political collapse of the Lebanese state. Representing a variety of opinions and interests, both Lebanese and foreign, the participants tended to divide along a single line of argument. The issue in debate seemed to boil down to whether the Lebanese system had to be drastically changed or merely reformed to accommodate new demands. The question was whether the system was legitimate or not. Some wished to see the Lebanese system remain more or less as it was, while others fervently wished to see it transformed. Those who wished to see it remain were inclined to exaggerate its virtues, and those who wished to see its demise expatiated on its defects.

The Shihab government had been installed, with American assistance, in the wake of the crisis of 1957–1958. All too typically, that crisis was produced by a convergence of domestic and regional processes and growing conflicts that both weak and strong alike sought to exploit for temporary advantage. Domestically, the issue was whether Lebanese democracy would continue to provide for the alternation in power of rival elite groups; and the central symbol of this struggle was the succession to the presidency. Regionally, the issue was whether Lebanon would fully identify itself with the Pan-Arab movement.

General Shihab provided strong leadership for the six years of his term, balancing Arab solidarity against Lebanese sovereignty and, for the first time, balancing elite interests against the needs of the rural poor. The Shihab government sought to strengthen the state and the state's control over economic development, internal security, and the formulation of foreign policy. While Shihab managed to inspire confidence in Lebanon's future, Shihabism as a policy of centralizing state power and redistributing the national wealth came under increasing attack. The conservatives wished to exploit the newly achieved stability to prevent further change, while the radicals feared that a continuation of Shihabist policies might stabilize the confessional regime. Shihab failed to inspire deep commitment to the Lebanese regime, as each of the major actors held in reserve the tacit right of secession from the political community.

But the Lebanese system did not collapse from domestic pressures alone. The burdens on the system were considerably increased by the escalation of the Arab-Israeli conflict beginning in 1967 and by the shift in the Arab balance of power that was the result of the Six-Day War. These additional difficulties, coming in the wake of efforts to dismantle the Shihabist structure of centralized authority, overwhelmed the administrative and security apparatus of the Lebanese state and paralyzed the parliament. The Lebanese state lost control of its own territory and became incapable of making any decisions without massive intervention on the part of some foreign power.

Whatever remained of law and order, of sovereignty and territorial integrity, collapsed with the violence of 1975 and the surfacing of the conflict between the Maronites and the Palestinians. The Lebanese civil war is dated from April 1975, and it has continued and even grown worse to this day. There is, moreover, no end in sight, as the solution to Lebanon's problems is tied to the solution to other regional problems, and as the possibility for domestic compromise depends upon the support of foreign governments.

In spite of the collapse of Lebanon into an extreme form of anarchy and violence, the semblance of constitutional legitimacy has been retained. Amin Gemayel clings tenaciously to his presidency. The cabinet exists and sometimes is convened in whole or part and even fails, officially, to agree. Lebanon is represented abroad by diplomatic officials. The Lebanese army still exists also. A serious debate continues over the revision of the constitution, as though the existing constitution determines the distribution of power, wealth, and authority. There is also renewed discussion of the next presidential election.

It is one of the supreme ironies of Lebanese political life that so many of its agonies have been linked to the problem of the succession to the presidency. Even when the presidency has been shorn of most of its power and certainly all of its prestige, its incumbency is still thought likely to be so central to any settlement that it will be fought over. Even though the presidency must be granted to a Maronite, all factions become engaged when the election nears.

The political process has declined into armed conflict, but still the Lebanese find themselves bound together by the parameters of the institutions that have broken down and by the demographic realities that define the dynamic social system to which they all belong.

The Lebanese civil war burst forth on the eve of the presidential election of 1976. The Israeli invasion took place on the occasion of the presidential election of 1982. Gemayel's term will be up in 1988. The six-year rhythm of Lebanese politics continues despite the breakdown of authority. The coming year will witness increasing efforts to identify the candidates of compromise and steadfastness, and all of the foreign and domestic players will place their bets. On the outcome of their maneuverings will depend the quality of the political life of Lebanon for the next six years: continued stalemate or precarious compromise.

The sovereign authority of the Lebanese government has been nearly extinguished but many players, both domestic and foreign, continue to cling to the illusion of legality as the basis for some kind of future arrangement. In the meantime, the country has undergone a de facto partition into cantons, or enclaves, into which the various religious groups or confessions have sorted themselves out. Moreover, even within the microgeography of this very small country, the location of the confessional cantons means everything. The Maronite canton is contiguous with neither Israel nor Syria. The two Shiʿite cantons are, respectively, contiguous with either Israel or Syria. The two Sunni cantons are heavily urban, on the coast, and laden with Palestinian refugees. The more important of the two is also surrounded by hostile Shiʿites, Maronites, and Druze.

Confessional diversity, cantonization, and the concentration of populations present insuperable obstacles to those who would control Lebanon from the outside as well as those who would seek some agreement with their fellow citizens. Neither Syria, nor Israel, nor France, nor the United States has been able to impose its will on the country. Those who have sought only to prevent solutions and to encourage disruption, such as Iran or Libya, have been the most successful. But even those who have tried to benefit from Lebanon's travail have been unable to control the outcome. At times it appears as though Lebanon is being wound slowly into a delicate Syrian web, but then Maronites, Druze, Shiʿites, and even Palestinians suddenly demonstrate their powers of resistance. With some American assistance, Israel imposed a treaty on Lebanon that seemed to define the future relationship of the two countries, but the treaty was never ratified and was eventually repudiated. It seems unlikely that any single power or any group of powers will succeed in imposing a political arrangement on Lebanon that the Lebanese do not wish to have. Instead, there persists a kind of negative unity that leaves the question of the future open and uncertain if still foreboding.

If there is any answer to Lebanon's problems, if there is any possibility of reestablishing order and tranquility, it will probably have to be an answer that is given by the Lebanese themselves. Of course, they will not be able to produce a solution that is vigorously opposed by Israel or Syria or the United States or the USSR or perhaps even Iran, but a major responsibility for their own fate rests with the people of Lebanon. It may well be that the Lebanese are not primarily responsible for the collapse of their state. It may well be that the primary cause of the political deterioration in Lebanon was the consequence of the Palestinian conflict, of Syrian irredentism, of Egyptian ambition, of Libyan trouble making, of Saudi caution, or of Iranian revolutionary fervor. Nevertheless, none of these forces determined how the Lebanese themselves would respond to these challenges.

For the most part, the Lebanese political elite responded to these challenges by attempting to reaffirm constitutional legitimacy while eschewing the use of sovereign force to protect the authority of the state. At the same time, the legitimacy of the state was under fire from at least two directions. The most important challenge to the Lebanese state came from the Palestinians and their Sunni allies who rightly accused the Lebanese government of seeking to remain neutral in the Israeli-Palestinian conflict. They demanded that government policy be determined by the ideology of the Arab national movement. The second challenge was less articulate but in the long run it has turned out to be at least as formidable as the first. The second was the challenge born of demographic change.

The challenge of Arab nationalism proposed a moral majority, representing the dominant culture and self-image of the Sunni Arabs, as the foundation of the new Lebanese political formula. It sought to bring Lebanon into line with the other Arab states. Its concept of democracy was inseparably bound up with its nationalism, populism, and state-building ideologies. In the face of the manifest presence of so important a moral majority, it argued that confessional pluralism, based on the absence of a majority, was illegitimate. The defect of the Lebanese system was that it took a small part of the Arab nation in place of the whole when it sought to define its own authenticity.

The challenge of demographic change did not and does not deny the validity of confessionalism in general. It rather denies the legitimacy of the particular confessional formula worked out some forty years ago. That formula was based on the assumption that the population of Lebanon was divided into two major groups, Muslims and Christians. It was also agreed that the Christians constituted a bare majority. Within each of the two major groups, one confessional group was considered to have precedence: the Maronites among the Christians and the Sunnis among the Muslims. Thus, the confessional system was supposed to work as long as there might be cooperation between the Maronites and the Sunnis. This understanding was upset by the fact that the Palestinian allies of the Sunnis made demands that the Maronites refused to accept, and by the fact that the Shi'ite community grew to become by far the most numerous among the Muslims.

As a result of these changes, Maronite-Sunni agreement became both more difficult to attain and less valuable once achieved. The Shi'ites became increasingly disinclined to subordinate themselves to Sunni leadership. They denied the legitimacy of both the existing confessional formula and alternate proposals based on the idea of a single political community. The alternative of a Maronite-Shi'ite cooperation has been mooted, but there remains the question of precedence within the system as a whole.

As the largest group among the majoritarian Christians, the Maronites claimed and received the leading position in the state as a whole. The Shi'ites now similarly constitute the largest community among the majority, which is now Muslim, so they demand a position comparable to that enjoyed by the Maronites heretofore. There are good and rational arguments that can be made for a Maronite-Shi'ite coalition, but there are competitive factions within each community that resist such an agreement if they cannot thereby improve their own positions. Besides, any such formula will require external support from Iran, Syria, and/or Israel, and it is not likely that such support will be forthcoming from all at once.

Twenty-five years ago, those who knew Lebanon best argued over the confessional system. Some said it couldn't work and others that it shouldn't. But now we find the experts turning to the confessional system as the only solution that is likely to win sufficient support to be viable. Now that the old system has broken down and with it the values that were to be preserved by that rigid formula, the same constitutional solution is being brought back as though it might restore those values. But a confessional system based on the precedence of the Shi'a will not be a merely pragmatic adaptation of the old system. The old system was also committed to a liberal political ideology and to the ideals of pluralist democracy. The critics of the old system are right to argue that the old elites betrayed those values, but we ought not be so naïve as to believe that the restoration of confessionalism under very different demographic conditions will restore the self-contradictory ideology of the old confessionalism.

The key to the changed political realities of Lebanon is the changed position of the Shiʿite community. It is not only that the Shiʿites are now the largest community in Lebanon, but also that their traditional ways of life have been profoundly disturbed, alien people have intruded into their traditional homelands, and their traditional leaders have either abdicated or been forced out of their positions. The Shiʿites of Lebanon are still weak, impoverished, and exploited by alien and fellow Shiʿite alike. Politically, they are divided and still in search of an identity that they can recognize. For the time being, the Shiʿites have been able to avoid submitting to any other group or subordinating their interests to the tactics of a neighboring country. It is impossible to predict whether they will long enjoy that modicum of independence and the window of opportunity that it affords and through which they may come to some sort of consensus among themselves. Much depends upon whether they can come to such a self-understanding and upon whether or not they can work things out with their fellow Lebanese.

This book deals with the question of the political destiny of the Shiʿite community of southern Lebanon and, thereby, with the fate of Lebanon itself. It provides a demographic and sociological analysis of the objective dimensions of the problem, but it also describes the resulting situation in human terms. The events that have occurred in Lebanon have been momentous, affecting global power politics, but they have been the work of a handful of often simple people. In order to understand the issues, and the strategies that make sense to the handful of actors on the ground, it is essential to have a grasp of the immediacy of the setting in which they find themselves. It is necessary that we suspend for the moment our own prepossession with self in order to see how things look from another point of view.

But empathy is not the same as sympathy, nor does it make any sense to identify with an adversary to the point of transforming one's consciousness of self. One cannot learn anything without changing oneself to some degree, nor can one make peace with an adversary without becoming a somewhat different person. But the point of so much of the conflict in Lebanon is precisely that the protagonists do not want to change or be changed. Learning and peacemaking are alike in that they necessarily involve changing ourselves. They differ in that we may learn alone, but we cannot make peace in isolation. But the best sort of learning is like reconciliation, in which it is not clear who causes the change in whom, and in which the respective identities of those participating become strengthened through self-consciousness. This is the kind of learning that I think you will find in this book.

I have known the author of this book for many years, since the time he first appeared in my office at the University of Chicago, an ambitious and intelligent young army officer, eager to learn about and to apply his analytical skills to the mysteries of Middle East politics. I wonder if he realized then just how much work it would take and how much he himself would change in the process. Far from a simple matter of acquiring some cultural skills or achieving professional competence or proficiency in the use of a specialized jargon, learning how to write this book took "a heap of living" in the Middle East as well as in the army of the United States. It is significant that the path he has taken fits neither the stereotype of the professional scholar nor that of the professional soldier, though he is both.

This is not the original thesis that Dick Norton thought he would write, nor is the Middle East the same place that it seemed to be when those dissertation plans were first discussed. Professor Norton did not set out to find the Shiʿites of southern Lebanon. In a sense, they found him; or rather circumstances threw them together. Professor Norton's service with UNIFIL was the context of his field research, and his duties as liaison with the indigenous population brought him into close, daily, operational contact with members of the Shiʿite community. But, if he did not originally plan to write on the Amal movement, Professor Norton was well prepared to transform experiences into scholarship and problem solving into analysis. He seized the opportunity to gain first-hand experience in what must have seemed to be one of the more remote parts of the Middle East; and that opportunity then seized him and allowed him to gain an unprecedented first-hand insight into one of the most important problems of our time.

The result is a truly unique book that could not have been written by anyone else. Those acquainted with things Lebanese will appreciate the understanding presentation and the importance of the content itself. Those who are relatively unfamiliar with the area will enjoy the lucidity of the argument and the intelligibility of the analysis. Above all, the book is pervaded by a sense of honesty and regard for the human beings whose tragic and dramatic story it presents. These are qualities to be highly valued especially in these times when many believe it will serve their interests to exaggerate or to simplify what is happening in southern Lebanon.

For the professional reader it hardly need be added that this is a study of a special case of political development. It is another one of those cases that does not fit the stereotype. It does not refute any theory, nor does it provide the basis for some entirely new conception of the developing world. What it does is enrich our understanding of the process of development by taking an entirely unexpected and surprising set of events and placing those events within an intelligible frame of reference. It gives a much deeper understanding of the limits of existing theory and of the ways in which we can apply what we thought we understood.

Leonard Binder
Los Angeles
November 1986

Preface

Terror, violence, conflict, carnage, chaos, cruelty, and mayhem are all evoked by the mere mention of Lebanon. For those who have known Lebanon in better times, and even for those of us who have known only a strife-torn country, the fact that Lebanon has come to be synonymous with bloodshed is a source of deep sadness. Lebanon, even in the worst of times, can be a remarkably seductive place. In my judgment, no other Middle Eastern country, perhaps no country in the world, is as enthralling as Lebanon. Its social and political complexity, the keen skill of its citizens in dealing with (and manipulating) foreigners, and its lovely climate and splendid food combine to imbue those who have known it—in good times or bad—with a sense of emotional attachment that is hard to shake. Lebanon entices and ensnares even the wary. Though the encounter is often bittersweet, it is long savored.

Remembrances of Lebanon clutter and dominate conversations with diplomats, journalists, businesspersons, and scholars who once lived there. This was brought home to me in May and June 1986 when I encountered a number of ex–Lebanon hands during a research trip to Egypt. Although recent events in Egypt, Libya, Israel, and elsewhere in the Middle East should have provided plenty of grist for conversation, it was never very long before the talk turned to Lebanon. Anecdotes, alternately horrific and enchanting, flowed, and frequent prognostication about Lebanon's fate exposed the continuing preoccupation of many of my interlocutors. As the reader has correctly deduced by now, I have not escaped this syndrome. I too have succumbed; however, I trust that those who read this book will find that my encounter with Lebanon has not prevented me from describing and analyzing its defects with candor.

I have striven for objectivity, but I hope that I have not so objectified the Lebanese that we lose sight of the humanity they share with all of us. Whether as social scientists or simply as frail members of the human race, we should not be so captured by our conceptual frameworks, or calloused by the dulling repetitiousness of violence, that we ever allow ourselves to forget that the Lebanese tragedy involves flesh-and-blood people. I know that these remarks will not be popular with some of the power realists of the world, or the commentators who would prefer to dehumanize Lebanon (even more than the Lebanese have done themselves), but we are all aware of the disasters that such perspectives have spawned.

In this book I attempt to help the reader understand the roots of the disintegration of Lebanon, but this is not intended to be a volume about the myriad ways that the Lebanese have found to destroy themselves and others. It is not that the killing should be ignored, fatalistically accepted, or condoned, but, without a rich sense of the social and political context in which the disorder has flourished, any account will be no more than lurid journalism. I reject the pungently racist, and transparently self-serving, perspective that seeks to explain the bloodletting in Lebanon as simply a direct result of primordially based enmities among a people who have somehow evolved defectively. On the other hand, I also reject the view of many apologists for Lebanon that the disorder flows directly from meddling and manipulation by external hands. Neither of these polar views captures the complexity or the reality of the rampant disorder. It is just not that simple, but this does not mean that it is inexplicable.

Sectarianism and external intervention have played an important part, but so have other factors that are hardly unique to an unfortunate Mediterranean republic. The conflict in large measure stems from issues of social inequality, injustice, and deprivation, and it has been fanned by the self-devoted ambition and poor political judgment of Lebanese leaders, who have all too frequently confused leadership with avarice.

The struggle for the political soul of Lebanon cannot be understood as simply the competition for power among Lebanese sects. As important, if not more important, are the struggles taking place within the sects, struggles that reflect contending visions of what Lebanon is, or should become. The latter phenomenon is starkly illustrated within the Shi'i community,[1] where the Amal movement's efforts to preserve a heterogeneous, if drastically reformed, polity are being seriously challenged by a collection of more radical Shi'is who seek to install Islamic rule in Lebanon. The severity of the challenge to Amal was well illustrated during Ramadan (May–June) in 1986, when about five dozen Lebanese Shi'i clerics issued a position paper calling for the creation of an Islamic regime as a cure for Lebanon's ills.[2]

The Shiʿa of Lebanon, the community upon which this book focuses, have the distinction of being deeply committed to Lebanon's
survival, even as their newfound aggressiveness has seriously complicated the task of reforming a discredited political system. The
Shiʿa have amply proven their potential for acting as a solvent upon
the old system of politics. Whether the future will find them acting
as a glue instead is one of the major questions remaining to be an-
swered. Whatever role the Shiʿa play, it is plain that the shape and
complexion of Lebanese politics will reflect their presence, in marked
contrast to the recent past, when they languished in quiescence.

My own exposure to the Shiʿa began in 1980, when I joined the
United Nations Truce Supervision Organization (UNTSO) as an un-
armed military observer. I did not venture to Lebanon for the purpose of studying Shiʿi politics; in fact, my unusual research opportunity bordered on the fortuitous. Having been seconded to the
UNTSO, I hoped to be able to use my free time to complete the field
research for a University of Chicago doctoral dissertation on the
politics of Palestinian nationalism; however, with a mere year of intensive Arabic (including the Egyptian dialect!) under my belt, I
found myself posted to southern Lebanon, where even fledgling Arabic speakers were at a premium.

Shortly after my arrival, and much to my surprise, I was given the
task of acting as a liaison between the United Nations Interim Force
in Lebanon (UNIFIL) and the local populace. I lived, more or less
continuously, from June 1980 to June 1981 in Kfir Dunin, a Shiʿi village not far from the border with Israel and within the portion of
south Lebanon under UNIFIL's control.[3] Much of my time was spent
mediating disputes, attempting to anticipate security-related problems, and doing what little I might to ameliorate the poor living conditions of the Lebanese under UNIFIL control (not always an easy
task, given UNIFIL's incredibly cumbersome bureaucratic structure).
By the very nature of my position, I spent many hours every week
visiting villages, drinking coffee, and partaking of the generous if
simple hospitality of peasants.

Of the approximately 1 million Shiʿis in Lebanon, about 40 percent live in the Jabal ʿAmil region in the South, a major portion of
which overlaps the UNIFIL area of operations. (Jabal ʿAmil is the region east of Sidon [Saida] and Tyre [Sur], which lies north of the
Galilee and south of the Shuf. "ʿAmil" is, by legend, the name of a
Yemeni tribe that migrated to the Levant in pre-Islamic times.) By
early 1980, it was obvious that the long docile Shiʿi community was
finding its political voice through the Amal movement. Therefore,

one of my first official acts, at the direction of UNIFIL, was to establish a liaison relationship with the Amal leadership in the South. Considering the pro-Iranian sympathies of the Shiʿis, as an American I frankly did not anticipate any great success in this endeavor. (At the time, the United States was deeply preoccupied with the hostage crisis and shortly before my arrival had tried and failed to rescue its diplomats imprisoned in Iran.)

As it happened, though, a leader of the Amal organization in the region, for whom I use the pseudonym "Abu ʿAli," proved himself to be a courageous and rare person who was willing—after a time—to accept me as an individual, rather than as an American. Indeed, I was not in Lebanon as a representative of the U.S. government, but as an official of a United Nations organization. (I was later to discover that the attitude of the Lebanese Shiʿis toward their Iranian co-religionists was much more multifaceted than my early and simplistic assumption had allowed.)

While we did not always agree, Abu ʿAli and I dealt with one another honestly and with great candor. After several months, I was enjoying unique access to the movement. I do not claim to have been admitted to the movement's innermost secrets, but I do claim to have enjoyed a glimpse of Shiʿi politics in Lebanon that few outsiders are likely to duplicate. In addition to taking part in very frank discussions with Abu ʿAli, I found that our relationship opened many doors. While not all Amal officials and members were as willing to trust me as Abu ʿAli was, most knew that he and I were on friendly terms; as a result, they were at least a bit more accessible than they would otherwise have been.

Throughout my sojourn in south Lebanon, I observed meetings, political rallies, *dhikir*s (Muslim services commemorating *shuhada'*, martyrs), and private social gatherings. Perhaps the apex of my exposure to Amal was reached when I was introduced to a number of the movement's financial backers during a very sensitive meeting in 1981. I was the only non-Shiʿi at the meeting, which had been convened to assess the movement's level of development in the South. At a time when relations with the *fida'iyin* were rapidly deteriorating, it was a vote of the highest confidence to permit me access to a group of men whose support for the movement was not generally known. It is a tribute to Abu ʿAli's courage that he was willing to accept the dangers inherent in our relationship, rather than choosing the safer route of ending it. Without seeking to be melodramatic, I think it is fair to say that if his most deadly adversaries had known the extent of our publicly observed friendship, neither one of us might be here to recall it. In fact, at our last 1981 meeting—a private luncheon in my honor, hosted by Abu ʿAli in his home—we both had cause to worry that it might be our last meal.

For my part, I have respected the confidences of a good and delicate man, who continues to stand up as a voice of reason and moderation. I wish him well, and I thank him for giving me an opportunity to see what I otherwise could not have seen.

Where possible, and where good sense and prudence permitted, I have identified my sources by name. Nonetheless, Lebanon is a very tough neighborhood, and in a number of cases—like that of Abu ʿAli—I did not feel that the value of complete documentation was so high that I could justify putting a person at risk by using his or her name. We are not dealing with a controversy in Whitehall or Washington, where providing the source of a quote merely poses potential embarrassment.

I returned to Lebanon in October 1982. My concern was to measure the effect of the Israeli invasion upon the Amal movement. During this last visit to Lebanon, I spent a considerable period of time with Abu ʿAli and through his good offices met several of the most important Shiʿis in Lebanon, including Mufti ʿAbd al-Amir Qabalan. Since then, I have managed to maintain occasional contact with a number of Shiʿi and non-Shiʿi Lebanese. As a direct result of my work in Lebanon and the publications I have produced, I have also been able to interview a number of prominent Lebanese parliamentarians, militia leaders, businesspersons, and government officials— some Shiʿis affiliated with Amal and others not. Since 1982, I have twice returned to the Middle East for extended research visits, but the dictates of physical survival have deterred me from returning to Lebanon.

Certainly it is fair to note that I still have many unanswered questions. I remain an outsider, but one who has sometimes been permitted to venture inside.

A.R.N.
West Point, New York
August 1986

Acknowledgments

I have been gifted with fine friends and colleagues, many of whom were generous with their time, intelligent in their advice, and candid in their criticism while this book was in various stages of completion. It is now my very pleasant duty to acknowledge the many debts that I have accumulated over the past few years.

Unfortunately, some who have made significant contributions will have to go unnamed, not for my protection, but for theirs. I am forever in the debt of a number of Lebanese who trusted my good intentions and took me into their confidence. It would be a serious betrayal if I were to name them here.

A number of diplomats, American, French, Israeli, Lebanese, Norwegian, and Syrian, shared their insights, perspectives, and complaints with me, always assuming that I would respect their confidences. I am grateful to all of them.

Brian Jenkins generously made the peerless facilities of the RAND Corporation available to me in September 1982, and as a result I was able to locate a number of documentary sources that would otherwise have eluded me. To Brian and his colleagues I express my appreciation.

A number of scholars have read and commented on various drafts of this endeavor, and their incisive comments have often helped me to keep my analysis on track. I am indebted to Fouad Ajami, Riad Ajami, James A. Bill, Louis J. Cantori, Peter J. Chelkowski, Juan Ricardo Cole, Richard Cottam, Evelyn A. Early, Iliya Harik, J. C. Hurewitz, George E. Irani, Daniel J. Kaufman, Farhad Kazemi, Nikki Keddie, Martin Kramer, Ronald D. McLaurin, Nikola Schahgaldian, Lewis W. Snider, and Drew Ziegler, for generously giving me the benefit of their scholarly and friendly counsel. Jerrold D. Green deserves his own sentence, because he has always been especially generous with his time and welcome advice, and when I most needed a good push to bring this book to completion he provided it.

Several of my former colleagues in the United Nations also played key roles. James Holger, probably the finest diplomat working for the United Nations, taught me that skilled diplomacy works, and on several occasions shared the warmth of the "pension Holger." Desmond Travers, fellow adventurer in UNIFIL, has become a dear friend and a valued adviser. Bjorn Odegaard, former deputy force commander of UNIFIL, now retired in Oslo, a courageous and unstinting officer, provided essential clout when I needed it. Timur Goksel, longtime press adviser for UNIFIL, and the keystone in whatever success UNIFIL has enjoyed in southern Lebanon, has always given me a fair and accurate assessment of the situation in the UNIFIL area of operations. If there were such a thing as a Most Valuable Player for international peacekeeping, Timur would be a leading candidate.

Several of my friends in journalism deserve special mention. Robin Wright, herself the author of a well-received book on the Shi'a, provided me an unusually sound accounting of several episodes in contemporary Shi'i politics. Tamar Jacoby, of the *New York Times*, forced me to learn how to squeeze a mouthful into 750 words, and in the process taught me a lot about good, tight writing. George Nader, whose *Middle East Insight* plays a unique role in writing on the Middle East, provided me a forum in which to publish very early versions of some of the chapters in this book. John Kifner, foreign correspondent *extraordinaire* for the *New York Times*, shared many of his sharp insights, as well as his good company.

I would be remiss if I did not also single out William Stanton, who in the midst of fourteen-hour days at the State Department still managed to find time for our friendship. His good mind, intolerance for nonsense, and ready wit are real assets to the Foreign Service corps of the United States.

Closer to home, I would like to express my relief that my department head here at West Point, Lee Donne Olvey, has among his many talents an extraordinary tolerance for eccentricity, as does his deputy, James R. Golden. Between the two of them, they have managed to sustain the delicate chemistry that makes the Social Sciences Department one of the finest places to work in the academic world. Barbara A. Thomas, the office supervisor in the department, has never failed to meet my many—too many—demands. She has earned my respect and loyalty. In the West Point Library, Charlotte R. Snyder has been a good-natured and persistent helper in finding all manner of strange publications, and the entire library staff has been consistently responsive to my requests.

I owe many debts of gratitude to employees of the University of Texas. Annes McCann-Baker, of the Center for Middle Eastern Studies, supported the publication of this book from the very onset. She has generously given of her time, and her help has often been instrumental in shaping this book. The copy editor of the manuscript, Kathleen Lewis, was incredible. She caught mistakes that even gifted Middle East scholars missed, and she deserves my deepest thanks for all that she did. I doubt any publisher could top the excellence of the editorial process at the University of Texas Press; if there are still errors in the text, they are likely to be mine.

Two organizations provided funding in support of this book. The Association of Graduates of the United States Military Academy helped with some modest funds to support my 1982 trip to Lebanon. The National Endowment for the Humanities awarded me a grant in 1986 that permitted me to tie up some of the loose ends in the manuscript. I am grateful to both organizations.

Some portions of the book originally appeared in my 1984 University of Chicago dissertation. The three members of my doctoral committee, Bernard Silberman, Marvin Zonis, and Leonard Binder, contrived to undermine all of the stereotypes about disinterested faculty advisers. Professor Silberman, not a Middle East specialist, kindly agreed nonetheless to suffer the esoterica of Levantine politics. Marvin Zonis helped me to give shape to the dissertation, and he was a stalwart and kind source of support. Leonard Binder helped me to see my subject matter with analytic lucidity and balance, and as a result I was able to clear away at least a bit of the muddle. My relationship with Professor Binder is one that I cherish, and if the mark of his influence is not always clear, it is because of my shortcomings.

I would also like to thank a number of publishers and journals for permission to use portions of articles and book chapters that I have written since 1981. *American-Arab Affairs, The Annals, Current History,* and *Middle East Insight* have provided me timely forums in which to publish some of my developing ideas and conclusions, and each journal has kindly permitted me to excerpt from my articles, as I saw fit. In 1982 I presented a long, but still preliminary paper on the Amal Movement at the annual meeting of the American Political Science Association (APSA). The APSA paper was subsequently published in *Political Anthropology,* and some parts of it appear here with the permission of Transaction, Inc., from *Religion and Politics,* copyright © 1983 by Transaction, Inc. I have also been able to draw several passages, with the permission of the publisher, from "Harakat Amal," in Azar et al., *The Emergence of a New Lebanon: Fantasy or Reality* (New York: Praeger Publishers, a division of Greenwood Press, Inc., 1984). In addition, both the Wilson Center, of the

Woodrow Wilson International Center for Scholars, and Yale University Press have graciously permitted me to draw upon material I originally wrote for them.

The superb translation of the Amal pact is the work of Barbara Parmenter, whose fine rendering of the pact is vastly superior to my own workmanlike translation. The translation of the Hizb Allah open letter is the capable work of the Joint Publications Research Service, which has once again placed an important, but hard to find, document in the public domain.

Lest there be any doubt, I would like to emphasize that, while I am proud to be a member of the West Point faculty, the arguments and conclusions I offer in this book reflect my views and not those of the United States Military Academy or any other institution or department of the U.S. government.

Finally, and most especially, I would like to thank my wife, to whom this book is dedicated, and my son, Tim, for their steady support, understanding, patience, and, most of all, their love. Without them there would be only empty pages.

Amal and the Shi^ca

An all too common scene. (Presented to the author, in 1982, by a senior
Amal leader.)

Southern Lebanon

MEDITERRANEAN SEA

LEBANON

Tripoli

Ba'labakk

Beirut

Zahla

SYRIA

Sidon   Jazzīn

al-Janub

Tyre

ISRAEL

Mediterranean

Sea

A rare 1975 photograph showing *(left to right)* Amin al-Jumayyil, the current president; Musa al-Sadr; and Pierre al-Jumayyil. (Used by permission of Jamil K. Mrowa and the *Daily Star*, Lebanon.)

1. Introduction

It is no small irony that Lebanon, now wrecked and wretched, was once put forth as a prototype that might be emulated by developing states. Respectable scholarly studies of just a dozen years ago cannot be read today without a shake of the head and a sense of the pathetic plight of this small Mediterranean country. Consider, for example, the following assertion by two Western scholars: "It is our contention that the Lebanese approach, while not wholly adequate and not exportable in toto, has much to offer other states confronting serious problems of religious, ethnic, and racial conflict."[1] Lest it be thought that only non-Lebanese failed to anticipate the looming dangers and inherent fragility of the Lebanese political system, we should note that the Lebanese themselves were often blissfully unaware of the explosions that were to come. Elie Salem, scholar and later foreign minister, marveled at the "flexibility" of the Lebanese system: "Lebanon is a country where one's first impressions are often proved wrong: it has been described as 'precarious,' 'improbable,' and as a 'mosaic,' but the flexibility of its system, the experience and shrewdness of its leaders, and the stability of its institutions have surprised all observers."[2]

If those writing before the bloodletting began often failed to anticipate even the broad outlines of what was to come, subsequent observers hardly distinguished themselves with incisive analyses. In short, more than a decade of carnage on the Lebanese killing-ground has obscured the real story in Lebanon—social and political change. Even before the onset of civil war in 1975, momentous changes were underway, changes that would upset the traditional distribution of political privilege and grossly complicate any attempt to write surcease to the violence that held the country in a deathgrip. Blinded by the dust of battles and skirmishes, we scarcely noticed the changes transforming the Lebanese body politic. True enough, journalists, diplomats, and, to a lesser extent, academics churned out reams of articles, dispatches, reports, and monographs, but the very conditions that have hidden change have also served to discourage probing analysis. Considering the volume of blood and ink that has been spilt in Lebanon, our appreciation of the whys and wherefores behind the conflict has been remarkably underdeveloped.

Indeed, our knowledge of this strife-torn country is strangely constricted in both time and space. Armed conflict is hardly a hospitable laboratory for the discovery of sociological verities, so it was always easier to accept crude political templates that often distorted more than they revealed, rather than to keep up with the shifting complexities of Lebanon. The favored template froze the Lebanese situation in the early days of 1975, and few commentators stopped to ask whether the "truths" of 1975 remained accurate in 1979 or 1982 or later, and fewer still considered whether the truths were applicable even in 1975.[3] Instead the conflict was blithely reported as one between Christians and Muslims, or between the right and the left (a dichotomy that was usually no more than an inaccurate synonym for Christians vs. Muslims). Unfolding events have all too often been interpreted within a framework that is of questionable accuracy.

A good example is the relationship between the "Muslims" and the Palestinian resistance. When the fighting began in the spring of 1975, the Maronite Christian militias were arrayed against a loose coalition of *fida'iyin*, Greek Orthodox Christians, Druze, and Shi'i and Sunni Muslims (although many Sunnis studiously avoided any involvement in the fighting). However, the fealty of the Lebanese to the Palestinian resistance was relatively short-lived. By the end of the 1970s, the Lebanese, including many erstwhile allies of the *fida'iyin*, were approaching unanimity in their opposition to the presence of any alien militaries—whether Syrian, Palestinian, or Israeli—in their country. The economically underprivileged and politically underrepresented Shi'i Muslims, formerly considered the natural allies of the Palestinians, were fighting pitched battles with the *fida'iyin* by the end of the decade. More than a few commentators and analysts failed to notice this important shift in alliance preferences. Some did not know any better, but others found "claims" of a shift in loyalties tantamount to heresy. I well remember a meeting of Middle East scholars in 1981, when the Lebanese situation was being described by senior scholars. Barring a few chronological details, their description seemed to be frozen in a 1975 time-warp. When I challenged the Muslims' fealty to the Palestinian resistance on the empirical basis that the *fida'iyin* had steadily alienated erstwhile supporters (especially the Shi'i Muslims), my challenge was condescendingly dismissed. After all, such a challenge was heretical on two counts: it impiously questioned the revealed truth inscribed in seminal works and it sacrilegiously impugned the ideological preferences of the speakers.

Furthermore, our understanding of Lebanon is mired in space, namely, the space defined by Beirut. To an extent that is seldom appreciated, reports, whether scholarly, journalistic, or diplomatic, were formulated from the vantage point of the capital. The reasons are not hard to fathom. No other city in Lebanon offered the conveniences of Beirut: telexes, restaurants, hotels, shops, . . . and sources. Journalists, often poorly prepared in the first place, found that the requisite column inches could easily be written from a relatively pleasant base like the Hotel Commodore in West Beirut. The Commodore is a remarkable institution, and a brief consideration will illustrate why some reporters never ventured far from its premises. Reasonably comfortable, with stellar rates to match the expense accounts of its patrons, the Commodore offered cold drinks, good food, wire service news tickers, telex facilities, its own supply of electricity, a swimming pool, and a multilingual staff. The well-stocked magazine shop in the lobby was itself an important news source, because it was there that the itinerant newsperson could, for a few dollars, buy a daily copy of the *Middle East Reporter*. The *Reporter*, a high-quality newsletter, is full of political gossip, analysis, and facts and has no doubt shaped many "original" reports from Beirut.

Prior to the momentous Israeli invasion in 1982, one could leave the Commodore at 8:30 A.M., travel to the PLO headquarters in Fakhani, perhaps stop by an embassy or two, look up a news source, and return by late afternoon to write an article, transmit it by telex in time to make deadline, and still have time for a few drinks, a dip in the pool, and a nice meal. There are exceptions, of course, but the typical journalist seldom found it necessary to travel to the Biqaʿ Valley, Kisruwan, or al-Janub (the southern province of Lebanon). Moreover, among journalists there is a generic aversion to being caught "out of pocket," which is to say, being stranded in one location when the hot story is happening elsewhere. For the few who strove to transcend the mundane regimen, and were willing to risk being stranded, there were many pitfalls.

Since 1975, Lebanon has been divided into a patchwork of fiefdoms and security zones controlled by militias, armies, and gangs.[4] Not only was it necessary to navigate a series of checkpoints operated by temperamental militiamen in order to reach any destination outside of Beirut (or, often, even within Beirut), but upon arrival at one's destination it was quite hazardous to travel without escorts, liaison officers, or authorized spokespersons. So even the adventurous, conscientious journalist who left the familiar comforts of Beirut usually did little more than "get a feel for the situation." Rare indeed was the reporter who would attempt to escape from this constrictive environment. The result was that reports from the hinterlands were seldom more revealing than those written in Beirut. To a large degree, the journalists' reportorial myopia only reflected the attitudes of the sophisticated Beiruti, who all too often could not have cared less about events occurring in a backwater like the South, for instance.

Furthermore, for most journalists posted in Beirut prior to 1982, the story in Lebanon was not Lebanon, but the Palestinian resistance. Lebanon was merely the stage upon which the Palestinian drama was played. While a large number of stories were filed with a Beirut dateline, many did not deal with Lebanon at all. Naturally, the journalist in the field was in large measure only responding to the orders of an editor and the interests of readers; the PLO was news, Lebanon was not.

Diplomats, especially American diplomats, had even less freedom of movement than their cohorts in the press corps. Legitimate security threats resulted in severe restrictions on the movement of diplomatic personnel, increasing the dependence of foreign service officers upon friendly sources—who often had their own desiderata and agendas. (For example, in 1980 U.S. embassy personnel were not permitted to travel south of Damur without the express permission of the ambassador.) Given the risks, it hardly comes as a surprise that many diplomats found the confines of Beirut, with its network of contacts and availability of creature comforts, an acceptable domain. As with the journalists, there were a few exceptional diplomats who recognized the cost of isolation and made every effort to move beyond the diplomatic circuit. One such diplomat, a Norwegian woman, knew Lebanon in great detail, but she was a very rare breed and was recognized as such by the press and diplomatic corps. When it is considered that much of the reporting—whether by the press or diplomats—was produced by a three-way synergism of journalist-diplomat-official, it is easy to understand how "truths" took on a life of their own.

Academics are a rather different case. Lebanon has hardly offered a hospitable research environment, and scholars intrigued by the politics of Lebanon often found it safer to study from afar rather than risk cherished myths by actually visiting the country. A few Lebanese scholars did produce useful and informative books on the 1975–1976 period, and Walid Khalidi has offered an elegant essay on the civil war and its aftermath, but by and large the scholarly cupboard is surprisingly bare.[5] By comparison, the work of the best journalists makes the scholarly offering seem especially paltry.[6] When the 1982 war resurrected interest in Lebanon, scholars found themselves discovering "new" facts that were sometimes new only to their cranial residences. Nor were the academic woods empty of opportunists. One scholar wrote a book about Israel's 1982 invasion based upon twenty-one days of field research and the friendly assistance of IDF (Israel Defence Forces) information officers.

Even for the adventurous, research opportunities in Lebanon have not exactly been abundant in recent years. The country has always been a magnet for conspirators, agents, and flamboyant bon vivants of various motives, but the onset of conflict multiplied the characters as well as the conspiracies (whether real or imagined). With ample evidence of duplicity, there was often good reason not to take people for what they purported to be. In short, prudence dictated caution in personal relationships with scholars who claimed to be researching political questions. One Fatah official alleged that 10 percent of the *fida'iyin* were agents—often unwitting—of outside powers. The accuracy of the charge is less important than the fact that it was made at all. Even questions that would seem innocent were often imbued with security ramifications. Whether the community of interest was the Maronite, Shi'i, or Palestinian, it could easily take several months to get answers to very basic—and seemingly benign—questions relating to population or social and political programs. Thus, many of our best Middle East scholars simply turned their attention elsewhere, rather than enmesh themselves in such a hostile research environment.

In 1982, when Lebanon exploded onto center stage, there was a remarkable shared ignorance about the country. Lebanese officials, who in many cases had long been absent from their country, frequently envisaged a Lebanon that no longer existed. Israeli officials were intent upon imposing a reality that fit neither the capabilities of their allies nor the sociopolitical realities of Lebanon. Meanwhile, the United States pursued an idyllic outcome that was most remarkable for the innocence it betrayed. All of these parties were to fail; they asked the wrong questions in 1982 because they understood poorly, if at all, what had happened prior to 1982.

The Evolution of Confessional Politics

We usually date the Lebanese state from 1943, when the unwritten National Pact (*Mithaq al-Watani*) established the current distribution of political office by confession on the basis of the population figures revealed by a problematic 1932 census. As a reflection of the 1932 figures, the Maronites were accorded the office of the presidency, the Sunnis the post of prime minister, and the Shiᶜa the position of parliamentary speaker. But, in point of fact, the modalities of the political system were well established long before 1943. For example, in 1841 Bashir III organized a confessional council of ten members (three Maronite, three Druze, one Greek Catholic, one Greek Orthodox, one Shiᶜi, and one Sunni) that represented the country's divergent social identities.[7]

In 1860, after Maronite peasants rose up against their Druze landlords, as many as 11,000 Maronites were killed over a period of several weeks. After the massacres of 1860, and under pressure from the British, Russians, French, and Austrians—each of which had their own Lebanese confessional client—the Règlement Organique of 1861 was acceded to by the Ottomans, the ostensible imperial power. The Règlement Organique provided for the establishment of a Representative Council to consist of two representatives of each major confessional community. The latter system was revised in 1864 to give greater numerical representation to the Maronites, Druze, and Greek Orthodox, but here again, confessional diversity was recognized. While the ratios changed from time to time, the formula remained.

By the beginning of the French Mandate in 1920, the dynamics of Lebanese politics were already well established. Patterns of identity, based on shared religion, geographic propinquity, and unique external ties, produced a political system in which politics and sectarian identities were inextricably linked.

Population Shifts

Unfortunately, Lebanon's confessional political system proved to be exceedingly fragile and unresponsive to demands spawned by population growth, as well as social, economic, and political changes. A decisive determinant of the system's fragility was the redrawing of Lebanon's boundaries by the French in 1920. While intended to enhance the state's viability, the expansion of Lebanon in 1920, from Mount Lebanon to Le Grand Liban (Greater Lebanon), had the effect of doubling the state's territory, but it also greatly complicated its political future. The enlargement of the state added the Shiᶜi Muslims of the South and the Biqaᶜ Valley; the Greek Orthodox, Armenians, and Sunnis of the coastal cities; and the Greek Catholics of the Biqaᶜ Valley. By expanding the confessional puzzle, it was assured that no one community would be preeminent. As the relative power of each communal group was reduced, the dual imperatives of internal alliances (as between the Greek Catholics and the Maronites, and the Sunnis and the Greek Orthodox) and external ties increased.

When we examine the political history of the past century and a half, we find that, until Lebanon achieved independence in 1943, there were periodic readjustments both in the ratios of confessional representation and in the allocation of specific offices. However, since the promulgation of the *Mithaq al-Watani* in 1943, there have only been modest adjustments, despite the fact that confessional birthrate differentials have significantly changed Lebanon's demographic profile. Not surprisingly, those confessions enjoying the highest socioeconomic status (SES)—such as the Maronite and the Sunni—have experienced diminishing birthrates, while those on the bottom rung—the Shiʿa—have experienced very high rates. This is not an astounding finding; we know that as SES increases, birthrates tend to decline. In addition, variations in migratory patterns have also worked against the Christian community as a whole, and in favor of the Shiʿi Muslims in particular. In other words, Christian Lebanese were more likely to settle outside of the country (particularly in western Europe and the Americas), while the Shiʿi Muslim migrants were more likely to return to Lebanon after a few years in the Gulf or West Africa.

It must be emphasized that precise population data are impossible to obtain in the present circumstances, but the skillful manipulation of limited data by demographers certainly indicates that the Christians have long since ceased to enjoy the 6:5 population advantage they enjoyed over the Muslims.[8] Indeed, while Lebanon's last census (administered in 1932) purportedly indicated that the Shiʿa comprised only the third largest community, following the Maronites and the Sunnis, it is now indisputable that they are the largest, constituting as much as 30 percent (or more) of the country's population. (For example, according to one calculation for the early 1970s, the average Shiʿi family size was nearly nine members, as compared to less than six in the case of Christian families.)[9] Taken together, the Muslims (Shiʿis, Sunnis, and Druze) probably represent 60 percent of Lebanon's population. All of the preceding demographic shifts, have—to reiterate the point—occurred without corresponding changes in the distribution of political power.

For the Shiʿi community, the principle of allocating political office by confession has fed a collective sense of deprivation, since the principle is widely equated with the historical numerical underrepresentation of the Shiʿa in political office. As Robert Melson and

Howard Wolpe observe, apropos of Lebanon: "The subordination of political institutions to the interests of particular communal groups tends to reinforce and politicize communal conflict."[10]

Another important population factor has been the influx of Palestinian refugees to Lebanon. About 100,000 Palestinian civilians fled to Lebanon following the first Palestine war in 1948. Through natural increases, this population numbered more than 200,000 by the onset of the civil war in 1975, of which more than half inhabited refugee camps. Although a fair percentage of those living outside of the camps, which is to say those Palestinians of higher socioeconomic status, managed to become integrated into Lebanese society, the camp populations never had that opportunity. Thus, the PLO found a steady stream of recruits in the squalid camps that were found in all of Lebanon's coastal cities. After the great disaster and humiliation of the Six-Day War of 1967, the militancy of the camp dwellers increased markedly. Simultaneously, Lebanon was used with increasing frequency as a base from which to launch attacks upon Israel, thus becoming embroiled in the crossfire of the Arab-Israeli conflict. Since most of the Palestinians were Sunni Muslims, they were viewed by many militants in the Maronite community as a dangerous threat to Maronite supremacy in Lebanon.

In 1970 and 1971, a second wave of refugees penetrated Lebanon, but this one was armed and angry, comprised as it was of the *fida'i* groups that had been expelled from Jordan. With the loss of Jordan as a base of operations, Lebanon became the only territory from which the PLO could operate with relative autonomy. More than any other single factor, it was the presence of a large armed and aggressive PLO in Lebanon that provided the spark that ignited the underlying tensions and grievances that defined Lebanese society.

Dimensions of Political Change

A dozen years of internal conflict, invasion, and civil disorder have intensified the socioeconomic forces that were changing Lebanon even before the civil war began in 1975. Carnage may have stolen the headlines, but the real story in Lebanon is the social and political change we usually associate with modernization. Vast numbers of Lebanese who were previously politically moot have now found their political voice and are no longer content to accept a political system that ignores their demands. The failure or unwillingness to recognize this dimension of change has been the defining characteristic of Lebanese governments for the past decade and a half. This recalcitrance, on the part of ruling elites, is the most important explanation for Lebanon's continuing susceptibility to meddling by foreign powers. Groups whose demands were not heard within the political system all too frequently found that external powers were willing to lend a hand (not to mention a gun).

As a result of increases in literacy, internal and external migration, exposure to the media, and occupational shifts away from agriculture and toward the services sector, even Lebanese dwelling in villages have transcended the isolation and malleability that we often glibly associate with nonurban populations. While Lebanese wax poetic about their pristine villages, such places are now only social history. Village, town, and city dweller alike have become increasingly assertive and, as a result, ever more available for political action.

While the people became politicized in Lebanon, a wide variety of political organizations competed for the growing pool of prospective recruits. Many of the most successful political movements appealed to the confessional (religious) identity that all Lebanese acquire at birth. The success of recruitment based upon primordial sentiments is hardly surprising. We have already noted that the Lebanese find it difficult to escape from their hyphenated identity as Sunni-Lebanese, Greek Orthodox–Lebanese, and so on. For years, even wedlock was politicized, since civil marriage was prohibited. From the citizens' identity cards specifying confession to the allocation of political rewards according to confessional formulae, it is impossible for people simply to be Lebanese.[11] However, the salience of such groups as the (Maronite) Lebanese Forces, (Shiʿi) Harakat Amal, and (Druze) Progressive Socialist party should not be allowed to mask the fundamental underlying factor—a profound broadening of the politically relevant population. This factor not only complicates relations between communal groups but within them as well.

The ranks of the politicized have swollen and the contours of politics in Lebanon have changed radically. Devoid of strong central political institutions, Lebanese politics have long been the domain of a coterie of political bosses known as zuʿama (singular zaʿim). Drawn from a few dozen families—twenty-six families have held 35 percent of all parliamentary seats since 1943—each zaʿim represented a clientele that traded its acquiescent political loyalty for the zaʿim's stock-in-trade political favors that were dispersed much in the style of Chicago ward bosses, but perhaps with more asperity. Power was passed from father to son as a political inheritance. Surnames like al-Jumayyil, Chamoun, Salam, al-Asʿad, Franjiya, Jumblatt, and Sulh appeared again and again on ministry portfolios. But the conflict in Lebanon—and the accelerating social and economic changes that accompanied it—has rendered the zuʿama increasingly irrelevant in contemporary Lebanon. Since the Israeli invasion of 1982, one of the more fascinating spectator sports has been watching an anachronistic political guard scramble to recover its control of fiefdoms that are now controlled, at least in part, by a new generation of leaders—often men with obscure family names. This is not to argue that the *zuᶜama* have lost all political significance, but the breadth of their influence—particularly in the Shiᶜi and Maronite communities—has been considerably narrowed.

The contenders for power have included political no-names such as Samir Jaᶜjaᶜ, the commander of the (Maronite) Lebanese Forces, and Nabih Berri, the leader of the Shiᶜi Amal movement. In temperament, social origin, and wealth these men are antithetical to the *zuᶜama* they seek to supplant. The Lebanese Forces were created in 1976 by Bashir al-Jumayyil, the scion of the founder of the Kataʾib (or Phalange) party, Pierre al-Jumayyil. While Bashir was certainly not a political unknown, the organization he created was manned, in large part, by the lower- and lower-middle-class Maronites from Beirut's eastern suburbs, who in most cases rejected the politics of the old guard (including the venerable Kataʾib party). As Lewis Snider notes in a remarkably pithy article, the Lebanese Forces is not just a militia, but a political ethos that rejected old-style politics as practiced by the Christian and Muslim establishment.[12] Since the assassination of Bashir al-Jumayyil in September 1982, the leadership has fallen to a group of young activists who are as staunch in their desire to retain a share of political power as they are committed to the protection of their community's Maronite identity.

Perhaps the most remarkable political transformation has occurred in the Shiᶜi community, which has recently been especially vocal in demanding its rights.[13] The most important Shiᶜi organization has been Harakat Amal (literally, the Movement of Hope)—the focus of this book. Amal was the creation of a charismatic and pragmatic religious leader, Musa al-Sadr, who quite purposefully and successfully challenged the authority of the established political bosses. Al-Sadr disappeared—he seems to have been murdered—during an enigmatic visit to Libya in 1978. His disappearance, the exemplar of the Islamic Revolution in Iran, and the punishing blows sustained by the Shiᶜa in the South have combined to invigorate the community with a sense of self that has long been absent. Amal is today led by Nabih Berri. Berri, a lawyer, was born in Sierra Leone of a trader family from south Lebanon, and upon his return to Lebanon lived for a time in the Beirut slums. His name evokes the contempt of *zuᶜama*, who deride his dearth of the traditional requisites for elite status. Nonetheless, it is Nabih Berri—and those like him—

who can speak for a majority of the Shi‘a, rather than discredited *zu‘ama*, whose clientele and influence nowadays often seem not to extend very far beyond their salons.

The combination of political fragmentation and external intervention has grossly exacerbated the difficulties facing any Lebanese government. The problem is not just to accommodate the demands of contending communities in a political milieu in which outside powers meddle at will, but to determine who speaks for each respective community or segments thereof. It is clear that pretending change has not happened is hardly likely to be a successful tactic, as President Amin al-Jumayyil has discovered to his disadvantage. Shaikh Amin, who was elected in September 1982 after the assassination of his brother Bashir, the president-elect, lacks a firm constituency in the Maronite community and apparently sought to placate his many Maronite detractors by declining to deal with the emergent leadership of the Shi‘a and the Druze. (It bears remembering that what is at stake is political power, of which the Maronites have more than their share in the view of the Shi‘a and the Druze.) Rather than deal with the likes of Nabih Berri, al-Jumayyil opted to turn to Kamil al-As‘ad, the Shi‘i Speaker of the Chamber of Deputies. However, al-As‘ad's constituency among the Shi‘a has shrunken to the point of disappearance, so the president's action did little more than feed the growing impression that he sought, above all else, to avoid any accommodation of the emerging social forces (outside of his own community, of course). The joint Shi‘i-Druze takeover of West Beirut on February 6, 1984, dramatically demonstrated the president's strategic misjudgment.

The processes of change that have brought newly politicized Shi‘is and Maronites to the political forefront (the Druze, despite their political prowess, still only represent about 7 percent of the population) portend significant realignments in Lebanese politics. The Sunnis, who long shared real political power with the Maronites, are numerically outweighed by the Shi‘a, and they lack the mass political organizations of either the Shi‘i or the Maronite communities. In fact, it is an interesting paradox that it is among the Sunnis—who enjoy high standards of social and economic development—that the *za‘im* institution persists most strongly. Most observers agree, if a new political formula can be agreed upon in Lebanon, that the Sunnis may well be the big losers—or the spoilers.

The process of reconciliation currently being erratically, and sometimes disingenuously, pursued will not succeed if it simply seems a vehicle for the *zu‘ama* to recapture political privilege. Reconciliation between the traditional leaders is, of course, not unimportant, but it is not enough. If blood-drenched Lebanon is to return to civility, the *zuᶜama* must make room for new leaders who voice the legitimate demands of their constituencies.

The emergence of these new leaders, and the social forces they represent, grossly complicates the Lebanon puzzle. It may well be that the puzzle is, for the time being, insoluble, given the haphazard fragmentation of the political authority (and the unfettered activities of Iran, Israel and Syria). But, if nothing else, it is undeniable that attempting to put Lebanon back together by resorting to an obsolete blueprint is doomed to failure. This dictum is nowhere clearer than in the case of the Shiᶜa, which we now examine in greater detail.

2. The Sources and Meaning of Change among the Shiʿa of Lebanon

Judging from some accounts, it would seem that the Shiʿa of Lebanon have suddenly sprung upon the political scene, in large measure as an echo of the revolution of 1978–1979 in Iran, but this is a self-deceiving perspective. In fact, the present activism of the Lebanese Shiʿa is the outcome of a long process of modernization. Evidence of the community's growing political importance loomed well before the historic events in Iran. It has also been tempting for many observers to present Shiʿi politics as an exotic blend of emotionalism, anger, and irrationality, but this, too, is a misleading view.

True enough, Shiʿism—especially the activist variant presently articulated in Iran—has been amply demonstrated to be a culturally validated idiom of protest that imbues its proponents with a potent and evocative symbolism. Yet, upon examination, the political program of the majority Shiʿi movement in Lebanon is far less concerned with issues of orthopraxy or apostasy than with political reforms of an "ordinary" and familiar sort. Thus, it is a central premise of this book that politics as practiced by the Shiʿa of Lebanon have been no more inscrutable or exotic than the politics of any other Lebanese community.

Shiʿi politics are not less transparent than any other form of politics, nor are the sociopolitical processes at work bereft of paradox and contradiction. We should not expect them to be. However, the key to understanding Shiʿi politics lies within the realm of good social science and the range of mundane political behavior, rather than in sensationalized images of crazed fanatics willing to obliterate themselves to gain a one-way express ticket to Paradise. The political goals of individual Shiʿis range from the banal to the sublime, but the meaning of Shiʿi activism is to be found in the context of Lebanese politics, in which deceit, courage, corruption, selflessness, and selfishness are qualities that have been distributed among politicized Shiʿis quite as randomly as among non-Shiʿis.

The Shiʿa are an often ignored and politically isolated community that has long stood on the periphery of the Lebanese economy and society.[1] In this chapter, the forces of modernization that have affected the Shiʿa are examined with a view toward illuminating the factors that have contributed to the emergence of the Shiʿa. Heavy emphasis is placed upon the Lebanese context, and particularly sectarianism in Lebanon, in order to demonstrate why the Shiʿa have found their political voice as Shiʿis and not in terms of alternative loci of identity. In subsequent chapters, the internal and external forces that have shaped the politicization of the Shiʿa are analyzed, as well as the organizations that have served as vehicles for their political mobilization.

An Ignored Community

Scholarship on the Shʿi community of Lebanon is notably sparse and superficial. The paucity of work on the Shiʿa is not altogether surprising though. Scholars tend to tread well-worn and well-tended paths, and in Lebanon most of those paths have wound their way through politically influential communities, namely, the Maronite Christians, Druze, and Sunni Muslims. Rare indeed is the political study of Lebanon that accords the Shiʿa more than passing mention. Indeed, for many authors the Shiʿi sect was no more than a curious artifact of the early succession struggles in Islam. Impoverished, underdeveloped socially, and underrepresented politically, Lebanon's Shiʿa hardly seemed to merit serious attention. A mid-nineteenth-century traveler, David Urquhart, described the Shiʿa as a listless, subservient people reveling in squalor, a description that many found apt even a century later.

> They are all in rags, except some of the Sheiks, and are all mendicants. They will come and stand round the cooking which goes on in the open air, and if one is asked to go and get some eggs, he will shrug his shoulders, and when told he will be paid for his trouble, he answers, "there is none." If another is asked to sell a sheep or a fowl, he answers, "it is not mine." The filth is revolting. It would seem as if they took a particular pride in exhibiting their rebellion against the law, originally proclaimed from Horeb and afterwards from Mecca, both in regard to their persons and the cleanliness of their villages.[2]

Even as recently as the 1950s, the Shiʿa seemed most notable for their invisibility and irrelevance in Lebanese politics.

Despite the fact that 1932 census data recognized the Shi'a as the third largest confessional grouping in the country, there was little incentive to study a community whose political clout was modest relative to its numbers. Albert Hourani's brief comments, in his 1946 book, well captured the sentiments of scholars who were to follow him. Hourani notes the backwardness of the Shi'a and their low standard of living and remarks, "Their first need is for a reformed social organization and improved economic conditions."[3]

For the most part, the community—or, more aptly, fragments of it—languished under the domination of a relatively small number of *zu'ama*, whose political power stemmed from land wealth and the political ineffectualness of their clientele. Urban and town-based merchant families such as the 'Usairans of Sidon, the al-Khalils of Tyre, and the al-Zains of Nabatiya gained their influence in the late nineteenth century when they acquired landed property or became *multazims* (tax agents) on behalf of the Ottoman rulers of the Levant. Other families, especially the al-As'ads of al-Tayybi or the Hamadas of Ba'albak, represented historically powerful clans or tribes (*'asha'ir*) who buttressed their traditional role by also becoming *multazims*. After independence these *zu'ama* dominated communal politics, winning Assembly seats and cabinet ministries again and again.

While the *Mithaq al-Watani* (or National Pact) of 1943 formalized the basis for the allocation of political office in the new republic and recognized the demographic share of the Shi'a by according them the third most important political office, the Speaker of the parliament, this was hardly a reflection of the political consciousness of the community. As Leonard Binder observes, the share of the Shi'i community was in fact the share of the traditional political bosses (*zu'ama*) who were its unchallenged power brokers.[4] Dominating their community economically, the *zu'ama* shrewdly translated this domination at election time by automatically delivering the vote of their pliant constituents.[5] Survival in such a system meant being a *zilm* (follower of a *za'im*), voting the prescribed electoral slate, defending the *za'im*'s interests and property, and affecting the proper respect for the patron.

Thus, the politically assertive and relatively united Lebanese Shi'i community that is evident today represents a recent and significant political phenomenon. This development is a product of a number of factors, including several decades of important socioeconomic change. The goal of this chapter is to analyze how the bonds of several centuries of political and social isolation were eroded by changes both mundane and dramatic.

The argument that frames this chapter is as follows:

1. By the 1960s, the Shiʿa were exposed to wide-ranging economic change and social disruption, the significance of which is partially anticipated by Karl Deutsch's work on social mobilization.

2. As the community's isolation was attenuated by the effects of changing agricultural patterns, increased access to the media, improved internal transportation networks, internal and external migration, and a deteriorating security environment, traditional political leaders became less capable of meeting the escalating needs and demands of their constituents.

3. Even before the onset of civil war in 1975, a wide variety of secular political movements vied for recruits from among the increasingly politicized Shiʿa; however, sectarian identity not only proved to be persistent, but was even enhanced by the distinctive characteristics of the sociopolitical setting of Lebanon.

4. In respect to Lebanon, the standard political science literature offers a false dichotomy in its treatment of the significance of rural versus urban residence for political participation. The posited effects of urbanization, including increased political participation, were equally evident in nonurban locales, leading to the conclusion that the urban-rural distinction has lost much of its meaning for political behavior in Lebanon.

5. The Lebanese case clearly shows that when dealing with states of modest geographic scale that are experiencing significant degrees of socioeconomic change, urban-rural dichotomies may mislead rather than inform.

6. As the insularity of the village has been demolished in the face of change both the village and the city have become important locales for political action.

7. Despite the persistence of sectarian identity and the continuing importance of the village-ideal in national political life, the success of a distinctively Shiʿi movement of broad appeal was hardly a necessary outcome. The community might easily have been fragmented among a number of locally based popular Shiʿi organizations and an admixture of "secular" parties espousing Shiʿi demands, and at times that has been the case. However, in large measure because of events originating outside of Lebanon, it was a broadly based communal reform movement that proved to be the most important mobilization agent of the Shiʿa.

Socioeconomic Underdevelopment and the Shiʿa

Population estimates for Lebanon are always risky—the last official census was conducted over fifty years ago—but virtually all informed observers agree that the Shiʿa presently constitute the largest single confessional group, representing at least 30 percent of the population, which is to say from 900,000 to 1 million members.⁶ Thus, the Shiʿi population now surpasses both the Maronite and Sunni sects that have dominated the republic since the attainment of self-rule in 1943. Lebanon's confessional political system institutionalizes a Maronite presidency, a Sunni premiership, and a Shiʿi Speakership in the Chamber of Deputies, all by virtue of the respective population shares established by the 1932 census. Should the Shiʿa succeed in demanding that the political system reflect their status as the plurality, it is clear that a substantial reallocation of political power in Lebanon would result.

The potential impact of changing population shares is well illustrated by a simple consideration of the allocation of parliamentary seats to the Shiʿa and the Maronite Christians. The present 99-seat Assembly, elected in 1972, includes 19 Shiʿi seats as opposed to 30 for the Maronites. Yet if the seats were allocated according to the realities of changed demographics, the Shiʿa would stand to gain as many as 10 seats while the Maronites would lose an equal number. And if parliamentary representation were to be split evenly between Muslims and Christians—a reform that has been on the agenda since 1976—the Shiʿa would claim the lion's share of the Muslim seats, much to the detriment of the previously dominant Sunnis, who now constitute only about 20 percent of Lebanon's population, and the Druze, who account for less than 10 percent. But numbers are no more a guarantee of political success than impoverishment, although both factors help to clarify the demands, if not the newfound assertiveness, of the Shiʿa. Moreover, I shall demonstrate that while increased political representation has been important as a communal issue, the Shiʿa have often been preoccupied by far less grand objectives, namely, the amelioration of their economic plight and the rampant insecurity that they have suffered, especially in al-Janub (the South), the Lebanese province bordering Israel.

Lebanon's Shiʿa have long been considered the most disadvantaged confessional group in the country. By most, if not all, of the conventional measures of socioeconomic status, the Shiʿa fare poorly in comparison to their non-Shiʿi cohorts. For example, using 1971 data, Joseph Chamie notes: the average Shiʿi family's income was 4,532 Lebanese pounds (lires) (L£; 3L£ = $1 in 1971), in comparison with the national average of 6,247L£; the Shiʿa constituted the highest percentage of families earning less than 1,500L£; they were the most poorly educated (50 percent with no schooling vs. 30 percent statewide); and the Shiʿa were the *least* likely, in comparison with their cohorts from other recognized sects,[7] to list their occupation as professional/technical, business/managerial, clerical or crafts/operatives, and the *most* likely to list it as farming, peddling, or labor.[8] In his 1968 study, Michael Hudson found that in the two regions where the Shiʿa predominate, al-Biqaʿ and al-Janub, the percentage of students in the population (about 13 percent) lagged by as much as five percentage points behind Lebanon's other three regions.[9] Riad B. Tabbarah, analyzing educational differentials, found that in 1971 only 6.6 percent of the Shiʿa had at least a secondary education, compared to at least 15 percent and 17 percent for the Sunnis and the Christians, respectively.[10] Citing official Lebanese government statistics for 1974, Hasan Sharif found that while the South had about 20 percent of the national population, it received less than 0.7 percent of the state budget.[11] Sharif's description of the underdevelopment of the South illustrates the conditions under which many Shiʿis have had to live.

> The south has the fewest paved roads per person or per acre. Running water is still missing in all villages and towns although water pipes were extended to many areas in the early sixties. Electricity networks were erected at about the same time, but they are inoperative most of the time. Sewage facilities are available only in large towns and cities. Outside the larger centers telephone service is completely absent except for a single manual cabin which is usually out of order. Doctors visit the villages once a week and sometimes only once a month. Clinics are maintained only in large villages and do not function regularly. Hospitals and pharmacies are found only in the larger population centers. Elementary school is usually run in an old unhealthy house provided by the village. Intermediate schools were introduced to the large towns in the mid-sixties.[12]

Based on my fieldwork in Lebanon from 1980 to 1982, Sharif's description is still essentially correct. While there have been some minor improvements, the conditions depicted are for the most part at least as bad as noted and in many respects have only been exacerbated by years of conflict and social disruption.

Transcending Political Irrelevance

The impoverishment of the Shiʿi community is irrefutable, but impoverishment, in and of itself, does not explain how or why so many "sackfuls of potatoes" (to use Marx's cruel metaphor) transcended their political underdevelopment. Notwithstanding the political activities of the *zu'ama*, who purported to speak for their respective segments of the community, the Shi'a as a group have long been marked by political quietude and even irrelevance for politics in Lebanon. For the student of political change, certainly one of the central questions—if not the fundamental one—is by what process do people become politicized. This process of change, its dynamics, speed, and intensity, is at the very core of political development.

How and why did the previously nonparticipant Shi'is find their political voice? I argue the Shi'is' political emergence is the result of a two-step process. The first step, the "why" of the process, may be simply described as the social and economic uprooting of the community. As we shall see, a consideration of the socioeconomic changes that have recently taken place in Lebanon helps us to understand the increasing availability of the Shi'a for political action, without, however, explaining the direction or shape of such action. An uprooted population is only potentially politically significant; its latent significance is only realized when the uprooted are mobilized or recruited for political action. Thus, the second step, the "how" of the process, may be called the political mobilization of the Shi'a. The details of the political mobilization of the Shi'a are discussed in the next chapter. For the present, the emphasis is upon the first step of the two-step process by which the Shi'a broke the bonds of social isolation and economic deprivation.

As I shall demonstrate, the Shi'a were, by the late 1960s, buffeted by the winds of modernization, winds that uprooted the Shi'a and rendered them ever more available for political mobilization. Even before the onset of open warfare in 1975, Lebanon was undergoing profound and wide-ranging socioeconomic changes. While these changes did not originate in armed conflict, they were accelerated and exacerbated by the societal disruption and civil upheaval incidental to conflict. It may seem—at first glance—counterindicative to consider anarchy and internal warfare as concomitant to the process of political modernization, but the case of Lebanon certainly illustrates the extent to which years of chaotic bloodletting may vastly broaden the politically relevant strata in a country.

While the process has been gruesome in the extreme, it is nonetheless clear that many once quiescent Lebanese have emerged from civil conflict and invasion insistent that their demands be addressed and their circumstances improved. Naturally, these developments have not been restricted to only one confessional community; they have affected virtually every confessional group in the country.[13] Internal conflict, invasion, and disorder have intensified the social and economic ferment that began even before the civil war in 1975.

Gradual educational advances, increased travel inside Lebanon and abroad, wider exposure to the press and television, the decline of agriculture and the expansion of the service sector—all of this greatly changed life in villages and even urban slums. People who were once nearly irrelevant to the political system are now increasingly determined to assert their political will. Observers have often failed to notice this most important result of the conflict in Lebanon, focusing instead on the epiphenomenal aspects.[14] This lacuna, however understandable, ignores the extensive, and probably permanent, structural changes that have occurred in the Lebanese political system.

Years of conflict and accelerating social and economic changes have also rendered the *zuʿama* increasingly impotent. The Shiʿi community—long under the thumbs of six *muqataʿjis* (feudal families), the Asʿads, Khalils, Zains, ʿUsairans, Haidars, and Hamadas—started to shake loose of their control in the 1960s, if not earlier. By the 1970s, the combination of change and conflict pushed forward a new generation of political leaders who were more sensitive to the demands of their new constituents. It is now germane to take a closer look at the processes of change and conflict that have had such telling effect within Lebanon.

The Social Mobilization of the Shiʿa

No political system is immune to change, yet many political studies and even works specifically treating political development ignore or underemphasize the dynamics of change.[15] Two articles by the distinguished anthropologist Emrys L. Peters nicely illustrate the perils of taking a narrow view of political change. Peters conducted fieldwork during the early 1950s in a Shiʿi village in south Lebanon. While he recognized that individuals might move from one social stratum to another, he failed, as he acknowledges in the later article, to recognize that the social strata might be reordered as a result of differential acceptance of educational, migration, and agricultural opportunities. The high-status "Learned Families" that seemed to comprise a village elite in 1952 had been denuded of political power when Peters returned several years later, in large part because they failed to adapt to changing social, economic, and political environments.[16] Peters' articles serve as useful reminders of the literally upsetting quality that change might engender, as well as the tendency of even a master of fieldwork to fail to anticipate the full impact of change.

Indeed, there have been precious few serious attempts to explain the sources and significance of change in modernizing societies. This is hardly surprising; just as change is a most important challenge for political leaders, whether they be Shiʿi shaikhs or Maronite presidents, political change has proven to be a most difficult puzzle for social scientists as well.

An exemplary, if still flawed, attempt to account for the impact of change is found in the work of Karl W. Deutsch. In an important 1961 article, Deutsch elaborated the concept of "social mobilization," an ambitious attempt to explain how socioeconomic changes unleash social forces and expand the politically relevant strata in a population,[17] and in so doing pose new challenges for political leaders and political systems. As we shall see, Deutsch's construct is incomplete in that it does not explain how socioeconomic changes are transformed into political ones. Yet his work serves as a useful conceptual first step toward understanding the significance of change in Lebanon.

Social mobilization, in effect, has two dimensions: first, it summarizes and indicates the process of change "which happens to substantial parts of the population in countries which are moving from traditional to modern ways of life." (Deutsch cautions that social mobilization is not identical with the "process of modernization as a whole.")[18] In effect, social mobilization is the process by which a population becomes *available* for modernization, which we may call the actual process of adopting new political commitments and patterns of behavior. Second, it loosely speaks to the expansion in demands that characterizes modernizing societies.

As an indicator of change, the concept subsumes a wide range of variables that, when measured over time, signal the extent of the changes that are taking place in a given country. Thus, Deutsch counsels that we pay attention to the following clusters of change: exposure to aspects of modern life (e.g., the media, consumer goods, and technology); changes in residence, in particular, rural to urban migration; occupational changes, such as shifts away from agrarian employment; rising literacy rates; and changes in income.

The consequences of social mobilization are described by Deutsch as follows: "In whatever country it occurs, social mobilization brings with it an expansion of the politically relevant strata of the population."[19] He adds: "Social mobilization also brings about a change in the quality of politics by changing the range of human needs that impinge upon the political process. As people are uprooted from their physical and intellectual isolation in their immediate localities, from their old habits and traditions, and often from their old patterns of occupation and places of residence, they experience drastic changes in their needs."[20]

Social mobilization is not only a process in which people break away from old loyalties, but one in which existing patterns of political behavior may lose their utility. Once "uprooted" from their old identities, people experience new needs and pose new challenges for their government. If these challenges are unmet, as has been the case in Lebanon, they raise the specter of political turmoil. As William Foltz notes: "It is no small tribute to Deutsch's article that well before Huntington raised the spectre of 'political decay' or Kasfir demonstrated the necessity and willingness of some Third World governments artificially to restrict political participation, Deutsch was attempting to *measure* the likelihood that particular governments would find themselves in such parlous straits."[21]

Taking Deutsch's concept as his inspiration, Michael Hudson examined social mobilization phenomena in Lebanon; his 1968 book offers persuasive, if sometimes circumstantial, evidence that the country was—in the late 1960s—undergoing rapid but uneven social mobilization that posed serious challenges and dilemmas for the "precarious republic."[22]

While reliable data are scarce, especially by confession, the limited available data continue to point to important socioeconomic changes in Lebanon over the past several decades. Particularly noteworthy are changes in employment and residence patterns, changes that are central to Deutsch's concept of social mobilization and can reasonably be inferred to have disproportionately affected the Shiʿa.

For example, from 1960 to 1980, the percentage of the total labor force employed in agriculture—the most common occupational category for the Shiʿa—declined from 38 percent to 11 percent, with most of those displaced moving to the urban-centered services sector, which increased its share of the labor force from 39 percent to 62 percent over the same period.[23] The reasons for these occupational shifts are complex, but, in addition to the dislocations incidental to warfare, they include stagnant prices for cash crops (tobacco and sugar beets); an increase in capital-intensive citrus-crop cultivation; a relatively high rate of growth in the labor force (3 percent per annum in the 1970–1980 period); an uncertain and dangerous security environment (especially in al-Janub and al-Biqaʿ, agrarian areas accounting for well over 50 percent of the Shiʿi population—the remainder are found in Beirut and its suburbs); and a decisive lack of budgetary support for the primary economic sector from the government and the private sector (the respective rates were 2.3 percent of the state budget in 1973 and 2.3 percent of total bank credits in 1974).

Not surprisingly, the result has been a growing impoverishment of the small freeholder, who typically owns three hectares or less and accounts for about three-quarters of the rural population (one 1973 estimate shows an annual per head of household income of 500L£ for agriculture, as compared to 1,100L£ in industry and 8,060L£ for the services sector). By the late 1960s—well before the onset of serious fighting—56 percent of those engaged in agriculture in south Lebanon took second jobs, usually as laborers.[24] The latter statistic is remarkable in that the majority of those seeking supplementary employment were landowners. Coupled with other important if less dramatic changes, such as a doubling of per capita energy consumption in the period 1960–1979, Lebanon was experiencing changes of the sort anticipated by the social mobilization construct.

The decline of the agrarian sector has been an important impetus for internal migration, usually to Beirut and its environs, as well as for external migration (for the Shi'a, typically to West Africa and the Arab Middle East), a factor not considered by Deutsch. Assuming a population of 3 million in 1980, some 6 percent of the males in the Lebanese work force were migrant workers in the Arab countries,[25] and the total of those working abroad who intended to return to Lebanon may have exceeded 25 percent of the total work force. Even before the events of 1975, about 40 percent of the population of predominantly Shi'i south Lebanon and about 25 percent of the population of al-Biqa' had migrated.[26]

Internal migrants—often landless, poorly educated, and unemployed—typically found that the Beirut slums offered only squalor and misery. In reality, relatively few transcended a transient status, a factor that was to prove very significant in shaping their political mobilization. On the other hand, external migrants tended to be somewhat better educated, and while the slum dwellers often had no choice but to maintain their village-based political alliances, the external migrants typically stepped into new political alliances in their overseas locations. Significantly, all of the Lebanese communities in Africa are led by Shi'is. Unlike earlier waves of Lebanese emigrants who relocated permanently in the Americas and Europe, the Shi'a found themselves in societies in which barriers of color or nationality ensured that they would eventually return to Lebanon. Thus, the overseas Shi'i population was not cut off from Lebanon, but instead maintained close ties to home. One result of these persistent ties was that the migrants became an important source of funds for political movements that would recognize and preserve their newly achieved socioeconomic status.

From Social Mobilization to Politicization

Deutsch discusses the consequences of social mobilization, namely, "an expansion of the politically relevant strata of the population"[27]— in other words, the notion that social mobilization has as one of its primary results politicization.[28] But, while Deutsch asserts that as increasing numbers of a population are socially mobilized its demands will eventually be translated into increased political participation, it is nowhere made clear in his important body of work how such a translation occurs. As Jerrold Green remarks in a noteworthy synthesis, "Unfortunately, we are told little about the mechanics of this increased politicization and participation. Deutsch merely asserts that they evolve, with implicit references to democratic theory for an understanding of the dynamics of such evolution."[29]

The causal connection between social mobilization and political participation was tested by Jorge Dominguez. Examining early-nineteenth-century data for Chile, Mexico, Venezuela, and Cuba, Dominguez found that social mobilization was not a reliable predictor of political participation; instead, "Political participation depended on leaders and organizations acting upon a fairly inept, non-civic mass."[30]

In his trenchant critique of Deutsch, David Cameron decries the assumption of social determinism, "That is, that political mobilization is the result or end product of certain types of social cleavage and social change."[31] Although he seems confused as to whether Deutsch's argument concerns "social" or "political" mobilization, Cameron's lack of terminological clarity does not weaken his central point, which is that the goals, resources, setting, and, most important, the very existence of a mobilization agent will determine whether the potentially politicized are actually inducted into politics.

> The traditional view of mobilization conceives induction as passive and inevitable. Little attention, if any, is given to the organization or behavioral pattern into which an individual is inducted. Yet it is obvious that induction is impossible without the existence of an organization which is seeking new members. Likewise it is plausible that the extent of induction may be affected by the organization itself. Through its recruitment policies, its promotional drives, and its ability to create a favorable image of itself, to espouse in its rhetoric solutions for current exigencies, and to adapt its organization to the existing social infrastructure, a new political movement may either succeed or fail in attracting new members.[32]

In short, by tending to treat politics as the dependent variable, Deutsch underemphasizes, even ignores, the widely different means by which the newly politicized may be brought into—or, for that matter, excluded from—the political system.

Furthermore, Deutsch ignores the international environment, which, as Lebanon so poignantly illustrates, may influence both stability and rates of change within a society[33]—and hence, the susceptibility of a population to political mobilization. Thus, the explanatory power of Deutsch's work on social mobilization lies in its treatment of the process that only acquires meaning in the context of politics.[34] This reality is well summed up by Leonard Binder's observation that social mobilization, as presented by Deutsch, ends where political mobilization begins.[35]

The Persistence of Sectarian Identity

In Lebanon, social mobilization was making ever larger numbers of Shi'is available for political action (i.e., for political mobilization), and I have already emphasized that the form of their political activity would depend upon the context in which they were recruited. That context would be defined by the characteristics of the Lebanese political system, as well as three developments (considered in the following chapter) originating outside of Lebanon: the Islamic Revolution in Iran, the disappearance of a popular Shi'i cleric, and a significant shift in Israeli retaliatory practices.

Clearly, not all of the Shi'a succumbed to recruitment along confessional lines, but over time large numbers did. That the Shi'a might act as Shi'i-Lebanese and not as Lebanese was not wholly unanticipated in the social science literature; the persistence of "primordial sentiments" is well recognized.[36]

Under some circumstances, the end result of the modernization process is the emergence of a shared nationality; indeed, this was the thrust of Deutsch's book *Nationalism and Social Communication*.[37] But, Deutsch recognized—some argue belatedly[38]—that in some political settings, apropos of Lebanon, the social mobilization of a population would lead not to assimilation, but to differentiation: "the same process may tend to strain or destroy the unity of states whose population is already divided into several groups with different languages or cultures or basic ways of life."[39]

The most obvious explanation for the relative solidarity of the Shi'a is the commonplace that it is nearly impossible to escape from one's confessional identity in Lebanon. Whether one looks at the meager success of secular political parties,[40] or the durability of confessionally based militias, evidence of the persistence of sectarian identity is hard to avoid. The successful Lebanese *zuʿama*, as well as the organizations that have challenged their authority, pay heed to the dictum offered by Fuad Khuri: "political arrangements remain valid insofar as they reflect sociological realities."[41]

Even among the sophisticates of Beirut, it is hard to find a person who cannot identify associates by confession. Not that fervent religiosity is necessarily widespread, of course, but religious identity defines one's primary social organization, through which political security is maintained.[42] Differentiation by sect is also reinforced by distinctive cultural realms and behavioral norms: religion, personal status law, dress, diet, and even tonsorial preferences.

None of this is to assert that there has been no incipient class structure emerging in Lebanon; but where class consciousness seems to exist, it is overlain (and obscured) by primordial identities. In fact, as Iliya Harik correctly claims in the case of the Lebanese (and Iraqi) Shiʿa, objective socioeconomic conditions and primordial sentiments so overlap that it is difficult to disaggregate one from the other.[43] The depressed economic status of the Shiʿa provides a basis for defining the communal reference group, but it has not led to significant class-based participation across confessions.

In his important study of two Beirut suburbs, Shiyya and Ghobeire, Khuri found that class identity sometimes defined minor aspects of culture, such as meal times and entertainment styles, as well as the use of living space within residences, but class per se was the "least important instrument of [political and social] organization."[44] As he notes, "In the West, social class is a determinant of organizational variation; in the Middle East it is a determinant of behavioral variation."[45] Huntington and Nelson's observation is thus very much to the point: "Where politics is organized largely on communal lines, issues and loyalties are likely to cut across both urban-rural boundaries and class differences, so that the categories of peasant, migrant, and worker are less likely to provide a basis for collective political action, although there may still be a salient interplay of opportunities for mobility and collective organization."[46]

The collective confessional consciousness of the Shiʿis was even further enhanced by the widespread—and not unjustified—belief that they have suffered the costs of the continuing conflict in Lebanon far more grievously than other groups in the country, and with very little to show for their grief. The Shiʿa were forcefully displaced from their homes in the South, and from the districts that fate placed on the "Christian" side of the Green Line in Beirut. In addition, Shiʿi men were the foot soldiers and cannon fodder of "leftist" forces during the civil war. We are clearly dealing with a case in which "primordial sentiments and objective socio-economic conditions . . . produce a reinforcing effect."[47]

As for the several hundred thousand Shiʿis who settled, both permanently and temporarily, in and around Beirut, it is now well acknowledged that urban residence does not necessarily erase sectarian identities and often has quite the opposite effect.[48] As Hudson remarks, "the crucible of Beirut does not appear to be molding less particularistic Lebanese citizens. . . . Urbanization appears to fortify, rather than diminish Lebanese parochialism. . . ."[49]

This fortification of parochial identity is not difficult to understand. The Shiʿi migrants were largely tenant farmers, sharecroppers, and agricultural laborers from al-Janub and al-Biqaʿ who had been forced off the land by the potent combination of war, declining agricultural incomes, and the decline in labor-intensive farming. Poorly educated, unskilled, and lacking in financial resources, they "tended to swell the ranks of the semi-employed sub-proletariat in the [Beirut] *bidonvilles* and suburbs."[50] Furthermore, unlike suave Sunni businessmen, the Shiʿa were often depicted by Beiruti compatriots in terms that neatly mimicked the racism of a Jim Crow bigot. I have heard cultured Maronite women refer to "those people" with an unmistakable disdain that one preserves for creatures, not people. In her study of Burj Hammud, a Beirut suburb, Suad Joseph describes Armenian attitudes toward the Shiʿa as follows: "The Muslim is pictured as dirty, untrustworthy, rapacious, sexual. In Borj Hammoud [Burj Hammud] this image is applied to the Shiʿites. The Shiʿite is represented as a constant threat to Armenian females."[51] Obviously, unbecoming stereotypes are held not only by Armenians and Maronites; but when they coincide with sociological distinctions between the settled and the transient, they illustrate sharply drawn cleavages (which have widened in the ensuing years).

As Michael Johnson argues in a persuasive study, the Shiʿi migrants to Beirut (as well as their objective allies, the Palestinian refugees) remained largely outside of the city's patron-client networks, which were dominated by Sunni Muslim *zuʿama* and *qabadayat* (political henchmen).[52] Cut off from the urban clientelist system, the migrants "continued to maintain relatively close ties with their villages of origin and with the political patrons or *zuʿama* of their home districts."[53] Thus, even as the Shiʿa moved away from the village, the village remained the locus of their political relationships. However, the value of these village-based political relationships with the *zuʿama* was declining simultaneously.

The Shiʿi *zuʿama* were proving to be increasingly ineffective in meeting the needs of their clients. They were unable to ameliorate the deteriorating security environment that gripped the villages (especially in al-Janub), and there is no evidence that they made any serious (or even semiserious) attempts to improve the conditions under which the urban poor lived. Indeed, on the latter count, there was little incentive for the Shiʿi *zaʿim* to work for the betterment of his slum-based clients. To do so would only attenuate the links between the migrants and their village, and hence their *zaʿim*. Thus, like their fellow sufferers, the Palestinian refugees, the urban Shiʿa were cast adrift in a turbulent political sea.

Even if the new urban dwellers of the early 1970s sought to cut village ties and become political participants in the new urban setting, Lebanon's electoral laws made it difficult, even impossible, to do so. (The complicated and lengthy legal process involved in an attempt to shift voting rights from one constituency to another effectively forecloses the possibility for most Lebanese.) In Burj Hammud, where the Shiʿa numbered as many as 80,000 by the early 1970s, only four or five hundred actually voted where they lived.[54] Khuri notes that, while only 17 percent of Lebanon's population remained rural after the migrations of the fifties, sixties, and seventies, these important demographic shifts remained unrecognized in the electoral law.

> A citizen, irrespective of where he was living or for how long, was required to return to his home-town to exercise the right to vote. Shifting voting rights from one constituency to another is a complicated procedure that requires a court decision. Had the electoral law been amended to give 17 percent of the parliamentary seats to the rural areas and 83 percent to the urban areas, the political structure of Lebanon would have been turned upside down. As it was, however, the electoral law helped to bind the voter to his village. . . .[55]

Like chickens being brought home to roost, urban dwellers were transported to their villages so that they could cast their vote for their patron, sometimes in anticipation of favors to be received and sometimes for cash payment. Touma al-Khouri provides a memorable literary picture of "The Election Bus[es]," used to return voters to their villages, in his short story: "It was the election season. Like eggs whipped up into a froth, the villages were in a turmoil of excited activity, their alleyways as busy as beehives. Buses rushed continually up and down in droves, transporting voters from towns and villages, from every farm, hamlet and homestead."[56]

Thus, the village followed the villagers into the city in both the social and the political realms, and the city never ceased to be closely linked to the village[57]—a state of affairs well illustrated by the vernacular query *Aslak min wein?* (Where are your roots?).

One result of the close linkage of the urban with the rural has been that the villages of southern Lebanon have been at least as important as Beirut's urban quarters and the surrounding poverty belt as a spawning ground for the political mobilization of the Shi'a. This may be mildly surprising, even taking into account the extraordinary security situation in the South, especially since some of the fundamental tenets of modernization writings claim an important relationship between urbanization and manifestations of increased political activity (i.e., participation).[58] In order to reconcile this apparent divergence between the empirical and the theoretical, it is pertinent to review some representative arguments on the meaning of urbanization for political development.

Urbanization

Daniel Lerner treats urbanization as the first phase of modernization and claims: "It is the transfer of population from scattered hinterlands to urban centers that stimulates the needs and provides the conditions for 'take off' toward widespread participation."[59] For Lerner, modern society "is distinctively industrial, urban, literate and *participant* [emphasis in original]."[60]

Karl Deutsch equates, in large part, the very process of change that transforms a society from traditional to modern ways of life with urbanization. Thus, as already noted, to measure social mobilization he proposes variables such as "changes in residence," "changes from agricultural occupation," and, specifically, "urbanization." As a society experiences greater social mobilization (hence, urbanization), we are told to expect an expansion of "the politically relevant strata of the population,"[61] which in turn leads to "increased political participation."[62] Finally, Huntington makes the point most directly: "Urbanization, increases in literacy, education, and media exposure all give enhanced aspirations and expectations which, if unsatisfied, galvanize individuals and groups into politics."[63]

Obviously, the object here is not to trivialize the work of other scholars, but to make an important theoretical point, as well as one with respect to Lebanon. The special meaning of urban residence for political participation has been lost in Lebanon, not necessarily because of faulty theorizing, but because for Lebanon the urban-rural distinction has lost much of its meaning.[64] In a country of 4,015 square miles, a country in which major urban centers can be reached

by road from even the most remote villages in three hours and usually much less, a country in which external migration (and return) is
a tradition, and in which brutal pulses of violence have propelled
cycles of internal migration, the vast preponderance of the population is psychically nonrural in outlook. What the Lebanese case
seems to suggest is that Iliya Harik is quite correct when he suggests
that the concepts "urban" and "rural" communities are less analytically useful in the context of political development than the
work of Deutsch and others suggests.[65] As Antoun and Harik note in
an important work on rural politics and social change, "We have seen
that characteristics of modernization, such as literacy, exposure to
mass media, political participation, rationalization of production
and administration, and higher living standards, may occur at the
village level as well as in urban communities."[66]

The Lebanese case is not unique. In his analysis of rural participation in the Iranian revolution, Eric Hooglund finds that young village
men who commuted to the cities for work were decidedly "urban" in
many of their activities and attitudes. (It is instructive that Hooglund is dealing with villages that lie within a forty- to fifty-kilometer
radius of large cities, whereas there is no village in Lebanon more
than sixty kilometers from Beirut, Sidon, Zahle, Tripoli, or Tyre.)
Hooglund's description could easily—save a few details—be applied
to Lebanon:

> Almost all have relatives living in cities, and their familiarity
> with urban life is as extensive as any native's. They exhibit a
> great interest in national developments, which are often topics of
> conversations in social gatherings. They certainly consider them-
> selves better informed than their fathers, and do not hesitate to
> make their views heard among village elders. Listening to the
> newscasts on radio is a pastime. During the revolution, many be-
> gan to read the newspapers regularly and most have continued
> this habit on an irregular basis. Throughout all of 1978 these
> young men were aware of political developments and by the end
> of the year had become as politicized as any other group.[67]

That it is difficult to be very precise with the limited data available for Lebanon is a major understatement; however, the data certainly do not contradict the impressions garnered in my own fieldwork; if anything, the data seem to underemphasize the level of the
politicization of the "rural" Shiᶜa in particular, and of the Lebanese
in general. For example, with respect to the extent of urbanization,
recent World Bank calculations show that 76 percent of Lebanon's

population is urban,[68] yet I argue that this figure underrepresents some aspects of urbanization and overrepresents others. If by urbanization we mean exposure to aspects of modernity, such as technology, media, consumer goods, monetary exchange, and education, then Lebanon is nearly completely urbanized, despite the attachment of the Lebanese to their mythical pristine villages. In point of fact, such villages are social history in Lebanon.[69] Isolated, bucolic villages are not merely uncommon in Lebanon, they are a rarity. As Harik has observed, "In many respects, Lebanon is one big suburb of Beirut."[70] For reasons that are well expounded by Khuri, the isolated village, safe in its customs and traditions and unaffected by the dynamics of modernity, is a vestige of dusty ethnographies. "Generally speaking, no community (village, suburb, or city) in Lebanon today has physical boundaries corresponding to its sociocultural limits, although this is a matter of degree. What emerges is a phenomenon in which social groups transcend territorial boundaries, a phenomenon more characteristic of suburban than city or village traditions."[71] Khuri's work, published in 1975, is even more relevant in light of the changes that have taken place since its publication.

Even the simple peasants—and the peasants that I have known are anything but simple—belie any image of isolated bumpkins blissfully ignorant of the larger world. While conservative in many social matters, the villagers evince a reasonably well developed understanding of what the world outside the village offers in both positive and negative terms. No doubt, this sort of argument might be made about villagers in locales outside of Lebanon, but in Lebanon several unique factors tend further to reduce the sociopolitical distance separating the urban from the rural sector. For example, circular migration patterns, in which sons go abroad to make their fortunes but return to their villages for regular visits and often to settle down for life, mitigate the insularity of the village. One estimate for 1983 is that 35 percent of the Lebanese work force is presently abroad, and 50 percent of the total work force has been abroad at one time or another over the past decade.[72] In one wealthy village, which I would argue is typical of its genre, the summer population is at least double the winter population. This is a result of Shiʿi merchants returning for their annual vacations from their businesses in Dakar and Abijan. Migrants returning home, whether permanently or not, bring with them new technologies, new ideas, and new styles, and by their very presence they symbolize the connection of the village to the external world.

Another factor leavening the urban-rural cleavage is education. In

1979, close to 100 percent of primary school age children actually attended school (the comparable figure for secondary school was 50 percent). These are rather remarkable figures considering the circumstances, and they reflect the widespread understanding in the country of the instrumental significance of education. Sons *and* daughters of illiterate and marginally literate peasants and shopkeepers are being educated. While the quality of the village elementary school may vary greatly—admittedly, some schools seem to be quite poor—it is clear that education is widely viewed as an essential precondition to making one's way in the world (i.e., outside the town or village). Under the most difficult security conditions of the late 1970s and early 1980s, children were still being educated. In this regard, it is noteworthy that education received more funding than any other item in the Lebanese state budgets for 1981 and 1982. (One of the reflections of the deadly deterioration that has occurred in Lebanon since 1982 is the fact that many children are no longer being sent to school because of the dangers, and many schools that operate do so only intermittently.)

Finally, the ever-present threat of violence plays an important role in reducing village insularity. One pays attention to the media for sound reasons of survival. Contacts with urban dwellers are not just casual or social, but are often the effect of population displacements incidental to war. For example, as a direct result of Operation Litani, Israel's 1978 invasion, south Lebanon's population fled almost en masse to Beirut and its suburbs. The flow was often reversed, as refugees from Beirut took shelter with relatives in the South and throughout Lebanon. Warfare disrupts the living, and it forces even "simple" villagers to acknowledge events far beyond the fields where they spend many of their days. The villagers may disdain politics, especially violent politics, but, even as they disdain, they are becoming politicized.

On the other hand, the urbanization figures for Lebanon do seem to overstate certain factors. Both in practice and by design, Lebanon's political system is not dominant at the center, but at the periphery.[73] The target for resource demands may be Beirut, but the locus of political participation is often in the village, where citizens vote, maintain familial relationships, and return in times of peril. While the city sometimes provides an alternative locus for political action, in Lebanon it tends to supplement rather than replace the village as the appropriate locus for political action. Thus, the suggestion "that rural-urban conditions be viewed as a continuum, not a dichotomy" seems to be especially apt for Lebanon.[74]

Political Participation

As we have seen, a long-standing reflection of the political under-development of the Shi'i community has been the persistence of patron-client ties between the *zu'ama* and the Shi'i peasantry. At election time, Shi'i voters—like many Lebanese—would typically cast their vote for their *za'im* or his designated candidate with little or no regard for political programs (which were generally scant at best anyway), ideology, or even the qualifications of the candidate. Participation in politics was mobilized rather than autonomous, and deferential as opposed to deriving from any sense of civic responsibility.[75] However, one important effect of the continuing modernization of the Shi'i community has been a significant loosening of the ties between the *za'im* and his clients. In his seminal essay on the *zu'ama*, Arnold Hottinger notes that real power was slipping out of the hands of the *zu'ama* as early as the beginning of the 1960s, largely as a result of the growth of the state bureaucracy that provided as services many of the political goods that the *zu'ama* dispensed as favors.[76] With widespread residential dislocation, shifts in the organization of the economy, and the deteriorating security situation in the South, the *za'im* found it steadily more difficult to meet the ever more complex needs and growing demands of his clients. (Unfortunately, the state has not been able to keep pace either.)

Political institutions are conditioned by tradition and culture, but they do not persist only because they are traditional. People participate in politics (and hence in political relationships) for instrumental purposes. As the utility of traditional clientship declined, and as the state proved incapable of redressing their demands, the Shi'a, like their fellow Lebanese, sought alternative means of overcoming socio-economic inequalities. Naturally, when people claim that they want a more effective political voice, they mean that they want to be heard, that they want to participate in shaping their destiny. The concern is not about political participation, it is about the instrumental objectives of participation. Many of the newly recruited Shi'is were rejecting a traditional political system that was deaf to their demands for security, education, health services, and employment.

By the 1960s, individual Shi'is were becoming ever more assertive in claiming their political voice. Secular parties such as the Lebanese Communist party (al-Hizb al-Shiyu'i) as well as a distinctively Shi'i movement were enjoying important recruitment successes. Youth, social, sports, and cultural clubs were springing up throughout the Shi'i areas. Government-licensed family associations, which provide welfare and benevolent services to members, as well as assistance in securing employment, were being organized at an unprecedented rate among the Shiʿa. Family associations are found in both rural and urban settings, and they duplicate many of the services typically provided by a *zaʿim*. Samir Khalaf reports that, although the Shiʿa only accounted for 12.8 percent of the family associations licensed during the 1930s (for a total of 5), they accounted for 47.2 percent (or 77 associations) by the 1960s.[77]

Civil War as a Crisis of Participation

A perennial concern of social scientists is the manner in which emerging social forces are best dealt with by the fragile governments that rule the states of the Third World, and much of the so-called developed world as well. Should these social forces be quashed, contained, controlled, accommodated, or some combination thereof?[78] We have, in recent times, witnessed the attempt to quash them in El Salvador and the Philippines, with uneven results at best. Samuel Huntington's counsel that they be contained is only too evident, and David Apter's prescription for what Green calls "pseudoparticipation" has failed in Ghana, Egypt, and, most recently, Pahlavi Iran.[79]

Indeed, there are no easy choices; however, in a state such as Lebanon where the very definition of the government is premised on the fixed distribution of political power, the choices are not only hard, they are also few. The causes of the civil strife in Lebanon are not solely internal, but to the extent that they are, they represent in part the demand that political power and state resources be reallocated. In no uncertain terms, what we have witnessed over the past decade in Lebanon is what Myron Weiner and his associates term a "participation crisis," and one of the major protagonists in the crisis has been the Shiʿa. "A participation crisis can be defined as a conflict that occurs when the governing elite views the demands or behavior of individuals and groups seeking to participate in the political system as illegitimate. . . . What distinguishes a participation crisis from other developmental crises is that the demand, whatever the specific content, also includes the right to share power."[80]

In effect, by the late 1960s, the Shiʿi community's social mobilization appeared to be overdetermined. While the Shiʿa still lagged behind other confessional groups on standard measures of socioeconomic status, evidence of keen socioeconomic change, and hence social mobilization, was clear. But, as we have seen, the translation of potential politicization into political action is dependent upon the availability of mobilization agents. As noted above, in his critique of Deutsch, David Cameron attacks "the traditional view of mobilization" that conceives political induction as passive and inevitable.[81] Cameron's emphasis on the "mobilizing agent" directs our attention to the means by which the socially mobilized are inducted into politics.[82] Extending Nie, Powell, and Prewitt's emphasis on organizations as mediators,[83] Cameron examines how a mobilizing agent or organization adapts its ideology to articulate and give meaning to local discontent and how it appropriates "to its own benefit the resources of local society by penetrating and adapting to its purposes the organization infrastructure already existing in society."[84]

A number of mobilizing agents, especially the Communist party and the Communist Action Organization (Munazzamat al-ʿAmal al-Shiyuʿi), competed in the early 1970s with a reform-oriented populist movement led by an Iranian-born cleric, the Imam Musa al-Sadr, for Shiʿi members. Referring to the 1970–1971 period, Walid Khalidi notes: "The Shiite phenomenon was best reflected in the deep penetration of Shiite areas by radical, and particularly the Marxist, political organizations. It was also reflected in the increasing militancy of Musa [al-]Sadr, the populist head of the Shiite religious hierarchy, against the regime."[85] To an extent that is not widely appreciated, the race to mobilize the Shiʿi community during the early 1970s was a race between secular creeds and a distinctly sectarian movement. This is not to say that there were not programmatic similarities, though. For both trends—secular and sectarian—the existing confessional system was anathema to the extent that it preserved the political control of the privileged at the expense of those denied equitable access to the political system. (There were significant divergent perspectives with respect to two issues: the role of religion and religious law and the choice of preferred external allies.)[86] By the end of the 1970s, the secular trend was in retreat.

Thus, Lebanon's governing elites—unwilling to accommodate the Shiʿi demands and unable to quash, contain, or control them—soon found that the newly politicized Shiʿa were readily recruited by a wide range of opposition parties and militias that offered the promise of social, political, and economic advancement, as well as the accoutrements of enhanced status—namely, money and guns, not to mention the opportunity to strike against the symbols of the governing elites.

Only since the late 1960s have the political horizons of the Shiʿa begun to encompass the state as such. Until then, the Shiʿa resided on the margins of the polity, and for most of their modern history the "Lebanese Shiʿi community" was something of a misnomer, given the community's fragmentation and its domination by six powerful families. With the modernization of the Shiʿi community, the control of the Shiʿi *zuʿama* has been seriously challenged and decisively supplanted by a number of militias and political parties. The most successful challenge has been mounted by an essentially populist political movement of protest and reform, a movement that has demanded that the Shiʿa be provided the most basic human rights: sanctity of hearth and well-being of kith and kin, as well as equal rights as Lebanese citizens. It is to emergence of that organization, Harakat Amal, that we now turn.

3. The Political Mobilization of the Shi⁽ᶜ⁾a

Notwithstanding—indeed, in spite of—their social, political, and economic underdevelopment, the Shi⁽ᶜ⁾a of Lebanon were not isolated from the processes of profound change that were affecting Lebanon as a whole by the early 1960s. As noted in chapter 2, sectoral shifts in the economy pushed peasants away from labor-intensive farming into low-paying jobs in the services sector in the Beirut suburbs or into unemployment. While infrastructure—roads, wells, telephone lines, and electrification—remained only poorly developed in the regions where the Shi⁽ᶜ⁾a predominate, transportation between the village and the city became more accessible. The media, especially radio but also newspapers, reached an increasing number of previously remote locales. While their schools continued to be inferior in quality and number to those available to other Lebanese, education, especially at the elementary level, became more readily available. Shops opened in villages that had never known them before. Men who would previously have followed the footsteps of peasant fathers migrated to Beirut or abroad. The Shi⁽ᶜ⁾a, like their compatriots, were caught in the throes of change. They were being torn away from familiar settings and associations, and as this was happening the strains on the traditional political system increased sharply. In short, by the 1960s, ever larger numbers of Shi⁽ᶜ⁾is became potential recruits for political movements (mobilization agents) that could translate their inchoate politicization into political action. While largely unnoticed outside of Lebanon, the Shi⁽ᶜ⁾a were beginning a political awakening that would play an important role in shaping the destiny of Lebanon in the 1970s and 1980s.

In point of fact, the effects of change in Lebanon were first felt at the leadership level. As Michael Hudson notes in his seminal 1968 book *The Precarious Republic*, one of the most interesting develop-

ments of the post—World War II period was the gradual modernization of the Shiʿi political leadership.[1] Nonetheless, there was nothing deterministic about the direction that the awakening would
follow. Given the absence of a well-developed movement or party
that could appeal broadly to the community, it is hardly surprising
that the Shiʿa lent their numbers to a wide variety of political organizations. For people long under the heavy thumbs of the *zuʿama*, who
controlled land, wealth, and access to the political system, the appeal of party slogans pledging equality, improvement in social and
health services, and better conditions of employment and housing
was obvious. Thus, quite a large number of Shiʿis joined the Lebanese Communist party and other antiestablishment organizations
such as the Communist Action Organization (Munazzamat al-ʿAmal
al-Shiyuʿi).

Moreover, the secular, antiestablishment parties based in Lebanon
did not have the field to themselves. Many Shiʿis, impressed by the
similarities between their plight and that of the Palestinian refugees,
joined various *fidaʾi* organizations, as well as parties that were closely
affiliated with the Palestinian resistance. Sizable numbers of Shiʿis
joined the Arab Liberation Front and the Popular Front for the Liberation of Palestine, as well as the Arab Nationalist Movement and
the pro-Iraqi and pro-Syrian branches of the Baʿth party. But it should
be noted that not all members were motivated by political principles—many joined organizations-cum-militias simply to win a
salary. (By the late 1970s, it was probably impossible to find a Shiʿi
village or quarter where stories about unemployed *shabab*—young
bloods—departing one day to join a militia and returning a few
weeks later sporting a Kalashnikov rifle and/or pistol and a wad of
Lebanese lira were not told.) No single party was overwhelmingly
successful in the recruitment of Shiʿi members, and, in retrospect, it
is the relatively broad ideological spectrum covered by the organizations that seems noteworthy.

Juxtaposed to the secular parties and the *fidaʾi* groups was a distinctively Shiʿi sectarian movement led by a cleric, al-Sayyid Musa
al-Sadr (who came to be known to his followers as Imam Musa). This
movement, known today as Amal, was only in its incipient stage in
the early 1960s, yet it has, in large measure, come to dominate Shiʿi
politics in present-day Lebanon. Through a combination of good for-
tune and astute leadership, it has submerged many of its competitors. While the founder of Amal has not been heard from since he
disappeared during a 1978 visit to Libya, al-Sadr's formative influence is irrefutable. For that reason, it is important to consider the
career of this "giant" (as he is often characterized by his followers).

Imam Musa and the Mobilization of the Shi'a

Musa al-Sadr was born in Qum, Iran, in 1928, the son of an important religious leader, Ayatollah Sadr al-Din al-Sadr. He attended secondary and primary school in Qum and college at the Tehran Faculty
of Law and Political Economy. He did not intend to become a cleric,
planning to pursue a secular career. It was only upon the urging of
his father, who feared for the preservation of Iran's Shi'i institutions,
that he discarded his secular ambitions and pursued an education in
Islamic jurisprudence (*fiqh*). Initially he studied in a Qum *madrasa*
(religious school), and while still in Qum he edited a magazine,
Makatib Islami (Schools of Islam), which is still published in Iran.
One year after his father's death in 1953, he moved to Najaf, Iraq,
where he studied *fiqh* under the Marja' al-Kabir Muhsin al-Hakim.

He first visited Lebanon, which he claimed as his ancestral home,
in 1957 (his great-great-grandfather reportedly had fled Lebanon for
Najaf). During this visit he made a very strong and positive impression on his co-religionists in Lebanon. Following the death in 1958 of
the Shi'i religious leader of the southern coastal city of Tyre, al-Sayyid
'Abd al-Husain Sharaf al-Din, he was invited by the Shi'i community of south Lebanon to replace the deceased mufti (chief expounder
of religious law). In late 1959 or early 1960, he moved to Tyre, with
the active encouragement and support of his teacher and mentor,
Muhsin al-Hakim. One of his first significant acts was the establishment of a vocational institute in the southern town of Burj al-
Shimali, which was constructed at a cost of half a million Lebanese
pounds (c. $165,000 U.S.) with monies provided by Shi'i benefactors,
the Ministry of Education, and bank loans. The institute would become an important symbol of his leadership; it is still in operation,
providing vocational training for about 500 orphans under the watch-
ful eyes of Musa's sister, Rahab al-Sadr.

A physically imposing man of intelligence, courage, personal
charm, and enormous energy—one of his former assistants claims
that he frequently worked twenty hours a day—al-Sadr attracted
a wide array of supporters, ranging from Shi'i merchants making
their fortunes in West Africa to petit-bourgeois youth. Musa al-Sadr
set out to establish himself as the paramount leader of the Shi'i
community, and his arrival could not have been more timely. He did
not single-handedly stimulate the community's political consciousness, but he capitalized on the budding politicization of the Shi'a,
invigorating and rationalizing it.[2] At the time of his arrival, there
were a number of indicators of incipient political organization, including a remarkable expansion in family associations, small politi-

cal discussion groups, and other social organizations of portentous significance.[3]

What Musa al-Sadr did bring to Lebanon, in addition to his other considerable attributes, was the ability to stand above a fragmented and victimized community and see it as a whole.[4] For an Iranian, Lebanon is a country of modest size indeed. While the Lebanese might speak of "distant" Lebanese towns as if they were foreign countries, al-Sadr was unimpressed by the minuscule distances that separated the South from the Biqa' Valley and Beirut. Despite the sometimes palpable sociological differences among the slum dwellers of Beirut, the peasants of the South, and the clansmen of the Biqa', he succeeded in giving many Shi'is an inclusive communal identity.[5] Furthermore, he reminded his followers that their deprivation was not to be fatalistically accepted, for, so long as they could speak out through their religion, they could overcome their condition. As he once observed, "whenever the poor involve themselves in a social revolution it is a confirmation that injustice is not predestined."[6]

He arrived in Lebanon as a Persian, but he was soon accepted—legally and emotively—as a Lebanese (President Chehab bestowed Lebanese citizenship on him in 1963). Karim Pakradouni notes that upon arrival he "murdered the Arabic language," but by 1975, although he still retained a Persian accent, he spoke the language with an elegance that matched his personal grooming and demeanor.[7] He well understood the affective potential of religion and its symbols. He shrewdly recognized that his power lay in part in his role as a custodian of symbols, and he exploited his custodianship to good effect. His fiery speeches at mass gatherings and rallies were sprinkled generously with allusions to the central symbols of Shi'ism. Addressing the 'Amiliyya College on the commemoration of 'Ashura in 1974, he characteristically placed his movement in apposition to the martyrdom of Imam Husain at Karbala.

> In fact, a great sacrifice was needed to shake consciences and stir feelings. The event of Karbala was that sacrifice. . . . Imam Hussain put his family, his force, and even his life, in the balance over against tyranny and corruption. Then the Islamic world burst forth with this unprecedented act of his, this revolution.
>
> This revolution did not die in the sands of Karbala, it flowed into the life stream of the Islamic world, and passed from generation to generation, even to our day. It is a deposit placed in our hands so that we may profit from it, that we draw out from it as from a source a new reform, a new position, a new movement, a new revolution to repel the darkness, to stop tyranny, and to pulverize evil.

Brothers, line up in the row of your choice: that of tyranny or that of Hussain. I am certain that you will not choose anything but the row of revolution and martyrdom for the realization of justice and the destruction of tyranny.[8]

Under Imam Musa's considerable influence, religious commemorations became vehicles for building communal solidarity and political consciousness. In villages with no memory of public commemoration of ʿAshura, or other significant events on the Shiʿi calendar, Imam Musa's appearances often spawned their inception. Most important, he placed Shiʿi demands in a culturally authentic context that bred support for the movement he led.

Above all else, he was a pragmatist, as one of his close associates never tired of reminding me. The record of his political alliances certainly betrays a deep-seated pragmatism. It is both a tribute to his political skill and a commentary on his tactics that several well-informed Lebanese should have commented that nobody knew where the imam stood. At one point, for instance, he backed Fatah against al-Saʿiqa (the guerrilla organization created by his Syrian ally), leading one Syrian official to note: "We suddenly realized that our friend and ally, Imam Musa, was a check that bounced."[9]

His followers today often characterize him as a vociferous critic of the shah, but it was only after the October War of 1973 that his relations with the shah deteriorated seriously. In the fall of 1973, he became a vehement critic of the shah, accusing him of suppressing religion in Iran, denouncing him for his pro-Israel stance, and describing him as an "imperialist stooge." However, for more than a decade he had maintained close, even cordial ties with the Pahlavi regime, and, during his visits to Tehran in the 1960s and early 1970s, he was warmly received. Shahpur Bakhtiar goes so far as to claim that he was dispatched to Lebanon by the shah in furtherance of a scheme to create a pan-Shiʿi union encompassing Iran, Iraq, and Lebanon.[10] There is no convincing evidence to support the latter assertion, but there seems little doubt that the shah did provide significant funding to support Imam Musa's efforts in Lebanon (some believe that the source of their falling out was monetary rather than moral or political). Whatever the source or sources of the relationship's failure, it is patent that Imam Musa was not averse to hedging his bets. Thus, as his relations with Iran deteriorated after 1973, he improved his relations with Iraq, from which he may have received significant funding in early 1974.

Like the Maronites, the Shiʿa are a minority in a predominantly Sunni Arab world; for both sects, Lebanon is a refuge in which sectarian identity can be preserved and security ensured. It is not surprising that many Maronites saw a natural ally in Imam Musa, especially before he organized his own militia in 1974. Imam Musa was a reformer, not a revolutionary. He sought the betterment of the Shiʿa in a Lebanese context. He often noted, "For us Lebanon is one definitive homeland." Despite his appreciation of the dramatic demographic shifts that had made the Shiʿi community the largest plurality in Lebanon, he declined to call for a new census. Musa al-Sadr recognized the insecurity of the Maronites, and he acknowledged their need to maintain their monopoly hold on the presidency. Yet he was critical of the Maronites for their arrogant stance toward the Muslims, and particularly toward the Shiʿa. He argued that Lebanon's Maronite-dominated governments had neglected the South since independence and had rendered the Shiʿa a "disinherited subproletariat in Lebanon."[11]

Imam Musa was anti-Communist. As two scholars writing in 1974 observe, "according to him, Marxism's negation of God is not so much in its open atheism, as in its effacing the individual and denying his freedoms. His position may be summarized in two sentences he often repeats: 'we are neither of the right nor of the left, but we follow the path of the just (al-sirat al-mustaqim)' and Quranic verse: 'He who sleeps while having a needy neighbour is not considered a believer.'"[12] After the bloody fighting of 1975 and 1976, he accused the Communists of exploiting sectarianism in Lebanon, and of hypocritically warning that "Islam is in danger" in order to mobilize support.[13] But one suspects that his opposition to the Communists was not only on principled grounds; the various Communist organizations were among his prime competitors for Shiʿi recruits.

While the two branches of the Baʿth party (pro-Iraqi and pro-Syrian) were making significant inroads among the Shiʿis of the South and the Beirut suburbs, he sometimes appropriated their pan-Arab slogans. Although the movement he founded, Harakat al-Mahrumin (Movement of the Deprived), was aligned with the Lebanese National Movement (LNM) in the early stages of the Lebanese civil war that began in 1975, he found its Druze leader, Kamal al-Jumblatt, irresponsible and exploitative of the Shiʿa. As he put it to Pakradouni, the National Movement was willing "to combat the Christians to the last Shiʿi." He imputed to Jumblatt the prolongation of the war: "Without him, the war in Lebanon would have been terminated in two months. Because of him, it has been prolonged two years and only God knows how long the encore will last."[14]

It was hardly consistent with his political stance that he should have deserted the LNM in May 1976, when Syria intervened in Lebanon on the side of the Maronite militias and against the LNM and its *fidaʾi* allies. But despite the fact that he was a friend and confidant of Syrian President Hafiz al-Asad, he mistrusted Syrian motives in Lebanon. It was, in Imam Musa's view, only the indigestibility of Lebanon that protected it from being cut up by Syria. Nonetheless, the Syrians were an essential card in his very serious and deadly game with the Palestinian resistance.

He claimed to support the Palestine resistance movement, but his relations with the PLO were tense and uneasy at best. During the 1973 clashes between the *fidaʾiyin* and the Lebanese army, Imam Musa reproached the Sunni Muslims for their chorus of support for the guerrillas. On the one hand, he chastised the government for failing to defend the South from Israeli aggression; but on the other, he criticized the PLO for shelling Israel from the South and hence provoking Israeli retaliation. As he later noted, speaking retrospectively: "The problem was not one of *fidaʾiyin* infiltration but of launching rockets and grenades against Israel across the South. This is something that is totally impermissible. The launching of rockets and grenades is not at all a revolutionary *fidaʾiyin* action. This also means that Lebanon is in a state of war with Israel. Who is opening the fire? This is not important. The gist of the matter is that the Lebanese territory became a base for launching missiles and grenades."[15] He consistently expressed sympathy for Palestinian aspirations, but he was unwilling to countenance actions that exposed Lebanese citizens, and especially Shiʿi citizens of the South, to additional suffering. Given the chronic weakness of the Lebanese army and its relative inferiority in arms and numbers to the IDF (Israel Defence Forces), it could only be inevitable that Musa al-Sadr would demand restraint from the PLO and hence emerge as its adversary.[16]

After the 1970 PLO defeat in Jordan, the bulk of the PLO fighters relocated to south Lebanon, where they proceeded to supplant the legitimate authorities. Imam Musa prophetically warned the PLO that it was not in its interests to establish a state within a state in Lebanon.[17] It was the organization's failure to heed this warning that helped to spawn the sharp eventual alienation of their "natural allies"—the Shiʿis—who actively resisted the *fidaʾiyin* in their midst only a few years later. He is reported—reliably I believe—to have stated that "the PLO is a factor of anarchy in the South. The Shiʿa are conquering their inferiority complex with respect to the Palestinian organizations. We have had enough!"[18] In private, he challenged the revolutionary bona fides of the Palestinians. He argued that they lacked a sense of martyrdom and that above all else the PLO was a military machine that terrorizes the Arab world, extorting money and mercy and the sympathy of world opinion. For their part, some PLO officials believed that Musa al-Sadr was a creation of the Deuxième Bureau (the Army Second—or intelligence—Bureau).[19]

But his unremitting opponent was Kamil al-Asʿad, the powerful *zaʿim* from the South—thrice Speaker of the National Assembly (most recently from 1968 to 1984)—who quite accurately viewed al-Sayyid Musa al-Sadr (he stubbornly refused to say "imam") as a threat to his political base. Al-Asʿad saw himself—correctly it seems—as Imam Musa's singular target.[20] For Imam Musa and his followers, Kamil Bey epitomized all that was wrong with Lebanon's political system; while al-Sadr seldom criticized anyone by name, the target for his barbs was often all too clear. In his view, Kamil al-Asʿad was a political feudalist, a man whose political power stemmed from his skillful manipulation of confessional politics much to the detriment of the Shiʿi masses—and al-Asʿad was also a formidable competitor. The early 1970s was a period of serious jockeying for power between the two protagonists, and one of the prime arenas for the contest was the Supreme Shiʿi Council (al-Majlis al-Islami al-Shiʿi al-Aʿla).

In 1967, the National Assembly passed a law (no. 72/67)—with all but one of the nineteen Shiʿi deputies voting in favor—establishing a Supreme Shiʿi Council, which would for the first time provide a representative body for the Shiʿa independent of the Sunni Muslims. Until the founding of the Supreme Shiʿi Council, there was no position occupied by a Shiʿi that rivaled the Speaker of the National Assembly in terms of visibility and political influence. The Jaʿfari Tribunal, which handled matters of Shiʿi personal status law, was prestigious, but, by definition, clerical in personality and peripheral to politics (although the president of the Tribunal, Husain al-Khatib, did challenge al-Sadr for the chairmanship of the Supreme Shiʿi Council). The establishment of the council, with a mandate to articulate growing Shiʿi demands within the political system, introduced a new calculus into the distribution of political power.

The council actually came into existence on May 18, 1969, with Imam Musa as its elected chairman for a six-year term—a stunning confirmation of his status as the leading Shiʿi cleric in the country and certainly one of the most important political figures in the Shiʿi community. The council quickly made itself heard with demands in the military, social, economic, and political realms, including improved measures for the defense of the South, the provision of development funds, construction and improvement of schools and hospitals, and an increase in the number of Shiʿis appointed to senior government positions.

Imam Musa made good use of his new position. In the spring of 1970, after a particularly harsh retaliatory raid by Israel into south Lebanon, he organized a general strike to protest "the negligence and disregard shown towards the problems of south Lebanon, the dangers that threaten it, and the catastrophe to which it is exposed,"[21] and "to dramatize to the government the plight of the population of southern Lebanon vis-à-vis the Israeli military threat."[22] Al-Sadr denigrated the government for acting as a benevolent society and relief agency, only coming to the aid of its citizens after the fact with "Red Cross tents" rather than maintaining appropriate security within the country's borders. One week after the strike, and in response to it, the government created the Majlis al-Janub (Council of the South) which was capitalized at 30 million Lebanese pounds and was chartered to support the development of the region. Unfortunately, the Majlis al-Janub quickly became more famous for being a locus of corruption than for being the origin of beneficial projects.[23] The creation of the council was a victory for al-Sadr, but it was the formidable Kamil al-Asʿad who subsequently dominated its operation. As one observer reported, "certain people insist that to be helped by the Council of the South, one must hang Kamil al-Asʿad's picture in the house."[24]

The seesaw battle between al-Asʿad and al-Sadr for political influence and authority did not abate, but was vigorously pursued by both men throughout the early and mid-1970s. Of the nineteen deputies in the National Assembly, six maintained their support for the speaker, and hence for the political status quo, while thirteen adopted positions that were at least complementary to the position espoused by Imam Musa. On June 22, 1973, the thirteen signed an agreement in which they pledged to work to obtain the full rights of the Shiʿi community.[25] (The Shiʿi demands, which are discussed in the following chapter, were presented to the prime minister, Taqi al-Din al-Sulh, in July 1973.) By the end of 1973, tensions between the two sides had risen appreciably, in part over a pending change in the Supreme Shiʿi Council bylaws that would extend the term of the chairman from six years to his sixty-fifth birthday, thus more or less ensuring that al-Asʿad's bête noire would maintain his political vantage point. Al-Asʿad attempted to block the change, but, by November 1974, the council denied the National Assembly's (ergo, the Speaker's) jurisdiction over the matter and approved the change. In the intervening period, al-Asʿad's partisans in the National Assembly sharply criticized al-Sadr; in March 1974, henchmen of the Speaker physically attacked Deputy Husain al-Husaini, an important ally of al-Sadr, in the Assembly chamber. The next month, the Jaʿfari Mufti al-

Mumtaz, Shaikh ʿAbd al-Amir Qabalan, was assaulted in a southern mosque, purportedly by al-Asʿad's supporters.

One would have to say that al-Sadr won more of the battles with his foe than he lost, as in December 1974, when a by-election for a single Assembly seat was held in Nabatiya. The candidate backed by the imam, Rafiq Shahin, beat al-Asʿad's man by a two-to-one margin in a contest that was widely seen as a test of Imam Musa's popularity. But Kamil al-Asʿad was not without victories. Most significantly, he had wrested control of the Majlis al-Janub from al-Sadr, and he maintained his considerable influence over governmental functions, especially bureaucratic appointments—a most important fief.

From Reform to Rage

With the influx of thousands of *fidaʾiyin* in 1970 and 1971, following the bloody conflict in Jordan, the existing social and economic problems of the Shiʿa were compounded by a rapidly deteriorating security environment in the South. Although the army made a few attempts to control the Palestinian militants, it soon became clear that the political and social divisions among the Lebanese precluded any decisive measures to bring them under control. Thus, the Cairo Agreement of 1969, which was to limit the guerrillas' activities in and from Lebanon, served instead to license the establishment of a rump state. Clubs were quickly becoming trump, and while the Supreme Shiʿi Council served as a useful vehicle for the promotion of the community's interests (as mediated by Musa al-Sadr, of course), it was ineffectual in a milieu that was quickly becoming dominated by militias and extralegal parties.

With the Lebanese government unable to protect its citizens, al-Sadr began to make armed struggle one of the motifs of his campaign to represent and mobilize the Shiʿa. Following the 1973 October War, he declared that there was no "alternative for us except revolution and weapons."[26] In a February 1974 speech in the Biqaʿ Valley town of Bidnayil, he angrily declared:

> We do not want to clash with the regime, with those who neglect us. Today, we shout out loud the wrongs against us, that cloud of injustice that has followed us since the beginning of our history. Starting from today we will no longer complain nor cry. Our name is not *mitwali* [a name for the Shiʿa that has taken on a derogatory connotation]; our name is "men of refusal" (*rafidun*), "men of vengeance," "men who revolt against all tyranny" (*kharijun*),

even though this costs us our blood and our lives. Husain faced the enemy with 70 men; the enemy was very numerous. Today we are more than 70, and our enemy is not the quarter of the whole world. . . .

We do not want sentiments, but action. We are tired of words, feelings, speeches. . . . I have made more speeches than anyone else. And I am the one who most often called for calm. . . . From today on I will not keep silent. If you keep quiet, I will not . . . We want our full rights completely. Not only our posts, but the twenty demands [discussed in chapter 4] in the petition, and we will accept nothing else in exchange.[27]

Without a doubt, Imam Musa's most famous speech was delivered in the Biqaʿ Valley city of Baʿalbak, on March 17, 1974, before a crowd that an *al-Nahar* correspondent estimated at 75,000. Standing before his supporters, many of whom were armed, he castigated the government for failing to meet the most basic needs of its people. He noted that Baʿalbak, a city of 10,000, still only had one government school, which dated to the period of the French Mandate. School, he noted, is the beginning of the [life's] path, and "what kind of government is it when it puts an obstruction in the groundwork of the path?"[28] He assailed the government for being "niggardly" in its development and conservation of water resources. He recalled that thousands of Lebanese in the South and the North were deprived of national identity cards, and hence access to government services (not to mention the ballot box). He excoriated the army for not protecting the citizenry of the South. Declaring that "arms are an adornment of men," he asked all those in attendance to join in a vow to seize their rights or face martyrdom in the attempt. As several of al-Sadr's very closest advisers have told me, the imam felt that he no longer had a choice. Government neglect was patent, the Communists and the Baʿthis were tapping the frustration and anger of the Shiʿi community, and his earlier, more restrained efforts had borne little palpable success. The situation of the moment was well captured by his rhetorical query: "What does the government expect, what does it expect except rage and revolution?"[29]

It was at the March rally that Imam Musa launched his popular mass movement, Harakat al-Mahrumin (Movement of the Deprived). With his movement he vowed to struggle relentlessly until the security needs and the social grievances of the deprived—in practice the Shiʿa—were satisfactorily addressed by the government. As the prominent Lebanese historian Kamal Salibi recounts: "He even warned that he would soon have his followers attack and occupy the palaces and mansions of the powerful if the grievances of the poor and oppressed were left unheeded."[30]

Just one year later, al-Sadr's efforts were overtaken by the onset of civil war in Lebanon. By July 1975, it became known that a militia adjunct to Harakat al-Mahrumin had been formed.[31] The militia, Afwaj al-Muqawama al-Lubnaniya (Lebanese Resistance Detachments), better known by its acronym AMAL (which also means "hope"), was initially trained by Fatah and played a minor role in the fighting of 1975 and 1976. Overshadowed by the military might of his many competitors among the militias of the left, and somewhat discredited for his alleged duplicity in the August 1976 fall of a *fidaʾi*-held quarter of Beirut, known as Nabʿa, to the Kataʾib,[32] al-Sadr retreated to the South with a coterie of dedicated followers. While he remained active, speaking and otherwise buttressing his following, as well as traveling throughout the Middle East, his national reputation and his popularity waned substantially between 1976 and 1978. (There are reports that he played an important role during this two-year period arousing opposition to the shah among Iran's Shiʿa, but the specific nature of such activities is still somewhat obscure.)

As we have already noted, Harakat al-Mahrumin and its militia, Amal, were affiliated with the LNM and its *fidaʾiyin* allies during the first year of the civil war, but al-Sadr broke with his erstwhile allies when the Syrians intervened in June 1976 to prevent the defeat of the Maronite-dominated Lebanese Front. Four months before the Syrian intervention, President Sulaiman Franjiya accepted a "Constitutional Document" that Imam Musa indicated was a satisfactory basis for implementing political reform. The document—which called for an increase in the proportion of parliamentary seats allocated to the Muslims, as well as some restrictions on the prerogatives of the Maronite president—seemed to offer a basis for restoring civility to Lebanon. When combined with the prospect that the Syrian intervention would bring the PLO under control, there appeared to be genuine prospects for a new beginning. However, the opportunity to stop the carnage was more apparent than real. While the pace of fighting had decreased by the end of 1976, the violence continued, and reform—constitutional or otherwise—remained a distant prospect.

Musa al-Sadr's ability to mobilize his co-religionists prior to the civil war was certainly a bellwether of the increased politicization of the Shiʿa; however, it bears repetition that Imam Musa only led a fraction of his politically affiliated co-religionists. It was the multiconfessional parties and militias that attracted the majority of Shi'i recruits, and many more Shi'is carried arms under their colors than under the banner of Amal. And in war, as in peace, the Shi'is suffered disproportionately; by a large measure, they incurred more casualties during the civil war than any other sect in Lebanon. Perhaps the single most important success achieved by Musa al-Sadr was the reduction of the authority and the influence of the traditional elites, the *zu'ama*, but it was the civil war, and the associated growth of extralegal organizations, that conclusively rendered these political personalities anachronistic, if not irrelevant in the Lebanese political system.

Whatever he may have been, despite his occasionally vehement histrionics, the imam was hardly a man of war. Indeed, he once confided to an associate that he had never heard a shot fired in anger before he arrived in Lebanon. His weapons were words and symbols, and as a result his political efforts were short-circuited by the din of war. He seemed to be eclipsed by the violence that engulfed Lebanon. Ironically, it was his disappearance in 1978 that helped to retrieve the promise of his earlier efforts.

The Revitalization of Amal

Three events transpired in the ten-month period from March 1978 to January 1979 that accelerated the mobilization of the Shi'i community and contributed to the consolidation of the political influence of the Shi'a in a revitalized Amal (the name Harakat al-Mahrumin having fallen into disuse). In March 1978, Israel launched its first major invasion of Lebanon, Operation Litani; in August 1978, the Imam Musa al-Sadr disappeared during a still enigmatic visit to Libya; and, in January 1979, the Islamic Revolution in Iran toppled the shah. It was these three events that resuscitated Amal and enabled it to play an unprecedented—if possibly transient—role in Lebanese politics.

Operation Litani

The 1978 invasion by Israel, which claimed about 1,000 (mostly Shi'i) lives and destroyed a significant number of homes throughout south Lebanon, not only demonstrated the heavy human costs that the Israelis would exact from the residents of the South as a result of the armed *fida'i* presence, but also signaled the onset of an accelerated Israeli campaign aimed at alienating the Lebanese Shi'a from the Palestinians in their midst. After Operation Litani, the IDF moved far beyond all but the slimmest pretense of retaliation. Instead, Israel sought to keep the PLO (and its supporters) constantly on the defensive with a relentless series of air attacks, raids, kidnappings, and house bombings. Helped by the callous, arrogant, and shortsighted behavior of the *fidaʾiyin*, the Israeli campaign was a tremendous success. The IDF's guiding principle was confirmed by chief of staff General Rafael Eytan, when he declared: "We will continue to take action where we want, when we want and how we want. Our own self-interest is supreme and will guide us in our actions not to allow terrorists [i.e., the *fidaʾiyin*] to return to the border fence."[33]

A significant consequence of the IDF's offensive was that the residents of the South were constantly reminded that a continuing Palestinian presence in the region would preclude any surcease to the Israeli campaign. Villagers, particularly those living in areas adjacent to the border strip controlled by Israel through its ally and puppet, Saʿad Haddad, lived in fear of nighttime raids carried out against those who sympathized with the Palestinians or who were suspected of being members of Lebanese groups hostile to Israel or Haddad. Indeed, such raids sometimes cut a wide swath, as villagers found that by denouncing their adversaries they could enjoy the nectar of revenge and settle old feuds; more than a few political innocents suffered the unwitting IDF's heavy hand. In a typical raid, carried out in December 1980, Israelis, accompanied by Lebanese cohorts, attacked five southern villages, killing three in the village of Braʿshit in cold blood, wounding ten, and damaging or destroying fourteen houses.[34] Such raids had several important effects. First, in those areas where the Israelis and their agents moved with ease, activists affiliated with the LNM or the PLO either left or kept a very low profile, and as a result their recruitment suffered. Thus, the field was increasingly open to Amal, which the Israelis discovered early as a tacit ally. Second, heretofore apolitical villagers learned that the best protection against unwanted early morning visitors was affiliation with a movement (Amal) that would prevent "undesirables" from entering their villages.

In a number of towns and villages, local residents even established their own local security forces, which would patrol during the hours of darkness. Over time, these ad hoc militia groups tended to affiliate, or at least identify, with Amal. Third, the net result of the campaign was a clear and widening gulf between the Palestine resistance movement and the villagers of the South. A similar estrangement was developing simultaneously in the Shiʿi quarters of Beirut, where the guerrillas and their allies were fast wearing out their welcome.

By the late 1970s, it was commonplace, when visiting Shi'i villages, to hear all manner of vignettes in which Palestinians were
the villains and Lebanese the victims. Even the simplest peasants
adopted anti-Palestinian slogans. Rather than casting blame on the
Israelis—as had been the case in the past—the cause of the villagers'
plight was often said to be the Palestinian presence. More than a few
times I heard humble people in meager surroundings mutter "the
basis of the problem is the *fida'iyin*," whereas ten years earlier they
would have proclaimed "the basis of the problem is Palestine." This
alienation represented an important and easily understood success
for the Israeli security apparatus. However, it should be noted that it
was the intensity of the Shi'i villagers' feelings that was remarkable
rather than their originality. In fact, the roots of the villagers' disen-
chantment may be traced to the early 1970s, when some of the Shi'a
rallied in support of the Lebanese army after clashes between the
army and the *fida'iyin*.[35]

As the conflict in Lebanon progressed, the Shi'a were increasingly
isolated as a community. In the early stages of the civil war, the Shi'a
provided the cannon fodder for most of the groups aligned with the
PLO. Indeed, as a dispossessed people they were often and aptly described as the natural allies of the Palestinians. However, they increasingly became the communal victims of the Palestinian-Israeli
war for Palestine-Israel. In a mean dialectical process, the Shi'a found
themselves targeted by the Israelis for their geographic propinquity
to the *fida'iyin* and viewed with increasing contempt and suspicion
by the *fida'iyin*, from whom they attempted to distance themselves.
It needs to be stressed that Israel's campaign would not have been
nearly as successful had it not been enhanced by the unpopularity of
the *fida'iyin*.[36] The IDF's intensive campaign, beginning in 1978,
served to bring the latent contradictions and tensions to the surface,[37] and the resultant alienation of the Shi'a from the Palestinian
resistance served as a fertile context for the growth of an organization, Amal, that promised to fill a most basic need, security.

In large part spurred by the desire to protect their families, homes,
and villages, many Shi'is either joined Amal or actively supported it.
By 1980 and 1981, important clashes were taking place between
Amal on one side, and the *fida'iyin* and their Lebanese allies on the
other. Fatah officials struggled unsuccessfully and sometimes disingenuously to arrange a rapprochement between Amal and its most
visceral foes (such as the Iraqi-sponsored Arab Liberation Front and
the Libyan-funded Arab Socialist Union), but the imperatives of the
Shi'a and the *fida'iyin* were almost diametrically opposed. By the

spring of 1982, after particularly heavy fighting between the Palestinians and Amal, many Shiʿis were expecting a Shiʿa-*fidaʾiyin* war to erupt at any moment.[38]

The Disappearance of Musa al-Sadr

The second development that helped to reawaken the dormant Amal movement was the disappearance of its leader, the Imam Musa al-Sadr. After arriving in Libya on August 25, 1978, Imam Musa vanished under circumstances that remain mysterious. Most Amal leaders believe that Libyan leader Muʿamar al-Qadhdhafi is responsible for his fate. Such suspicions have not evaporated, as a chain of anti-Libyan skyjackings, kidnappings, and sundry other attacks on Libyan officials and facilities attest.[39]

Accompanied by two associates, Shaikh Muhammad Shahadih Yaʿqub and Shafi ʿAbbas Badr al-Din, Musa al-Sadr had arrived in Libya on August 25, 1978, for a visit of unspecified length and purpose. One of Imam Musa's close associates has indicated that the visit was in response to an invitation from al-Qadhdhafi, which al-Sadr accepted so that he could "advocate the return of peace to Lebanon and to work for peace."[40] Prior to his arrival in Libya, al-Sadr had visited Saudi Arabia, Kuwait, and Algeria, ostensibly for the same purposes.

According to a sympathetic account, the imam decided to leave Libya on August 31, 1978, the eve of the Libyan national holiday commemorating the September 1, 1970, revolution. During the visit, al-Sadr was met by the chief of the Libyan Foreign Relations Office, al-Sayyid Ahmad al-Shahati, and, presumably, al-Qadhdhafi. Libya's mercurial leader claims that Musa al-Sadr and his companions left Libya on an Alitalia flight bound for Rome, but his followers deny this and claim that he never left Libya. Their denial was borne out by an official Italian inquiry.[41] One senior associate, who told me he urged al-Sadr not to go to Libya, states that the Libyans sent three persons intended to pass for the traveling party, along with the party's luggage, on the flight to Rome.[42] At any event, Musa al-Sadr has not been heard from since, although occasional reports of dubious origins indicate that he is still alive.[43] Most impartial observers believe him to be dead, as do a good number of his followers when speaking privately.

Several explanations of the disappearance have been offered, but this is obviously a shadowy affair for which there will probably never be a definitive account. It is instructive at least to touch upon the proffered explanations though, since they each tell us a bit about the extent to which some have gone to exploit this bizarre incident, if not about al-Sadr's fate.

According to one version, al-Qadhdhafi had earlier provided 3 million Lebanese pounds (about $1 million) to al-Sadr for which he could not satisfactorily account. The money allegedly ended up in a Swiss bank account. As a result of this malfeasance, the Libyan leader had al-Sadr murdered or incarcerated. There are several reasons to doubt this report. First, Libyan monies have been distributed to a number of Palestinian and Lebanese organizations (e.g., the Ittihad al-Ishtiraki al-ʿArabi, the Arab Socialist Union) without any semblance of close or even cursory accounting. Second, al-Sadr's closest companions claim that he was deeply in debt ($2 million) when he disappeared, largely as a result of loans he had personally signed to operate the large Technical Institute in Burj al-Shimali (near Tyre). An examination of his personal accounts revealed very modest sums of money. Third, al-Sadr's life style was simple, though not ascetic, and there is no reason to believe that he would have hoarded money that might have been used to support his movement; after all, to the extent the movement grew, his stature grew as well. Furthermore, interviews with individuals who knew him, including some of his adversaries, have not produced even one accusation of corruption on his part. Finally, al-Sadr's followers claim that they told al-Qadhdhafi that, if he could substantiate any financial misconduct on al-Sadr's part, they would gladly agree to his imprisonment or even execution. In the words of a senior Amal official: "Regarding the money affair, we discard as absurd and untrue Qadhdhafi's claim that he had given the Imam any money and we have told Qadhdhafi that if he can prove that the money claim is true we would agree to his [Imam Musa's] imprisonment or even his execution. But all that came as a response from Qadhdhafi was that al-Imam departed from Libya to Italy, while all clues prove that he had never left Libya."[44]

Another version of the story has the shah of Iran employing his intelligence service, SAVAK, to eliminate al-Sadr, who apparently was playing at least a minor role in exciting anti-Pahlavi sentiment in Iran. There has traditionally been a very close relationship between Lebanese and Iranian Shiʿi religious leaders, particularly since many Lebanese shaikhs trained in the *madaris*—religious schools— of Iran (as Musa al-Sadr did for a short period). Furthermore, al-Sadr was not only an Iranian by birth, but he was linked by marriage to two of the major antagonists of the shah: the Ayatollahs Ruhollah al-Musavi Khomeini and Muhammad Hasan Tabatabaʾi (his niece is married to Khomeini's son, Ahmad; and one of his sisters is the wife of Sadiq Tabatabaʾi—the son of Ayatollah Tabatabaʾi; Sadiq is the brother-in-law of Ahmad Khomeini). Thus, there is a certain superficial plausibility to this variant of the story.

In fact, when the UN Interim Force in Lebanon (UNIFIL) was formed in the spring of 1978, Iran provided a battalion—reportedly well staffed by SAVAK agents—to the force. The Iranian unit was, according to a correspondent's report, busy "identifying and isolating followers of the anti-Shah leader, Imam Musa al-Sadr."[45] Nonetheless, while the shah may have had the motive and no doubt the means to eradicate al-Sadr, Imam Musa's followers as well as the current Iranian regime—both with every incentive to blame the shah—persist in placing the blame on al-Qadhdhafi's shoulders. As an Iranian official noted in 1980, "we consider the Libyan Government directly responsible for the mystery that continues to hover over this matter."[46]

Yet another version of the disappearance saga is offered by Shahpur Bakhtiar, to whom the shah handed power when he left Iran in December 1978. Bakhtiar claims that al-Sadr was sent to Lebanon by the shah in furtherance of a scheme to create a Shiʿi state consisting of Iran, Iraq, and Lebanon. They subsequently fell out over the failure of the shah to disburse a promised $500,000, which other sources indicate represented monies for the construction of a hospital in Tyre. However, Bakhtiar claims that the one responsible for the disappearance was not the shah but Khomeini, for whom al-Sadr was a very strong and dangerous competitor.[47] Especially well-informed observers have noted that even after the triumph of the Islamic Revolution, there was real fear that the "Amalists would take over the revolution."

Interestingly enough, the latter explanation is given credence by one of al-Sadr's close associates, a man who was directly involved in investigating the disappearance, who believes that the imam was murdered as a result of a Syrian-Libyan-Iranian plot. He adds that al-Sadr and Khomeini did not like one another, clerical and personal ties notwithstanding. (Yet another knowledgeable individual indicates that Khomeini seemed positively disinterested when a prominent Egyptian journalist inquired about Musa al-Sadr's disappearance.) According to the former associate, it was the Syrians, and particularly Foreign Minister Khaddam, who urged al-Sadr to accept the Libyan invitation; obviously, it takes a rather substantial inferential leap to arrive at a full-blown assassination plot, but there are intriguing aspects to such a possibility.[48]

Another plausible version of the episode links it to Imam Musa's growing opposition to the armed Palestinian presence in south Lebanon, and in particular to the strained relations between the Shi'i movement and the *fida'i* factions backed by al-Qadhdhafi. 'Aziz 'Umar al-Shunaib, a former Libyan diplomat to Jordan, who defected to the Hashemite Kingdom, asserts that al-Qadhdhafi tried to impose a new political line on Imam Musa, who was executed when he demurred. According to al-Shunaib's version, the same fate had been prepared for PLO chairman Yasir Arafat because of his deviation from a rejectionist line vis-à-vis Israel. The former ambassador names three aides of the Libyan leader—Ahmad Ramadan, Bukabir Hannish, and Khalifah Hannish—as the assassins. The bodies of the imam and his two confederates were reputedly buried south of the Libyan coastal town of Sidra, near a farming project run by a cousin of the colonel. Al-Shunaib claims to have substantiating documents, but to date they have not been made public.[49] Others who have followed the saga indicate that al-Qadhdhafi had a deep dislike for Imam Musa; once during a meeting between the two, the Libyan feigned falling asleep while the imam was speaking to him in order to demonstrate his disrespect. Yet, while it does not seem out of character for al-Qadhdhafi to have had a hand in liquidating al-Sadr, the case, so to speak, remains unclosed.

While the mystery of Musa al-Sadr's fate remains, his disappearance has been of enormous symbolic importance to Harakat Amal. His persona has been elevated to that of a national martyr for many of Lebanon's Shi'a. By 1979, his face had been added to the panoply of posters that testify to the multitude of causes and movements in Lebanon. The movement's newspaper, *Amal*, uses a picture of Imam Musa on its masthead and regularly reprints his speeches and commentary (usually accompanied by additional photographs). From time to time, movement members identify themselves as "Sadriyyin." Most of the younger members of Harakat Amal wear a button or a pendant with al-Sadr's visage on it, and some even sport silk-screened t-shirts depicting him. In a country with precious few contemporary heroes, Imam Musa has achieved a special degree of fame.

Had Imam Musa passed quietly from the scene, it is likely that Shi'i politics in Lebanon would have been far more fractious than they have been. While his followers applaud his humanity, selflessness, and staunch commitment to Lebanon's "disinherited" and to Lebanon itself, Musa al-Sadr's detractors point to his tactical shifts of alliances, the witting or unwitting role he played to the benefit of "counterrevolutionary" institutions and interests (i.e., the Deuxième Bureau, the Army Second Bureau), and his political ambitions. Hence, had he continued his efforts in Lebanon, it is unlikely that he would have been able to repair or surmount the fissures that divided him from the Shiʿi *zuʿama* and their followers and from many of the groups that were affiliated with the LNM. While his disappearance has not eliminated the divisions, it has made them somewhat irrelevant. Many Shiʿis find in the vanished imam a compelling and culturally authentic symbol for the expression of their discontent with the cruel malady that they have had to suffer. Al-Sadr's disappearance has complemented and fed a political mood and has been propitious for the crystallization of the populist movement, Harakat Amal.

More than a few Amal leaders concede that a *mish mawjud* (not present) imam is no doubt of greater value for the political mobilization of the masses than one who is "present." Not only did the imam's mysterious disappearance make it much more difficult for adversaries to criticize the movement that he represents, but his "occultation" is plainly reminiscent of the Shiʿi dogma of the hidden imam (*al-Imam al-Ghaʾib*), a fact that lends further authenticity to the only wholly Shiʿi political organization in Lebanon.[50] As one thoughtful movement member conceded, the disappearance of Musa al-Sadr is "the single most important thing" that has happened for Harakat Amal.

The Islamic Revolution

There is no question that the victory of the Islamic Revolution in Iran keenly affected the Shiʿa of Lebanon. The deposing of the shah in January 1979 served as an important exemplar, demonstrating what a pious, well-organized, and motivated *umma* (Islamic community) could accomplish in the face of oppression and unjustness. Furthermore, the new regime in Tehran promised to be an important source of material and political support.

The links joining Jabal ʿAmil Shiʿis with their co-religionists in Iran have a long and distinguished history, as Michel Mazzaoui reminds us: "In fact, the chapter on the establishment of Shiʿism in Iran after the rise of the Safavid dynasty in the early sixteenth century cannot be written with direct reference to the role played by ʿAmili scholars from south Lebanon who flocked into the country as soon as the new regime gained military and political control."[51] In the ensuing centuries, many Lebanese Shiʿi shaikhs received their clerical training in Najaf, Iraq, which came to overshadow Jabal ʿAmil as a center of Shiʿi scholarship. After the 1920s, when Qum became an important center of religious education, Lebanese Shiʿi ʿulama (scholars of the Islamic religion) were trained there as well.[52]

More to the point, several Amal officials were to play an active role in the recent unfolding events in Iran, and a number of Iranians, including Ayatollah Khomeini's son, Ahmad, and his brother-in-law, Sadiq Tabatabaʾi, received military training in Lebanon under Amal's auspices.[53] Most notable, perhaps, is the example of Mustafa Chamran, an American-trained engineer and an Iranian by birth, who was the director of the Burj al-Shimali Technical Institute until 1979, when he departed for Iran to become chairman of the Supreme Defense Council in the new Islamic Republic. While it is not illogical to presume that such a well-placed official would have been of immeasurable assistance in securing substantial assistance for Amal, the mysterious death of Chamran in 1981, reputedly in a plane crash on the Iraqi front, casts some doubt on such presumptions. Many Lebanese affiliated with Amal believe that Chamran's death was the work of persons or parties affiliated with Khomeini's regime who saw Chamran as a dangerous competitor. Thus, it may well be the case that popular notions about extensive and consistent support flowing from Tehran to Amal are somewhat inaccurate. This qualification is lent support by the Islamic Republic's subsequent assistance to "authentic" Islamic organizations in direct competition with Harakat Amal, a subject treated in more detail in chapter 6.

It is important to distinguish between the specific political results of the Islamic Revolution, which produced what I choose to call the "Iranian exemplar," and the broader sociopolitical phenomenon of Shiᶜism (or, more generally, religion) as a refuge for those who find themselves isolated or excluded from the political system and who find in religion a familiar collective identity as well as a vehicle with which to pursue political objectives.

The phenomenon of "Islamic revival" is neither new nor homogeneous. Despite the earlier predictions by scholars that secularization would "devour the phenomena of religious political parties,"[54] it is now patent that such forecasts were at best premature. As I have argued in a comparative study of Islamic protest movements in Lebanon and Syria, such movements are not part of "a monolith lurching across the Middle East, but they represent an admixture of natural histories, programs, and prospects."[55] In Syria, the previously dominant Sunni Muslims have clung to Islam as a means of legitimizing their often violent *political* campaign against the ᶜAlawi regime of Hafiz al-Asad. In Lebanon, where the very essence of *politics* is the sect, the Shiᶜa have sought their *political* rights in a movement that serves as a touchstone of their identity as Lebanese-Shiᶜis. In both of the foregoing cases, the idiom of protest is Islamic, in part at least, because secular idioms have failed.

Yet there can be no denying that the Iranian exemplar is a powerful inspiration. But many commentators and scholars have failed to note that the typical Lebanese Shiʿis—like many of their Muslim cohorts throughout the *umma*—have a bifurcated view of the Islamic Revolution. On the one hand, there is a recognition that it did exemplify what a pious, mobilized Muslim community could accomplish; on the other hand, it is not widely touted as a model for Lebanon. In brief, the Islamic Revolution is more important for its emotive significance than for its institutional form. Many of the same Lebanese who extol the exemplar roundly and freely condemn and excoriate the excesses of the revolution (e.g., summary executions, torture, and other depravities), as well as the anachronistic political vision of many of its principal personalities. For the Muslim mainstream in Lebanon, there was no indication, at least through mid-1986, that Lebanese Shiʿis or Sunnis would care to transplant the Islamic Revolution to Lebanon; indeed, many Lebanese Muslims are both contemptuous and fearful of what they sometimes describe as "Khomeini-ism." This is not to deny that many Lebanese Shiʿis see Lebanon as a part of the *umma*, but a part that is to be preserved, not replaced by an Islamic entity. The important point, qualifications aside, is that the events in Iran have served as an important spur to the political mobilization of the Shiʿa in Lebanon, without being a model for emulation for the majority of the community.

Musa al-Sadr in South Lebanon. (Presented to the author, in 1982, by a senior Amal leader.)

4. The End of a "Natural Alliance"

As indicated in chapter 3, Harakat Amal has to a large extent been the beneficiary of a number of circumstances that it did little to foster. There was nothing deterministic about the emergence of Amal or an organization like it. Had Musa al-Sadr returned from Libya, or the shah prevailed in Iran, or the *fida'iyin* comported themselves less antagonistically and more compassionately with their host Lebanese, the past few years might have produced very different patterns of organizational development among the Shi'a. The movement was rescued from obscurity because it offered a hero, an exemplar, and the promise of security for Lebanese Shi'is who had tired of paying *diya* (blood money) and blood on behalf of Palestinians, Israelis, and non-Shi'i Lebanese. This chapter elaborates on the manner in which the security environment bolstered Amal as an organization and as a locus of Shi'i identity. While the focus of this chapter is south Lebanon, it should be noted that events in the South reverberate throughout the Shi'i community. The South *qua* Jabal 'Amil is the spiritual epicenter for the community, and, just as important, the extensive familial ties that link Shi'is throughout Lebanon tend to foster a keen degree of concern with events in the South. Thus, the clashes and conflicts that occurred in the South were often rehearsals or encores of similar patterns of violence in the Beirut suburbs.

Amal as a Vehicle for Communal Security

Although the divergence of *fida'iyin* and Shi'i interests was hardly a novel development of the late 1970s, it was only at that time that the Shi'a engaged in concerted opposition to the armed Palestinian presence. Whether wealthy or impoverished, educated or illiterate, worldly or provincial, the Shi'is came to direct their animus toward the *fida'iyin*, whom they blamed for exposing their families, homes, and livelihoods to constant danger. No doubt, there have been many culprits in the Lebanese tragedy, but it was the *fidaʾi* who was visible and held culpable.

Even the Amal leadership, which had long striven to maintain at least the appearance of amiable relations with the *fidaʾiyin* and their allies, was becoming increasingly outspoken in criticizing its erstwhile allies. The remarks in early 1982 of Nabih Berri, who has served since early 1980 as the leader of Amal, as to the heavy price paid by the Shiʿa accurately reflected the communal mood: "The people of the south, including the Shiʿa, have given the Palestinian cause more than all the Arabs combined have given it. They have given the cause their land, their children, their security, their orchards—everything but their honor and dignity."[1] Yet Berri's comments were also very restrained in comparison to the vehement opinions one would hear in the villages of the South in the late 1970s and early 1980s.

The villager, for whom Berri's language no doubt seemed subdued, often put the matter more directly: "We gave the Palestinians everything and they gave us back insults, corpses, and a lesson in corruption." One *mukhtar*, speaking contemptuously of the PLO, told me that *al-thawra al-filastiniya bitsir al-tijara al-filastiniya bi-Lubnan* (the Palestinian revolution becomes a Palestinian business in Lebanon), a reference to the PLO's alleged infidelity to its central aims. The people had lost their patience, and with every incident, every clash, and every insult, the appeal of a populist movement that promised security to peasant, worker, farmer, and teacher grew.

We tend to view events through familiar structural prisms, so much of the early attention devoted to Harakat Amal stressed the fact that the Shiʿa had simply organized themselves in a paramilitary organization that was challenging many of the other paramilitary groups that populated the Lebanese scene.[2] But such notions understate the significance of Amal. As a combatant force, the movement was often overshadowed by its adversaries; even its leaders were quick to recognize its military weakness: "If you go by arms, ammunition and equipment, we are probably the weakest party in Lebanon: The smallest organization is probably better armed and better equipped than we are, but our strength lies in our ability to make the people, the masses, carry out our orders, and they do it because they know we are out to meet their demands."[3] While the preceding observation by Berri somewhat overstates Amal's military weakness, it does highlight the movement's real strength: its capacity for transcending raw military power and, having done so, exerting substantial political influence in Lebanon.

In the South, where Amal has drawn much of its strength, and nurtured its growth, the actual membership—as opposed to the number of sympathizers—has been incredibly small. In one major Shiʿi village, only 90 persons even held membership out of an active male population of over 1,500. In two other important villages, only 30 to 40 were officially members. Yet each of these villages was considered an Amal stronghold. The point is not that the significance of the movement has been exaggerated, but that we have to consider Amal in its wider meaning—as a political statement to which the Shiʿa affiliated ideationally, if not always officially.

In more than a few villages in al-Janub, residents identified themselves as Amalists, yet they often had no official connection with the organization. Of course, for more than a few villagers the best politics were no politics at all, a feeling that is well summed up in the folk proverb *Raʾih al baqir ahsan min siyasat al-bashar* (the intellect of a cow is better than the politics of the people). But politics, especially in violent variants, were impossible to escape. Thus, it was quite common to encounter a village, replete with posters depicting Imam Musa and the Ayatollah Khomeini, where the *mukhtar,* village notables, and the peasants voiced the mottoes that so well exemplified Amal, and yet discover that Amal officials, who had every reason to claim a large membership in the village, could not claim one registered member. When the villagers say, "I am with Harakat Amal," they are merely confirming that Amal's populist message is striking a fundamental and authentic chord.

While the Amal leadership advocated the restructuring of the Lebanese political system, the villagers' fundamental objectives were focused locally. In a word, they sought "security." Hence, the appeal of a movement that called, without equivocation, for the reestablishment of the legitimate government and its institutions (and especially the army); for the support of the Palestinian struggle *in* Palestine *not* Lebanon; and for the disarming of militias, thugs, and marauders that have proliferated in all parts of the country.[4]

It was from the villages and towns that Amal drew much of its strength, but at the same time derived its weakness. Merchants, the small agrarian middle class, and overseas Shiʿis were important financial supporters of the movement. For example, the wealthy Shiʿi citrus growers of the southern coast (especially those south of the Rashidiya refugee camp) were ardent contributors to the movement; yet beyond an occasional meeting (which in itself could be dangerous), their active participation in Amal affairs outside their respective villages was nearly nil. (Having attended several private meetings between Amal leaders and their communal benefactors, I can testify to the very rudimentary nature of the movement in 1980 and 1981.)

Dependent as it was on a geographically diverse base of support, of which the basic unit was the village, Harakat Amal was only infrequently capable of concentrating coercive military or political power. Thus, in al-Janub in particular, Amal was defensively oriented. This was certainly true through 1981.[5] In short, Amal was usually at a decided disadvantage when it had to confront its adversaries on their terms. Only in early 1982 did Amal's readily mobilizable military potential begin to approach that of its enemies.

Arguably, it is not even accurate to speak of one Harakat Amal. For every village where pro-Amal sympathies predominated, there was a separate Harakat Amal. The result was an organization that accurately claimed wide support, but that often was unable to translate its affective force into effective control over its members and their activities. Indicative of this lack of control is the following candid comment made by an important movement leader: "Remember that Amal is a movement. Thus, direct orders can often not be given. Instead leadership must be a combination of persuasion, moral example, and the like."[6]

While not lacking in funds or weapons, the movement's infrastructure remained underdeveloped. Beset by constant clashes with its Lebanese and Palestinian adversaries, many of its most competent leaders spent the vast preponderance of their time quelling armed clashes and attempting to maintain at least the fiction of a brotherly relationship with the overtly less hostile segments of the Quwat Mushtarika (Joint Forces, a military command under Fatah's domination that brought together PLO and LNM fighters). Organization-building efforts were further stalled by the simple fact that many of the principal leaders continued to pursue a livelihood (usually out of necessity). Personal security was also a major preoccupation. Many leaders lived in villages that, while internally secure, were located adjacent to military positions manned by the Quwat Mushtarika. In one extraordinary case, a key leader in the South lived in a house that was less than two hundred meters from a military position that had apparently been sited for the express purpose of intimidating and observing him. (This man's constant vulnerability was driven home to me in June 1981, when he and I were besieged in his home by *fida'iyin* who believed—incorrectly—that we were engaged in some clandestine activity. Elements of the Quwat Mushtarika sacked and burned his home some months later.)

The movement was much less vulnerable in the Beirut suburbs, especially in its Ghobeire stronghold, where larger concentrations of

Shi'a and the self-contained nature of the community facilitated both the growth of the movement and the exclusion of "aliens." (One Ghobeire resident bragged that *"fida'iyin* and leftists do not dare to enter.") Hence, in a violence-ridden environment like Lebanon of late, it was the degree of geographical integrity of respective Shi'i population clusters that largely determined the extent of Harakat Amal's "official" or public growth.

In the South, as a result of the absence of a well-integrated organization, the label "Amal" was sometimes free for the taking. For many Shi'i villagers, the movement's name was merely a synonym for any collective self-defense activity carried out in the village. This, in itself, was a persuasive if ambiguous indicator of the degree to which Harakat Amal had come to be seen as the quintessential Shi'i organization. The Amal name was adopted, in at least a few cases, by local *shabab* who found that it provided them and their activities a certain legitimacy that they could not otherwise have. Furthermore, many Shi'is who had previously belonged to the ALF or any of the several Communist organizations tested the wind and found that the time was propitious for a change of labels. This latter tendency was serious enough that, in the spring of 1981, Harakat Amal temporarily suspended its recruitment activities, at least in the South, because of the well-founded suspicion that it had recruited quite a few members of questionable loyalty and background. (Lest the reader be misled, it is germane to note that while, in the early 1980s, the parties of the "left" were being overshadowed progressively by Amal, successful recruiting campaigns were conducted by the Lebanese Communist party right up to Israel's invasion of 1982.)

The characteristics and developments described above are neither surprising nor dysfunctional for an emergent communally based organization such as Amal. However, the movement's weak infrastructure had made it potentially vulnerable to co-optation by those who could manipulate the same symbols as Amal, that is, the Shi'i clergy. The leadership that replaced Imam Musa in Amal is nonclerical. While contacts with Shi'i religious leaders were assiduously maintained, there was little evidence of any day-to-day participation in Amal by individual shaikhs. There are those within the movement who espoused the closer integration of Amal with the Shi'i clergy, but they seemed to have little effect before 1982.[7] However, in early 1982, there was some evidence to indicate that the Mufti Muhammad Mahdi Shams al-Din, deputy chairman of the Supreme Shi'i Council (Imam Musa is still officially the chairman), was challenging Nabih Berri for the leadership of the Shi'a—and doing so successfully.

While this particular power struggle was short-circuited by the Israeli invasion, it was, as we shall see, reinitiated following the June invasion.

On the local level, a few shaikhs who were sympathetic to Amal's security objectives were nonetheless reluctant to concede a leading role to its secular leaders. Apparently taking the Iranian mullahs as their role models, several of these men took a direct role in organizing village chapters of Amal replete with militia and security activities. One colorful case involved the southern village of Siddiqine, where the local shaikh, incensed because his house had been bombed by pro-Iraqi elements, took matters into his own hands. Ignoring movement representatives in the village, he directed and apparently led the village militia. When Amal officials attempted to bring the maverick shaikh under control, he refused to concede their authority. It was only after Mufti Shams al-Din, at the behest of the Amal leadership, convinced the shaikh of Siddiqine to cooperate that he began to do so, and then only grudgingly. Contemptuous of the right of secular officials to represent his constituency or direct his efforts, the shaikh remarked: "I am Siddiqine and Siddiqine is me."

The Movement's Security Agenda

With the plethora of militias and political groups in Lebanon, there has been a surfeit of political programs replete with prescriptions for curing the country's ills.[8] Before examining Amal's contribution to this crazy quilt of political platitudes and proposals, it is pertinent briefly to discuss the reasons why it is difficult definitively to present the political program for Amal—or any other political grouping for that matter.

Most obviously, among the early casualties of any war are the grand ideals for which people believe that they fight. The Lebanese conflict that began in 1975 was different only in that the idealism of the participants faded with astonishing rapidity. While each of the many militias that fought in the conflict could—to a greater or lesser extent—claim some semblance of a political rationale, the (il-)logic of the conflict quickly reduced the basis for individual campaigns and clashes to military pragmatism. Wars start with objectives writ large, but they are fought for objectives writ small. Indeed, even the tactical rationale for specific clashes was arguable, given the large number of violent incidents sparked by affronts at checkpoints, killings or kidnappings of friends and relatives, or merely the opportunity to loot and pillage.[9] War becomes its own justification, and those engaged in it have little time or inclination to reflect on their collective future. Thus, in an environment of near anomie, prescriptions for eradicating the conditions that engendered the conflict often must wait until the combatants exhaust themselves (or each other), or until decisive results (i.e., "victory" and "defeat") are achieved.

It is important to recognize that Harakat Amal was, before the 1982 invasion, acting on two complementary agendas: one, implicit and publicly unacknowledged by its officials, and a second, explicitly enunciated agenda. Before turning to the latter in chapter 5, it is germane to elaborate the movement's implicit or hidden agenda.

As we have seen, at the local level the primary motive for joining or supporting the movement was—plainly and simply—to find some relief from the rampant insecurity that gripped much of Lebanon. As the increasingly serious and frequent Amal–Quwat Mushtarika clashes of 1981 and 1982 indicated, the primary threat to the Shi'i community's security was perceived to emanate from the *fida'iyin* and their supporters in the Lebanese National Movement.[10] Since the presence of Palestinian fighters and their allies was seen as an invitation for Israeli attacks, villagers were understandably opposed to the location of *fida'i* positions in their midst. Furthermore, not only was there the ever-present fear of Israeli strikes, but all too often the propinquity of the *fida'iyin* meant the expropriation of agricultural lands, communal property, and privately owned buildings, not to mention exposure to constant coercion and physical intimidation. (These unsavory side effects were, of course, not restricted to locales occupied by the *fida'iyin*, but were only one symptom of the devolution of coercive power to armed groups and paramilitary groups throughout Lebanon.)

The frequent Israeli raids, artillery bombardments, and air strikes dictated the dispersion of *fida'i* positions; otherwise, the Palestinians would have been even easier targets for Israeli guns. But the dispersion of Palestinian resistance forces fed the anxiety, resentment, and resolve of those who paid the heaviest price—the villagers. Accordingly, as Harakat Amal gained strength, it only further limited the freedom of action of the *fida'iyin* and rendered them ever more vulnerable to enemy attacks. Thus, Amal's implicit agenda that aimed at denying the *fida'iyin* access to the Shi'i community could only weaken the *fida'iyin*. It is hardly surprising that the consequences of the growth of Harakat Amal were recognized by both movement officials and leaders of the various organizational components of the Quwat Mushtarika. Those groups that were most directly threatened by the resurgence of Amal pursued an aggressive campaign to stifle and even eliminate the movement. In particular, the Jabhat ʿArabiya, which because of its close association with the Baghdad regime of Saddam Husain was anathema to the pro-Iranian Amal, and the various Communist factions that were prime competitors for Shiʿi recruits were among the most militant in their opposition to Amal.

While Fatah officials recognized the threat represented by a strong Amal, they also recognized the imperative of maintaining at least the appearance of good relations with the most important movement in the Shiʿi community. Hence, Fatah strove to avoid any overt involvement in open hostility to the movement. For their part, Amal officials were quick to express their distrust of Fatah, which they believed was instigating anti-Amal activities, but they also recognized the temporary utility of the largest PLO group as a *wasita* (mediator). In fact, Fatah was unquestionably the preeminent organization in the Quwat Mushtarika, and the only group that was capable of even attempting to impose any discipline on Amal's adversaries. The significant, if transitory, importance of a relationship with Fatah was illustrated in late March 1980, when bloody street battles erupted in Beirut between Amal, on the one side, and the Jabhat ʿArabiyya and al-Tanzim al-Shaʿbi al-Nasiri (Popular Nasirite Organization), on the other. The fighting, which left twenty-seven dead, so alarmed Yasir Arafat (leader of Fatah and chairman of the PLO Executive Committee) that he interrupted his attendance at the Fourth Fatah Congress, then in progress in Damascus, and returned to Beirut to mediate the conflict.

By the summer of 1980, two tendencies with respect to the armed Palestinian presence in Lebanon were discernible within Harakat Amal. The more moderate tendency, stemming from sympathy for the Palestinian cause and a recognition that the *fidaʾi* presence was not likely to be terminated soon by a peaceful solution, held that Amal's enemies were those who were affiliated with despicable governments (Iraq and Libya). For those espousing this point of view, Fatah was not only a useful *wasita*, but a worthy ally. The second tendency, which even in 1980 clearly represented the mainstream in the South, held the Palestinian fighters and *all* foreign interlopers responsible for the continuing troubles in Lebanon. According to the latter perspective, any relationship with Fatah (or any *fidaʾiyin* organization, for that matter) was merely tactical and transitory.

Despite the public posturing of Amal's officials and the staunchly pro-PLO line of the movement's weekly organ, *Amal*, the delicate partial entente between Amal and Fatah steadily deteriorated between 1980 and 1982. Clashes occurred with increasing regularity and all but the pretense of amity vanished. While Fatah officials attempted to maintain a modicum of control over Harakat Amal through local joint security committees (which in practice it dominated) and various forms of pressure and intimidation, the movement's geographic dispersion, diffuse leadership, and a rapidly growing public support rendered such attempts increasingly ineffective.

One corollary of the movement's hidden agenda that bears noting is the public support that it expressed frequently (prior to 1982) for the deployment of the Lebanese army throughout Lebanon. While the LNM and the Lebanese Front represented alternative legitimacy structures, Amal firmly committed itself to the reestablishment of the central government's authority—an essentially conservative position that seemed to serve well the interests of a constituency that sought security *plus* a fair share of political rewards. Amal's stand on the deployment of the army did not endear it to its enemies, for whom the army continued to be a Maronite-dominated force that was opposed by definition to the National Movement (and its Palestinian allies).[11] Amal's support of the army further emphasized to the Quwat Mushtarika the antithetical quality of its position. Thus, suspicions grew that the movement (or at least segments of it) was no more than a stalking horse for the army's intelligence bureau, the Deuxième Bureau. (While Amal's support certainly warmed some hearts in the Lebanese army, it is not clear that the army directed or buttressed Amal to any significant extent, although there seemed to be frequent contacts between functionaries of Amal and the Deuxième Bureau during the pre-1982 period.)

In addition to supporting the army, the movement sought to associate itself with any program or institution that symbolized legitimate governance in Lebanon. Furthermore, it seized every opportunity to compel the government to extend its authority. As previously noted, one consistent focus for Amal has been governmental indifference to the plight of those living in al-Janub. A palpable symbol of that neglect has been the Majlis al-Janub (Council of the South). Originally chartered in 1970 to foster economic development, the council had languished corruption-ridden. Amal made the council a constant target for criticism and protest and, in September 1980, occupied the council's offices in Sidon, preventing its employees from entering the premises. Simultaneously, Nabih Berri announced a series of demands, including the more timely and adequate compensation of those who had been displaced or who had suffered property damage due to hostilities. The movement threatened to take over the operation of the Majlis al-Janub if its demands were not met.[12] A more lucrative political target could hardly have been chosen. By attacking the council, Amal raised an issue of widespread concern, forced the feeble government of Salim al-Huss to take—or at least purport to take—a keener interest in the welfare of its citizens, and astutely identified itself with a legitimate governmental function.

The Syrian Connection

The relationship between Amal and Syria has been an interesting one. Well before Musa al-Sadr broke with the LNM in 1976, when he supported the Syrians against his former allies, he had established close ties with Hafiz al-Asad. Later, when Amal enjoyed its re-surgence in the wake of Imam Musa's disappearance, the movement received weapons "via" Syria,[13] and the Syrians played a role in train-ing the Amal militia, especially since 1980. Berri affirmed his move-ment's relationship with the Damascus government in February 1982, when in an enunciation of Amal's goals for Lebanon he in-cluded "the definition of special military, security, economic, and cultural relations between Lebanon and Syria, and the specification of Israel as Lebanon's arch-enemy."[14]

The Amal-Syria relationship served as yet another proof of the danger that Amal represented for the Quwat Mushtarika. Since the June 1976 Syrian intervention on the side of the Lebanese Front, re-lations between Syria and Fatah (and its allies) had been frosty in the best of times,[15] and Amal's good relations with Syria could only add venom to ongoing conflicts. From the perspective of Hafiz al-Asad, Amal was a useful device with which to temper, thwart, and even control the actions of those groups that lay outside of his sway, in particular, south of the "red line" delimited by Israel. Thus, in an area from which Syrian forces were excluded and in which direct Syrian influence was limited, a resurgent Amal serving its own in-terests might also serve those of Damascus.

Prelude to the Israeli Invasion

In early 1982, relations between Amal and its adversaries further de-teriorated as widespread skirmishes broke out in a number of south-ern villages. Fighting erupted in Beirut and in sixteen villages in al-Janub in April. According to an Amal account, elements belong-ing to or aligned with Fatah conducted a ten-hour bombardment of the Technical Institute in Burj al-Shimali during the April fighting.[16] These serious clashes represented an important watershed for sev-eral reasons. When the fighting was brought to a halt, Amal forces—

for the first time—remained in control of several formerly disputed villages.[17] While the movement was far from being a well-oiled military organization, it showed significant tactical skill, even to the extent of mounting diversionary attacks and feints. Most significantly, through the auspices of the Syrian-dominated Higher Coordination Committee (comprised of representatives from the PLO, Amal, the LNM, and Syria), it was agreed that the PLO "should henceforth not involve itself in Lebanese internal security matters" but should concentrate on "strategic security." No one really expected the PLO to observe the agreement, but its very promulgation served as an indictment.

In the months preceding the Israeli invasion, the contradictions separating the Quwat Mushtarika from Amal had become highly visible. The deteriorating character of the relationship was well illustrated by the contrasting statements of Salah Khalaf (he is often referred to by his *nom de guerre,* Abu Iyad, usually identified as the second-in-command of Fatah) and the leading Shiʻi cleric, Mufti Muhammad Mahdi Shams al-Din. When Khalaf was asked in December 1981 about Fatah's relationship with Amal, he replied, "In fact, there is no conflict between the [Palestinian] resistance and the Amal movement. Indeed relations are good."[18] Commenting on the same subject, just two months later, Khalaf had clearly lost his patience with Amal: "We address our brothers in the Amal movement, not the schemers in Amal, but the brother nationalists whom we know take the initiative in the Amal movement and participate in the joint command and the joint forces in the south so that we can prevent all evil elements and schemers in various areas from scheming in southern Lebanon. We reaffirm that we are concerned about the Amal movement . . . so that they will be with us in the same trench, within one joint command."[19]

Following the April fighting, Mufti Shams al-Din offered his first public criticism of the *fidaʾiyin* and the LNM. The strongly worded statement, which follows, was widely interpreted as an important hardening of the Shiʻi (and Amal) position. "The Supreme Shiʻi Council urgently asks *those responsible in the Palestinian resistance and the Nationalist Movement* to stop the shelling of the villages immediately, to pull the gunmen out of them and to withdraw the weapons directed at them. The continuation of this situation portends grave consequences for the entire Arab situation. The people of the south are now facing Arab bullets, which are supposed to be directed at Israel, and are being displaced from their homes not by Israelis but by fellow Arabs [emphasis added]."[20] Even Nabih Berri, who had previously adopted a conciliatory and circumspect public stance,[21] did not hesitate to contradict the PLO leadership's claims that Palestinians were not involved in the April clashes.[22]

The 1982 clashes removed even the dimmest prospect of a reconciliation between the two sides. But given their contending objectives, that can hardly be viewed as a startling revelation.

"They want to extinguish the light of God in their mouths and the fulfillment of His light, although [al-Sadr] detested the nonbelievers." This poster depicts many of the charges leveled against Musa al-Sadr by his competitors and enemies. Among the epithets are "Kataʾibist," "Palestinian," "Communist," "rightist," "leftist," and "pro-Shahist."

5. *Contradiction versus Consistency in Amal's Politics*

The political stance (more accurately, stances) adopted by Amal contains elements of consistency and contradiction. Contradiction in that, despite the fact that Amal is essentially a sectarian movement, owing its vibrancy and prominence to a heightened sense of co-identity among the Shiᶜa, it has concurrently called for an end to a political system grounded in sectarianism (which is to say, a system based upon the allocation of political privileges in accordance with sectarian criteria). Thus, we find the movement denouncing confessional politics, even as it has shown itself to be adept at playing by the rules of confessional politics. Although Amal's leaders might defend their seeming deviations as temporary concessions to the realities of the moment, it is hardly surprising that many of Amal's competitors and adversaries have accused the movement of duplicity and hypocrisy as a result of this contradiction between action and rhetoric.

Of course, all of this begs the question as to whether the abolition of the distribution of political offices by confessional criteria would diminish the confessional factor in Lebanese politics. Indeed, there may be less of a contradiction than first appears between the reallocation of sectarian privileges to the benefit of the Shiᶜa and the abolishment of the present system as a whole. In other words, given the great fortification of communal identities in Lebanon in the mid-1980s, it seems more rather than less likely that Shiᶜi voters, or any Lebanese voters for that matter, would remain deeply conscious of the confessional factor. Thus, it is at least a fair assertion that Amal—as the leading Shiᶜi political movement—could easily afford to promote a reform of Lebanese politics that would put more power in absolute vote tallies, rather than in allocative confessional formulae that have been made obsolete by differential population growth.

Unfortunately, any discussion of profound and comprehensive political reform in Lebanon remains sadly premature. In the meantime, it remains a matter of fact that Amal has become increasing adamant in its demands for Shiʿi political rights. The Shiʿa share a deep resentment of their political underrepresentation in Lebanon, and Amal has accepted several programs that would have the effect of redistributing political power to the detriment of the politically dominant Maronite community and to the advantage of the Shiʿa. Most recently, on December 28, 1985, Nabih Berri was a signatory (along with Walid Jumblatt representing the Druze and Elie Hubaika representing the predominantly Maronite Lebanese Forces) of a stillborn agreement negotiated in Damascus that would have increased Shiʿi representation in parliament, while simultaneously reducing the power of the presidency—an office, the reader will recall, that has been traditionally reserved for a Maronite.

If there has been one consistent thread running through the political literature of Amal, it is the movement's commitment to Lebanon as a distinct and definitive homeland. This position clearly distinguishes Amal from its radical Shiʿi opponents, who have viewed Lebanon as a compartment in the Islamic *umma* that they seek to transform into an Islamic republic. Even a cursory reading of the Amal charter alongside the political program of Hizb Allah (both of which are reproduced in the appendices) reveals the sharp distinctions separating the two perspectives.

The Political Program

Although Amal's immediate concerns and activities have been shaped by the rampant insecurity and chaos that have beset Lebanon, a state of affairs to which Amal has made its own deadly contributions, it is a mistake to presume that the movement is quintessentially a militia formation.[1] Amal began as a reform-oriented political protest movement, and such it remains. In the heat of armed confrontations and clashes, Amal's political program has sometimes been obscured by the imperatives of the moment, but the program remains, undergirding and defining the movement's activities. Upon examination, it is clear that the political program—first enunciated in 1974—has been marked by a fair amount of clarity and a generous ration of pragmatism.[2] We shall explore the program in some detail, noting a few instances in which it has been clarified by observable behavior; just as interests and goals define action, so does action reveal and verify interests and goals.

Briefly stated, Harakat Amal is a self-consciously Shiʿi movement for which the reinvigoration of Shiʿi orthopraxy is a stated goal. However, it does not seek to establish an Islamic or Shiʿi state in

Lebanon, and it has consistently extolled the virtues of Lebanon as a state in which religious toleration has been a historical landmark. The Iranian model of the guardianship of the jurisconsult (*wilayat al-faqih*) has been expressly rejected by many of the movement's leaders, yet they have taken pains to declare their respect for Ayatollah Khomeini, whom Nabih Berri has diffidently referred to as "my master." Given the vitality and the emotive appeal that the rival and more radical Hizb Allah has continued to demonstrate among a significant minority of the Shi'a, Amal has been compelled to play a delicate game of claiming to be a bona fide Shi'i movement, while promoting a program that Iran has found significant cause to criticize. Amal's dilemma has been exacerbated in the ongoing climate of utter despair that has prompted many Shi'is to look to radical Shi'ism for the answers that more moderate political leaders seem unable to provide.

Yet, in private and public statements, Amal has continued to espouse the survival of a definitive, independent Lebanon capable of self-defense, a Lebanon that is a member of the family of Arab states. The movement affirms its support for a parliamentary system of government, albeit a significantly reformed one. While ethnic diversity and reciprocal tolerance between sects are seen as a redeeming characteristic of Lebanon, Amal rejects the application of sectarian quotas, which is to say, the present system of confessional politics and the elites the system has spawned. Perhaps most significant, when and if the Lebanese enjoy a return to civility, is the movement's demand that the government adopt a much more activist distributive role in the allocation of economic resources for internal development and social welfare purposes.

The Independence of Lebanon

Scholars have written at length about the artificiality of state boundaries in the Middle East, remarking accurately that the states of the region frequently lack ethnic validity and meaningful natural histories. The region's map reflects boundary demarcations—more often than not—drawn by external actors in order to facilitate domination rather than to engender indigenous self-government. Yet one of the more interesting phenomena of the postimperialist era is the demonstrated durability of the state in the Middle East, while another is the moribund quality of pan-Arab unification ideologies.[3] Lebanon, like its neighbors, is a geopolitical product of an arbitrary decision, in this case, the 1920 redrawing of its borders by France; however, the Lebanese, like their neighbors, today widely accept what was once considered a capricious decision by a foreign overlord. Simply put, most Lebanese can at least agree about the delineation of the state's borders.[4]

Certainly the Lebanese Shi'a mirror the wider phenomenon. Harakat Amal is not a Shi'i movement devoid of nationality—in fact, it claims somewhat dubiously to be a movement for all deprived Lebanese—but a Lebanese movement representing the interests of Lebanese citizens who in most cases happen to be Shi'is. Amal defines itself, in its *Mithaq Harakat Amal* (Charter or Covenant of the Amal Movement), as a Harakat Wataniya (national movement) "that strongly believes in the preeminence of the nation, in the unity of the nation [*al-watan*], and in maintaining [the nation's] sovereignty intact."[5] The following excerpt from the covenant lucidly demonstrates the movement's commitment to the state:

> Our movement is completely devoted to national sovereignty and to independence in defining its own political course. It rejects any foreign mandate over the motherland, works toward preserving its territory and borders, and protects its dignity against subversion and slander. In this way, the nation will be able to determine its own fate without the intervention of malicious forces or special interests in any of its affairs.
>
> The sovereignty of the motherland cannot be achieved without according sovereignty to its citizens and protecting them from both political convulsions and capers and from restrictions on their free will and thought. Such sovereignty must be accompanied by a fusing together of the people in the tolerant melting pot [*butaqa*] of patriotism to produce a strong and healthy Lebanon embracing all her different cultures.

There is another angle to Amal's commitment to Lebanon's survival, and that is the candid recognition that the Shi'a must preserve Lebanon in order to preserve the social and political integrity of their community. In short, the Shi'a would pay a heavy price for any truncation of Lebanese territory or independence. Indeed, movement officials see the survival of an intact, independent Lebanon as a necessary condition for the very survival of Harakat Amal: "If the partitioning of Lebanon and the settlement of people [i.e., Palestinian refugees in Lebanon] cause significant damage to some, they would absolutely annihilate Harakat Amal."[6]

The movement has opposed any effort to proliferate alternative governmental structures, whoever the author of the scheme. There is good reason to believe the heavy fighting that took place in Beirut during April 1982, between Amal and militias affiliated with the

Lebanese National Movement (LNM), was precipitated by the LNM's attempt to elect local councils in West Beirut. The election of such councils was seen by Amal as a "form of autonomy" that might be preliminary to the partition of the country.[7]

Until the Lebanese army came to be viewed as an oppressor of the Shiʿa in the months following the Israeli invasion of 1982, it was viewed by Amal as a vestige of Lebanese legitimacy. In the two to three years preceding the invasion, Amal consistently supported the deployment of the army to the South, even if, as Nabih Berri once said, it is 100 percent Maronite.[8] The imperative that was at work is quite clear: issues of reform and sectarian balance in the army took a back seat when the survival of the Shiʿi community was at stake. The Lebanese army, ineffectual though it may have been, was a manifestation of Lebanese legitimacy, and thus served, at least, as a symbolic antidote to alternative authority structures that were being created in the South by the PLO and by Israel. Amal officials were shrewd enough to recognize that any step that reduced the power of its adversaries redounded to its benefit. Moreover, in the South, Amal has more or less consistently maintained cordial working relations with UNIFIL, following parallel lines of reasoning.

An Arab Lebanon and Its Foreign Policy

Amal officials have consistently identified Lebanon as an Arab state that shares the interests of its fellow Arabs. In this sense, the Amal position merely corresponds with one of the two poles of identity that were accommodated in the unwritten *Mithaq al-Watani* (National Pact) of 1943. In contrast to the Maronites, who sometimes portray themselves as descendants of the Phoenicians (thus denying an Arab ancestry) and who see Lebanon as a country in the Middle East but not of the Middle East, the Muslims (and the Greek Orthodox Christians, for that matter) have consistently viewed themselves as an Arab people living in an Arab state, and that Arab state is widely identified as Lebanon. Certainly the reconciliation of the two perspectives will require compromise from both sides, a quality that has not always been much in evidence.

Insofar as Amal is concerned, there has been a recognition that the "Maronite perspective" (and Maronite insecurities) must be taken into account. As a Shiʿi parliamentary deputy told me, "We want to reconstruct Lebanon with the Maronites, not in spite of them." However, the serious fighting of 1983 to 1986 has grossly complicated the road to compromise; by 1985, Amal officials were substantially less sensitive to the demands and requirements of their

Maronite opponents, and some, including Berri, were talking about the need to impose military defeat upon the Maronite militias.[9]

Another source of difficulties with the Maronite community has been Amal's espousal of a foreign policy for Lebanon that many Maronites find wholly unpalatable. For example, it has called for Lebanese nonalignment, specifically demanding that the country stand between the two international camps. While this perspective is not without a few Maronite adherents (e.g., the Neutral Lebanon Movement headed by Roger Edde), the Maronite community's tendency to look to Europe and the United States rather than the Arab world puts it at odds with Amal, and the Lebanese Muslim community in general.

Most important, though, is Amal's close relationship with Syria, a relationship that may be traced for more than a decade and one that poses a legion of real and imagined threats to Lebanon's independence, and not just in the eyes of the Maronite militia. There were times, especially when *pax* Americana seemed on the way to supplanting Syrian influence in 1982 and early 1983, when Amal attempted to distance itself from Syria, but it has since returned to the embrace of Damascus, taking its support wherever it could be found. In an important August 1985 speech in Ba'albak, which could not even have been delivered without significant Syrian assistance, given Syria's presence in the Biqa', Berri enunciated a perspective that was later inscribed in the ill-fated December 28 agreement: "There must be integration with Syria, by means of actual agreements in the economic, security, military, political, information, and educational fields. Let them not be afraid of Lebanon's sovereignty. Never be afraid. France, the beloved mother, did not lose its independence when it joined the EEC or when it signed the European security pact."[10] Clearly, many Lebanese find Syria much more threatening than the European Economic Community would be to its membership, and it is not without some justification that many have come to view Amal as a stalking horse for Syria. Despite these serious apprehensions, Amal's commitment to Lebanon's independent existence remains, and it is important that a calculation of shared interests not be confused with a willingness to submit to full-blown Syrian domination.

The movement purports to support the liberation of *al-Ard al-'Arabiya* (the Arab land) from foreign domination. Most particularly, this has been taken to mean the liberation of Palestine, a cause that Amal continued to espouse even as it violently opposed the armed Palestinian presence in Lebanon. The sincerity of such pro-Palestine positions should be viewed with a good dose of skepticism, as illustrated by Berri's reminder that "Palestinian blood is not more sacred than Lebanese blood."[11]

The movement's problems with the *fidaʾiyin* have not led to a corresponding diminishment of its distrust and almost sacred enmity toward Zionism. On more than a few occasions, I have heard Israel equated with Yazid, the historical enemy of Shiʿism and sponsor of Imam Husain's bloody end (in A.D. 680) and, more generally, Israel *qua* "Zionist entity" is seen as the enemy of both Lebanon and the Arabs. While the lay leadership of Amal has had its share of disagreements with the Shiʿi clerics (or "estrangements" as Berri once said), there is one subject on which there is very little contention—namely, Israel. In a statement that could easily have been uttered by Mufti Shams al-Din, Shaikh Muhammad Husain Fadl Allah, or any other Shiʿi religious leader, Nabih Berri notes: "Cooperation with the Zionist enemy is proscribed, as Imam al-Sadr taught us. He who is underprivileged on his land should support him who is deprived of his land as Imam Musa al-Sadr has taught us. Moreover, Israel is an absolute evil and whoever stands against it becomes in our view, one way or another, an absolute good."[12]

This does not mean that Amal is anxious to take the fight against Israel into Israel; it is too pragmatic in its politico-military assessments to do so. Indeed, the movement has been bitterly critical of the Arabs' willingness to fight Israel with Shiʿi blood and on Lebanese territory. Despite their extolling of *ʿUruba* (Arabism) and its causes, Nabih Berri and other Amal officials have indicated an abiding irritation with the Arabs' indifference to the plight of south Lebanon in particular, and Lebanon in general.[13] This factor has tended to fortify the movement's sense of its singular responsibility for its destiny, and as a result has further strengthened its identification as a uniquely Lebanese movement.

The Nature of Society in Lebanon

The Amal covenant portrays Lebanon as a pluralistic society in which the freedom and liberty of the individual must be preserved. In a dictum that students of U.S. constitutional law would not find unfamiliar, freedom is defined as a milieu in which the rights of the individual do not infringe upon the rights of others. Not unexpectedly, Amal, as a movement that identifies itself as the vanguard of the deprived, calls for "equal opportunities for all citizens." The state (*dawla*) is to be the vehicle for realizing "social justice in its progressive and complete meaning."

In the preamble to its working paper prepared for the October 1983 reconciliation conference, held in Geneva, Amal declared: "Lebanon is a democratic, parliamentary republic based upon respect of public freedoms, including above all the freedom of opinion and belief, and on the principle of division of authority, on social justice and equality of rights and obligations of all citizens, without privileges or discrimination. Lebanon has an economic system and general economic and developmental planning for the various capacities, requirements and activities of different sectors. It is the land of human dignity and civil ambitions."[14]

The Economy

In general, Harakat Amal has demanded that the government play a much more active role in the distribution of resources. Lebanon's free market economy, characterized by near-total government indifference to economic matters, is viewed as the culprit that has perpetrated the deprivation of the Shi'i community and nurtured the perceived concentration of wealth in the hands of *zu'ama* and their ilk. In a novel definitional twist, the movement describes the land-wealthy as feudalists ("Feudalism is the ownership of the property by the few")—a useful epithet, even if it is of dubious accuracy. Whatever the correctness of its definitions, the demands for the reallocation of economic resources would tend to undercut the political power of those described as "feudalists," and that—after all—is the name of the game for a movement that reflects, in part, the ambitions of the new Shi'i middle class.

A comprehensive set of Shi'i demands was promulgated in 1974 by the Supreme Shi'i Council (the reader is reminded that Imam Musa al-Sadr chaired the council and led Harakat al-Mahrumin at the time) and presented to the government in the same year.[15] The demands still stand as the nucleus of Amal's agenda in the economic realm, and for that reason they warrant listing in summary form. They include:

1. A call for the allocation of credits in the general budget to ensure that the regions develop at approximately the same rate. (The practical effect would be a major increase in funds allocated to underdeveloped regions, especially al-Janub and al-Biqa'.)
2. Prompt action on irrigation and water conservation projects. (A boon to the community with the largest number—both proportionately and absolutely—of farmers, i.e., the Shi'a.)
3. Granting priority to school construction in the under-

developed regions. (Rather than funding school construction at the same rate throughout the country.)

4. Creation of hospitals and clinics, also on an accelerated basis in the underdeveloped regions.

5. Improvement and construction of roads, particularly between Beirut and Tyre and between Beirut and Baʿalbak. (Both of these outlying cities being in the prime areas of Shiʿi population concentrations.)

6. Amelioration of the tobacco farmers' plight. (In practice, this means the restructuring or elimination of the state monopoly, the Régie des Tabacs, the focus of a famous demonstration in 1973 involving 10,000 petty planters.)

7. General improvements in agriculture with the preference for funding given to deprived areas.

8. Tourism projects in Tyre and Baʿalbak.

9. Comprehensive survey of mineral deposits in Lebanon.

10. New system of allocation for municipal funds.

11. Law of general amnesty on building code violations so that the inhabitants of the Beirut suburbs may benefit from water and electricity (which cannot, by law, be extended to the unlawfully constructed dwellings occupied by many Shiʿi migrants).

12. General improvement of conditions in the Beirut suburbs.

In addition to the preceding, the Amal charter calls for an end to interest lending, a demand that very few Amal officials seem to take very seriously. Indeed, upon my return to Lebanon in 1982, I met several Shiʿi bankers closely aligned with Amal, and not one of them seemed to have sacrificed any influence in the movement because the banks they worked for, and in one case owned, charged the prevailing rate of interest.

Reforming Politics in Lebanon

We may debate the extent to which external intervention in Lebanon has exacerbated and inflamed internal divisions, but there seems little debate that internal political divisions along sectarian lines have spawned a fertile environment for brutal conflict. For many Lebanese, whether Christian or Muslim, the political system's greatest fault is its enshrinement of sectarian division. Ironically, this may not have been the intention of the framers of the National Pact, who saw the pact as a means to attenuate rather than entrench sectarian considerations in politics. Independent Lebanon's first prime minister, Riad al-Sulh (a Sunni Muslim), is identified with this perspective.

> One of the principles of reform necessitated by the national interest of Lebanon is the confrontation of sectarianism and the eradication of its evils, since sectarianism obstructs national development and destroys the good name of Lebanon at the international level. Furthermore it poisons the relationship among the various spiritual groups which constitute Lebanon. We have seen how, in most cases, sectarianism was used as an instrument to secure private benefits or to weaken national life in Lebanon to the benefit of those who envy it, we are sure that once the national feelings which are apt to grow under independence and popular rule, once these feelings are accepted the people will then willingly agree to eliminate the sectarian system which weakens the country.
>
> The hour in which we are able to eliminate sectarianism will be a blessed hour and will represent a comprehensive national awakening in the history of Lebanon. With God's help we shall seek to have this hour in the near future.[16]

Obviously the "blessed hour" is still awaited, but al-Sulh's aspiration does not want for adherents.[17]

The preceding chapters have examined a number of factors that have reinforced the Shi'is' sectarian identity, yet, even as their particularistic identity has grown and even as the Amal leadership has demanded political equity confessionally measured, the leadership has also called for the abolishment of the sectarian equation in politics. In short, the movement has demanded immediate equity in a system that must eventually be eliminated. The coexistence of a practical program for the present and an idealistic program for the future is hardly a new feature of Shi'i politics. In 1974, even as Musa al-Sadr was demanding that the Shi'a be accorded eleven more senior government posts, he was also calling for the end of the confessional classification of bureaucratic posts so that specific positions would cease to be the fief of individual sects.

Nabih Berri has argued, consistent with the Amal covenant, that confessionalism has precluded the development of a Lebanese nationality and has been the root cause of the country's troubles. "This [confessional] hallucination that we have in our minds has made us behave like tribes instead of like people of one country. The 1943 National Pact that we created is a partitionist pact. It helped us to build a farm, not a country. . . . I say this Pact is the root of all of our troubles."[18] And: "Because here the economic and employment competition is built on a purely sectarian basis. Sectarianism is imposed on us. They are making us wear turbans and priests' robes and forcing us to think confessional."[19] Until early 1982, Amal called for the abolition of confessionalism "from the top of the pyramid to its base,"[20] excepting the top three political positions, only so long as necessary to demonstrate that deconfessionalism was working. By February 1982, the position had softened somewhat, although deconfessionalism was still proclaimed the ultimate goal: "The abolition of sectarianism must at least start in the army and in education, in the hope that this will lead to the total abolition of political sectarianism in Lebanon eventually."[21]

By 1985, as movement toward intercommunal reconciliation foundered, Berri's position hardened significantly. In August, he called for the creation of a presidential council, which would have the presidency rotated on a yearly basis among representatives of the six leading sects (the Maronites, Sunnis, Shi'a, Druze, Greek Catholic, and Greek Orthodox).[22] Once again, Berri demonstrated a penchant for sectarian solutions, even as he called simultaneously for deconfessionalism.

At first glance, the deconfessionalism position publicized by Berri is not complementary to the collective interests of the Shi'i community, which would stand to benefit from a reallocation of political positions and rewards proportionate to its share of the demographic pie. Nor has Amal always acted consistently with its declared objectives. For example, during the fall of 1980, it succeeded in forestalling the formation of a new cabinet for fifty-six days, because it had not been consulted about cabinet appointments or offered any of the four cabinet posts given to Shi'is. While the new cabinet under Prime Minister Shafik al-Wazzan was finally confirmed over Amal objections (as well as those of the Supreme Shi'i Council and the Front for the Preservation of the South), the episode illustrated that Amal would not abjure confessional politics, even as it called for its abolishment.

Two interesting factors are adduced to justify the call for jettisoning—albeit slowly—confessionalism. First and most important, it was the proliferation of parochial sectarian interests that, according to one Shi'i principal's interpretation, made the civil war possible and thwarted the cessation of violence. The second and related factor was voiced by an important Shi'i leader and Amal official, Hasan Hashim, who has argued that the outside powers—especially the East and West military camps—were able to exploit sectarianism in furtherance of their aim of controlling the Palestinian revolution. Hashim asserts:

Lebanon is a victim of the dirty political game laid out by the Eastern and Western camps.

All of the organizations active on the Lebanese stage (except Harakat Amal) were connected and affiliated with one of the Arab countries or an outside foreign power, and all of these groups and organizations were deeply and thickly involved in Lebanon and in the developments that took place in it.[23]

Thus, to leave the Lebanese political system unchanged is to maintain its vulnerability to meddling by outside powers. Obviously, there is a very good dose of truth in this analysis, but there is another side to the position, and that is the point noted from time to time in the movement's weekly newspaper, *Amal*, that the Shi'i sect is the only one lacking an outside sponsor; lacking a political sugar daddy, the Shi'a were unable to enjoy the advantages of the other sects.[24]

If Amal's immediate objectives may be understood, with justifiable cynicism, as crass jockeying for political power, the movement's longer-term prescriptions, if implemented, would amount to a reinvention of the political wheel in Lebanon. Amal officials may make a good case for eliminating confessionalism in politics, but it should also be borne in mind that this stance—sincere though it might be—is a means of undercutting the traditional confessional politicians, that is, the *zu'ama*. In fact, Amal's covenant equates the end of sectarianism with the end of the *zu'ama* system, which is often described as one of political backwardness.

At first glance, the successful elimination of confessionalism would seem to carry with it the seeds of Amal's demise, for to eliminate the sectarian label in politics would conceivably be a significant step toward buttressing the citizen's identity as simply a Lebanese. Thus, we might expect a significant erosion of the constituency for a movement that, notwithstanding its claims to the contrary, is in its essence a sectarian movement. However, none of the leading Amal officials is so naive as to expect a withering of sectarian identities, even in the event of the elimination of confessional formulae for the distribution of political offices. It is clearly expected that Amal will sustain its constituency, and the movement's proposal for the establishment of a system of proportional representation is clearly one that could work to its benefit, especially given the number of Shi'i voters. In addition, Amal has come out in favor of eliminating Lebanon's twenty-six electoral districts and creating a single national district, a proposal that would undermine those politicians with local bases of power and benefit a "national" political movement.

Although the Amal position has expressly excluded federalist or confederalist solutions,[25] such as the Lebanese Front has proposed from time to time,[26] the movement has been careful not to exclude the discussion of any political program. In short, it has striven to project a conciliatory pose that makes it a natural interlocutor for any party willing to discuss reform. Berri has stated that any changes that are undertaken should result from a dialogue among "all active forces in Lebanon without exception."[27]

It remains to be seen whether Imam Musa's political heirs prove to be more interested in short-term gains or in long-term ideals. This point is discussed in the closing chapter.

Nabih Berri.

6. The Israeli Invasion and Its Aftermath

For seven blood-spattered years, the Lebanese had awaited the final battle in the conflict that had wrecked and sundered their country. On the eve of the Israeli invasion in June 1982, many Lebanese had reached the end of their rope; they had had enough. Many Lebanese shared the belief that if only the Palestinian, Syrian, and Israeli interlopers (among others) would leave Lebanon, the Lebanese could solve the problems that divided them. Significantly, the motto "Lebanon for the Lebanese" was being uttered by both the Shiʿa and the Maronites, and many felt that their country had been victimized and plundered by all manner of external powers.

Yet all Lebanese recognized that they were unable to muster the means to expel the foreign forces from Lebanon. Hence, when the Israeli army invaded in 1982, ebullience and rejuvenated hopes spread throughout the country, for it seemed that the Israelis had succeeded in doing what the Lebanese were not capable of doing for themselves—namely, returning Lebanon to the Lebanese. As the smoke cleared in the fall of 1982, the Lebanese breathed a collective sigh of relief. Finally, the much anticipated "last battle" had come and passed. Lebanon would finally see peace, although few stopped to ask: "peace on whose terms?" The all-powerful United States had at last turned its attention to Lebanon, foreign armies would soon depart (as U.S. negotiator Philip Habib told President Sarkis in August 1982), and rebuilding and political reformation would soon commence. Lebanon's long night of agony seemed to be ending.

As we now know, the slender hopes were sadly mistaken. In the years following the June invasion, Lebanon displayed new levels of fractiousness and violence; the country seemed very far indeed from even a modicum of peace and civility. There is no simple answer for Lebanon's dilemma, neither in pundits' barbs nor in the social scientists' hypotheses. The answers lie both within and without Lebanon, as does the blame. In the cozy comfort of pontification, it is all too easy to dismiss Lebanon as a failed country—as a disaster that had long been waiting to happen—but such deterministic assertions ignore the impact of differential events and policies. This point rings especially true with respect to Harakat Amal, which serves as a useful lens with which to understand and interpret recent events, both within the Shi‘i community and in Lebanon as a whole. The sections that follow explore the interplay of factors that have conditioned the political mobilization of the Shi‘a since 1982. As we shall see, although Amal was rapidly gaining adherents and overshadowing its competitors within the Shi‘i community prior to the 1982 invasion, events since then have increased the prospect that the political mobilization of the Shi‘a will be a centrifugal rather than a centripetal process.

Surviving 1982

By early 1982, relations between Amal and the Fatah–dominated Quwat Mushtarika had passed the breaking point. After serious clashes in January and April, it was a foregone conclusion that the interests of the Shi‘a could no longer be reconciled with the *fida'iyin* presence. While the movement was still significantly outgunned by its opponents, tactical improvements and a militarily wiser leadership helped to make it an increasingly formidable military force. Even in the South, where Amal lacked the geographic concentration of its cohorts in the Beirut suburbs (its fighters were scattered from village to village), it compensated for its weakness by launching hit-and-run attacks and diversionary actions, while carefully defending village strongpoints.

It is likely that Amal's growing effectiveness against the PLO was a source of encouragement to the engineers of Israel's invasion, which was intended to emasculate the PLO, both militarily and politically; however, it quickly became apparent that Israeli planners grossly misinterpreted the longer-term meaning of Amal's militancy. The paucity of indigenous support for the *fida'iyin* did not translate into ecstatic, long-term support for Israel. No Amal leader of stature could accept an overt relationship with Israel or with its puppet, Sa‘ad Haddad. Nonetheless, there was no lack of understanding of the benefits of a tacit alliance. In fact, after hearing the definition of an "objective alliance," one key leader acknowledged that that was indeed a good description of the movement's relationship with the IDF and Haddad. Some reports have exaggerated the level of collaboration between the invading IDF and Amal, but it is clear that, especially in the first weeks of the invasion, residents of the South provided assistance in such matters as pinpointing *fida'iyin* arms caches or identifying leaders of adversarial groups. One leader even stated that, had Israel not invaded, a war between Amal and the *fida'iyin* was inevitable. It is no overstatement to claim that many southern Shi'is welcomed the Israeli invasion, but—it must be emphasized—they did so on the presumption that Israel would not linger in Lebanon.

The mood in the South was not neatly replicated in the other two Amal strongholds—Beirut and the Biqa'. It was only in the South that the Shi'a were constantly exposed to the deadly weight of Israeli military power, and it was only in the South that the fortunes of geography forced the Shi'a to choose between tolerating or resisting the Palestinian presence. It was the shortsightedness of the PLO, and in particular the preeminent Fatah, that helped to decide the matter. Notwithstanding an active Israeli military campaign to alienate the people of the South from the guerrillas, the obnoxious behavior of the *fida'iyin*, or their Lebanese allies, rendered the choice really no choice at all.

Outside of the South, Amal defined its adversaries more narrowly. Thus, south of Beirut, around Burj al-Burajinah, for example, fighting involving Amal tended to be against forces perceived as viscerally anti-Shi'a (or anti-Iran), such as the Iraqi-sponsored Jabhat 'Arabiya (Arab [Liberation] Front). In addition, many of the battles in the Beirut suburbs had less to do with political ideologies than with political recruitment, as in the case of many of the clashes with the Lebanese Communist party, which was finding that Amal was cutting into its membership base. The contrast in situations is well illustrated by the fact that while the Amal fighters in the South watched as the Israeli tank columns rolled by, those from Shiyya, Ouza'i, and Ghobeire mounted some of the most spirited and aggressive defensive actions against the invaders. For instance, the defense of the Khalda junction, which badly bloodied the attacking IDF, was largely by the Shi'a.

True, the invasion accomplished what Amal could not, namely, the expulsion of the *fida'iyin* from the South, but the glee of the Shi'a was short-lived as it became clear that for the cost of their suffering they might merely have witnessed the supplanting of one occupation force by another.[1] Furthermore, with the invasion Harakat Amal found itself faced with a new panoply of problems that, if not satisfactorily resolved, could well threaten the viability and even the survival of the movement.

Just as an earlier phase in the political mobilization of the Shiʿa by Musa al-Sadr was interrupted by the cascading violence of 1975–1976, so the events of the summer of 1982 seemed likely to short-circuit the renewed mobilization efforts that had commenced in 1978 and 1979 and gained impressive momentum in 1981 and 1982. At first glance, it even seemed that Amal's very *raison d'être*—communal security—had been obviated. While the Iranian exemplar and the disappearance of the Musa al-Sadr were very important mobilization symbols, the decisive factor pushing recruitment was the increasingly serious and violence-fraught estrangement of the Shiʿa from the Palestinian resistance movement. With the *fidaʾiyin* excised, the critical question to be faced was whether a membership fed by the attraction of collective security could be maintained when the imperative of collective security was much weaker or at least less obvious. Put another way, could Amal redirect its efforts so as to retain its primary leadership role for a politicized Shiʿi community, or would the organization prove to be an anachronism in whatever "New Lebanon" emerged?

In effect, the organization faced challenges at three distinct levels: from within the organization, from within the sect, and from non-Shiʿi actors in Lebanon's porous political system.

Internal Challenges

Amal was never a tightly integrated organization, and the possibility of organizational fissuring was always latent. The movement was as much an ideal, a sociopolitical state of mind, as it was a palpable, well-organized entity. In contrast to many of the other militias that populate Lebanon, Amal fighters were paid very little, and economic necessity led many simply to return to the process of attempting to earn a living, whenever possible. Not unexpectedly, given the movement's inchoate quality, there were keen regional splits that roughly corresponded with relative proximity to the Israeli (and Syrian) border. In addition to disparities born of locale, the movement subsumed a broad admixture of political perspectives and ideological preferences.

Amal always contained its share of agents and opportunists who were perfectly willing to return to patron-client relationships outside the organization. For these people, the movement's instrumental value was simply as a substitute for preferred patrons—whether this or that *zaʿim* or a competing political organization. Moreover, more than a few Shiʿis had merely found it astute, even advantageous, to support or join the movement rather than overtly to oppose it. Many of the latter category dropped away from Amal after June 1982, when this pragmatic rationale became much less compelling.

Further threats to the movement's viability were mounted by those who raised serious challenges regarding the political objectives of Amal, including questions as to its very authenticity as a Shiʿi movement. One such challenge was mounted by a member of the thirty-member Command Council, Husain Musawi. In July 1982, Musawi charged the movement's leaders with blatant collaboration with the invading Israelis and, apparently with Iranian support, attempted to reorient the movement to what he saw as its proper objective: the replication of Iran's Islamic Revolution in Lebanon. According to Amal officials, Musawi was subsequently expelled from the movement during the summer of 1982, although he may simply have quit. He is, as of mid-1986, ensconced in the Baʿalbak area, in the Syrian-controlled Biqaʿ Valley, where he leads the Islamic Amal Movement in apparent cooperation with a contingent of Pasdaran (Revolutionary Guards) dispatched by Iran to Lebanon in mid-1982. He has been implicated by some in a number of acts of political violence, including the 1982 kidnapping of the president of the American University, David Dodge, and the destruction of the U.S. Embassy in April 1983, although his specific role is still unclear. In November 1983, Musawi and his followers were the targets for Israeli and French air attacks launched by Jerusalem and Paris to retaliate for their suspected role in the October truck bombings of the French contingent of the Multinational Force in October (which was attacked the same day as the U.S. Marine headquarters, where 243 American soldiers died) and the bombing of an Israeli headquarters in Tyre in November 1983. In addition, two of Musawi's followers have been accused of attempting to assassinate Prime Minister Shafiq al-Wazzan in July 1983.[2] While Musawi's following is limited, his activities, buttressed as they seem to be by Iran and tolerated, even encouraged—at least until mid-1984—by Syria, have served to remove segments of the sizable Shiʿi population of the Biqaʿ Valley from the organizational grasp of the mainline Amal organization.[3]

Although Musawi's activities garnered a fair degree of notoriety, the more important immediate task facing Amal was to preserve its critical mass of moderate political personalities under one banner. To the latter end, the movement held a convention in mid-April 1983. The convention returned Nabih Berri, in office since April 1980, as president of the movement without serious opposition. It also approved a plan, drafted by Berri and his close associates, for the restructuring of Amal. The thirty-member Command Council was abolished and replaced by a sixty-member Political Bureau to be headed by retired Colonel ʿAkif Haidar. Haidar is a bright and energetic political moderate who is widely respected outside of the Shiʿi community, but he seems to lack the street popularity of several of the other Amal principals. Thus, while Haidar has been touted as the number-two man in Amal, it is unlikely that he would ever replace Berri.

Berri, whose survival instincts are known to be keen, has apparently sought to use Haidar as a counterbalance to some of his more serious competitors within Amal, and especially Hasan Hashim, who has emerged as his most serious rival within the movement. In the 1983 restructuring, Hashim emerged as the chairman of an Executive Council charged with carrying out the decisions of the Political Bureau. Hashim, from the southern village of Zahrani, enjoys considerable grassroots support in the South, where he is widely credited with actively aiding the resistance against Israel with materiel support, when many of the other Amal leaders were offering no more than tough words. In addition to Hashim, seats on the twelve-member Executive Council were given to Zakaria Hamza, Haitham Jumaʿ, and Ghassan Siblani (an American citizen). Most important, a Presidential Council was formed, and it is this organ that is charged with the day-to-day leadership of the movement. The Presidential Council is chaired by Berri, and members include Haidar, Hashim, Imam Musa's sister, Rabab al-Sadr (who lives in Tyre), and Mufti ʿAbd al-Amir Qabalan (one of the leading Shiʿi clerics).

One clear outcome of the convention is the confirmation of Berri's authority as the first among equals, but he is by no means the unchallenged leader. The reorganization eliminated a number of "pro-Iranians," who were critical of Berri's centrist politics and his unwillingness to emulate the Iranian Islamic Revolution model. Moreover, at least one official, who blatantly collaborated with the Israelis in south Lebanon, was subsequently dropped from the leadership structure. While it has been impossible to get a comprehensive list of Amal officials, it is noteworthy that Mufti Shams al-Din (of whom more below) seems to have ceased to play an official role. In private conversations, Berri indicated that one objective of the reorganization was to deemphasize the military aspect of the movement and enhance its potential for playing a more effective political role, specifically aimed at securing economic gains and improving the social conditions of the Shiʿa. To those ends, several seats in the Political Bureau and the Executive Council were to be given to technocrats (such as Haitham Jumaʿ and Ghassan Siblani).[4]

Berri's leadership style reflects his less than total authority. He leads less by direction than by cajolery and suasion. Internal bargaining and negotiation are a necessary precondition to decisions, and as a result it is often easier to decide not to decide than to provide positive leadership. In short, the imperatives of political—and physical—survival frequently are a source of intentional indecisiveness and a policy penchant for keeping all options open.

Shi'i Competitors

The postinvasion period witnessed the reemergence of a number of the traditional leaders who, while lacking sizable constituencies within the Shi'i community, still maintained important political ties outside of it. Of course, the most notable was Kamil al-As'ad, the Speaker of the Assembly (until his defeat in October 1984), but there were others as well, with familiar names like Hamada, al-Khalil, and 'Usairan. These *zu'ama*, often denoted "semi-feudal leaders" by their political opponents, were increasingly anachronistic figures in contemporary Lebanon. Their control of segments of the Shi'i community was tenuous even before 1975, as demonstrated by the successes of Musa al-Sadr in the early 1970s. The very processes of social mobilization that helped to make the Shi'i community available for political action had reduced its isolation and fragmentation and, concomitantly, the ability of a *za'im* to control respective segments of the community.

With few exceptions, the Amal leadership has been drawn from precisely those families that have not traditionally enjoyed political influence. No one better epitomizes this fact than Nabih Berri. Unlike the *zu'ama*, Berri cannot claim descent from a notable family. His personal natural history is a metaphor for many of his brethren, for whom the key to escaping the old politics and entering a new political era was migration. Berri was born in Freetown, Sierra Leone, of a trader father who, like so many other Shi'is from south Lebanon, went to West Africa to escape the stultifying economic system of the South. Berri returned as a child to his family's south Lebanon hometown, Tibnin. His family, while a fairly large one in south Lebanon, is noted neither for its wealth nor for its influence. For instance, his sister Zainib is married to the principal of the elementary school in Tibnin. Her husband also owns a petrol station in Tibnin; in 1981, her home was simply a room next to the lube bay (although she and her husband now live in more conventional quarters). In short, Berri is a man of petit-bourgeois origins, who lacks the flamboyant style and connections of his traditional competitors. One of Berri's prime rivals, a deputy who can claim all the trappings and lineage that Berri cannot, once sarcastically asked in my presence, "Who is this

Ibn Mustafa Berri?" (But, of course, he knew the answer only too well.) His rivals within the Shi'i community frequently note that his association with Imam Musa began only in 1974 and allude to his having been a member of the Ba'th party.

Berri is an easy man to underestimate. Colorless, at least in comparison to many of his political foes, Berri is a true newcomer to political prominence. He has the insecurities that one might expect of a man whose success is as much a surprise to himself as it is to his opponents, and his insecurities have bred an impressive instinct for political survival.

Berri is a lawyer, educated at the Lebanese University. At the university he was a campus politician, rising to the office of student body president. After graduating in 1963, he went on to the Sorbonne to continue his studies. While Musa al-Sadr was busy mobilizing followers in the 1960s, Nabih Berri was, like many of his fellow Shi'is, a member of the pro-Syrian wing of the Ba'th party. He also spent several of his adult years in West Africa and at least two periods in the United States between 1963 and the early 1970s (his ex-wife and six children still live in the United States, and Berri retains a "green card" that enables him to work there). Berri, unlike Husain al-Husaini (whom he replaced as the leader of Amal), is a model for the new Shi'i middle class—those who find old-style *za'im* politics stifling and oppressive. He is a man with sociological resonance. Much to the surprise of his adversaries, he has been able to maintain the support of a fair proportion of those Shi'is who have "made it," while also retaining the support of those who have not. (By the mid-1980s, he was fighting to retain the support of the latter category.)

The sociopolitical changes that have helped to engender Berri's growing influence have not escaped the notice of the Shi'i *zu'ama* and their allies, but they have hardly rushed to make room for the new claimants to power. As I shall explain below, attempting to ignore, or even turn back the clock of Shi'i politicization may be a compelling maneuver for those who have so much to lose, but it is also doomed. While adept gyrations and manipulations may keep the *zu'ama* off the endangered species list for a bit longer, it is very doubtful that they will ever recapture even a modicum of the influence and control that they once enjoyed. This judgment is not only applicable to the Shi'a, but especially to the Maronites, whose recent patterns of modernization sometimes seem to be strikingly parallel to those of the Shi'a.[5]

One of the more serious intrasectarian challenges to Amal's primacy in the leadership of the Shi'a, especially in late 1982 and throughout 1983, came from one individual, Mufti Muhammad

Mahdi Shams al-Din. Shams al-Din, formerly a principal in Amal (he was a leading member of the Command Council until 1983), is one of the most important Shiʿi clerics in Lebanon. In terms of institutional legitimacy, Shams al-Din's only real competitor is the Jaʿfari Mufti al-Mumtaz, ʿAbd al-Amir Qabalan (who, by way of contrast, has maintained close relations with Amal).[6] Since the disappearance of Musa al-Sadr, who led Harakat Amal while simultaneously chairing the Supreme Shiʿi Council, the two leadership positions have been split along secular-clerical lines. Husain al-Husaini, a parliamentary deputy, led Amal until 1980, when he resigned and was replaced by Nabih Berri. Subsequently, al-Husaini has aligned with Shams al-Din, who chairs the Supreme Shiʿi Council (while retaining the title deputy chairman, in deference to the missing Musa al-Sadr, who is the elected chairman until 1992). Al-Husaini's defeat of Kamil al-Asʿad, in the October 1984 election of the Speaker of the National Assembly, further enhanced both his and Shams al-Din's claim for communal leadership.

The details of the struggle for supremacy between Shams al-Din and Berri are elusive; nonetheless, it is clear that they view one another as arch political competitors. In early 1982, for example, press reports indicated that there was a power struggle between Berri and Shams al-Din.[7] The Israeli invasion seemed to push Berri closer to the mufti, although there was some controversy between the two concerning the extent to which Amal fighters should oppose the IDF. Berri, according to some informants, was pushing for a more aggressive role, especially in Ras Beirut, but he seems to have been successfully overruled by Shams al-Din. (As the political climate became more radical, in late 1983, Shams al-Din became a vociferous advocate of resistance to the Israeli occupation.) In the months following the invasion, the two men temporarily overcame or at least put aside their differences, but the competition resumed in 1983.

Although Berri gained some legitimacy through the active support of Shaikh Qabalan, who has called Amal the "backbone of the Shiʿi sect,"[8] Shams al-Din, emphasizing his role in an institution legitimated by the state, has shrewdly attempted to isolate Berri by dismissing him as just another militia leader, and hence merely symptomatic of the carnage that has gripped Lebanon. In early 1983, the Supreme Shiʿi Council announced that Shams al-Din had broken off all relations with the leadership of Harakat Amal.[9] The truncation of relations had the effect of placing the mufti above the fray, validating his prospective claim for the principal political leadership role of the Shiʿa while making him an attractive interlocutor for non-Shiʿi power brokers.

While Berri and his compatriots were fighting in the political trenches to preserve Amal's organizational integrity, Shams al-Din transcended the turmoil and joined other Muslim leaders in adopting what was called the "Islamic Position."[10] In collaboration with Mufti Hasan Khalid (Sunni), Shaikh Halim Taqi al-Din (Druze), former prime ministers Salim al-Huss and Saʾib Salam (both Sunnis), and other well-known Muslim figures, Shams al-Din signed a program that, upon examination, might easily have been published by Amal. The program declares the signatories' commitment to a definitive, independent Lebanon, a democratic parliamentary republic dedicated to freedom, equal opportunity, and social justice. They called for the abolishment of political confessionalism (while implicitly preserving differential personal status law among the various sects), and the rejection of any scheme to cantonize, decentralize, or partition Lebanon.

The point is that there are few substantive differences between the "Islamic Position" and that of Amal. Shams al-Din and Berri are not competing because of any significant disjunction in their political programs, but because they are jealous and even fearful of one another's power. Berri's constituency is in the street, but Shams al-Din's is with the respectable Shiʿi establishment, with those who are discomfited by the unruly and unkempt activists who have both numbers and guns. Thus, we find men like the wealthy businessman Muhammad Hammud and the Assembly deputies Latif al-Zain and Husain al-Husaini standing with Shams al-Din against Berri. As they see it, they are standing with legitimacy and for civility, two attributes that will elude Amal, in their view. In each case, the men grouped with Shams al-Din and the Supreme Shiʿi Council were early associates of Imam Musa.[11] To a man, they certainly recognize the crying need for political reform in Lebanon, but they seek to be the agents of reform; they want to manage it and shape it, as they must do if they are to avoid being submerged in the process. This is not a game of ego gratification, but an issue of political survival, and the final result, notwithstanding minor victories by each side, remains to be seen.

While Berri and Shams al-Din have been engaged in a struggle to determine the legitimate spokesperson for the Shiʿa, a process of factionalization has been under way that threatens to make the outcome of their struggle a moot point. In the three or four years preceding the 1982 invasion, Amal enjoyed increasing success in consolidating its control. However, the postlude to the invasion saw a reversal of the process.

While Israel's massive invasion was still in progress, Nabih Berri was serving as a member of the National Salvation Committee, formed to begin what will continue to be a very long and trouble-filled road toward national reconciliation. Although Harakat Amal could not openly support the election of Bashir al-Jumayyil in August 1982, it privately pledged support, as did the two major Shi'i religious leaders, Qabalan and Shams al-Din. Given Amin al-Jumayyil's less problematic résumé, Amal supported Amin's election on the presumption that he would move purposefully toward intercommunal reconciliation and political reform.[12]

Unfortunately, Shaikh Amin lacked a significant constituency in his own Maronite sect, where he competed unsuccessfully with his brother's organizational legacy—the Lebanese Forces. Unlike the 1958 crisis, when President Fuad Chehab widely promoted reconciliation on the basis that there had been "no victor and no vanquished," in 1982, the new president was confronted with an exuberant and seemingly powerful Maronite militia that was convinced it had won the war, if only vicariously. I well remember a conversation with an official of the Lebanese Forces in October 1982. The conversation turned icy when I suggested that there was plenty of blame to go around for all. In the view of my interlocutor, the Maronites had done nothing wrong whatsoever—his view was not uncommon.

Faced with an unyielding Maronite community, which resented Amin al-Jumayyil's assumption of the office that rightly belonged to the martyred Bashir, the new president was forced to spend much of his time casting worried glances over his shoulder. Furthermore, not only was his political survival at stake, but his physical survival as well, a fact that is well illustrated by periodic authoritative rumors concerning plots being hatched within the Lebanese Forces (in late 1983, the Lebanese Forces may have actively planned a coup d'etat). The president's daunting lack of support in the Maronite community was dramatically demonstrated in the spring of 1985 when his opponents in the Lebanese Forces launched an uprising (*intifadah*) to consolidate their authority and to state in no uncertain terms their unwillingness to defer to Amin.

The irony is that as Amin al-Jumayyil struggled unsuccessfully to gain a base of support within his own sect, he squandered the not inconsiderable support that he initially enjoyed among the Muslim communities. Rather than attempting to cultivate the cooperation of Amal's leaders, he proved to be much more comfortable dealing with the established *zu'ama* in lieu of their challengers. He chose to ally with Kamil al-As'ad, who as Speaker of the Assembly facilitated the election of both Bashir and Amin (it is rumored that the Speaker's assistance was not an act of charity—he may have been richly compensated, at least according to Lebanese Maronite informants). It is interesting and revealing that Kamil al-Asʿad enjoyed firm support among the Maronites, but almost none from his own community, an anomaly well illustrated by the fact that since 1976 he resided in Jabal Lubnan (Mount Lebanon, the Maronite's geographic locus) rather than Jabal ʿAmil (he is from the southern village of al-Tayybi). Not unexpectedly, the close links between the Speaker and the president helped to resurrect the old venomous rivalry between al-Asʿad and Amal.

In the fall of 1982, Amal had adopted a moderate stance, expecting that *al-sabr miftah al-faraj*—patience was the key to success. While it was recognized at the time within Amal that the movement had not yet surmounted its militia days, a number of initiatives were taken to broaden the movement's activities in the social welfare sphere, and thus to recapture its original essence as a sociopolitical reform movement. For instance, in the South it opened a series of Spartan, yet adequate clinics that were accessible to all citizens for a modest fee (with free care available when justified by need). The clinics were well planned and hardly seemed to be fly-by-night operations when I visited them in 1982. Although Amal's financial resources were limited, it also funded several community improvement projects, including the planting of nut-bearing trees and the paving of roads within villages.

The much derided and corruption-ridden Majlis al-Janub (Council of the South) at long last, and with much prodding by Amal, was finally given a chairman, Husain Kanʿan, who was at least nominally more interested in civic service than in self-service. Kanʿan was subsequently replaced by Muhammad Baidun, who is on good terms with Berri and is, unlike Kanʿan, actually from the South. Moreover, Amal's vitality received early affirmation when as many as 250,000 Shiʿis gathered in Tyre in September 1982 to commemorate the fourth anniversary of the disappearance of Imam Musa (a smaller but still impressive demonstration was later held in Nabatiya). Periodic strikes and local demonstrations also served as continuous reminders that Amal had sustained a significant—albeit reduced—base of support.

At the same time, the movement's principal officials merely expected evidence of good faith from the government in the form of relatively modest incremental concessions to Shiʿi demands. Sadly, the expectation was not met. The phoenix did not rise from the ashes; instead, the security situation deteriorated through the fall of 1982 into 1983.

By October 1982, fighting erupted in al-Shuf between the Druze militia and the Lebanese Forces that had reentered the region in order to consolidate the "victory." Israel, which occupied al-Shuf until its precipitous withdrawal in September 1983, seemed unable to stem the fighting. Indeed, credible reports indicate that the Israelis may even have facilitated the fighting.[13] Berri and his compatriots expressed support for the Druze, but provided little, if any, substantive support. Meanwhile, the army, acting at times in apparent sympathy with the Lebanese Forces, began a series of forays into West Beirut and the suburbs, arresting a number of Shiʿi militants (often on flimsy evidence) and attempting to disarm the Shiʿa. As one Shiʿi in Ghobeire told me in October 1982, "they see me as an enemy simply because I wear a beard, and because my wife dresses as a modest Muslim woman should. Everytime I approach an army checkpoint, I am afraid that I will be arrested." (This man has since quit Amal in order to join a more militant group that he believes will aggressively defend his rights.)

A key turning point in the deteriorating internal situation was the U.S. mediated agreement of May 17, 1983, between Israel and Lebanon. The agreement provided for serious restrictions upon Lebanese sovereignty, including limitations on its use of air space and the employment of its soldiers and weapons. Moreover, the agreement made no mention of United Nations forces, save a very modest observation role in the environs of the refugee camps, raising suspicions among many Muslims who feared the elimination of the international forces would give the Israelis a freer hand once out of the glare of world attention. A key impediment to the agreement's implementation was a secret side letter from Israel to the United States. The letter conditioned a phased and partial Israeli withdrawal from Lebanon upon a simultaneous withdrawal of Syrian and remaining Palestinian forces.

In retrospect, it seems clear that the May 17 agreement reversed Syria's waning fortunes in Lebanon. The appended conditions ensured the opposition of Syria, which objected to being equated to the Israeli invasion force, and provided President Hafiz al-Asad the decisive voice in determining whether the agreement would be implemented. Al-Asad leaped on the agreement as a potent symbol to mobilize anti-American and anti-Israeli sentiment. Lebanese resistance to the agreement, and to Maronite President Amin al-Jumayyil as well, was institutionalized in the National Salvation Front (NSF) that was formed in July 1983.

Although it is not well recognized, the agreement did succeed in one respect. In effect, but not necessarily by American design, the agreement served as a public relations rescue operation for Israel. By signing the agreement, the Israeli government could cast off the accusation of obduracy that had dogged it since the previous fall. Defense Minister Moshe Arens accurately noted that the agreement was a no-lose proposition for Israel. If implemented, Israel would maintain an infrastructure of control in south Lebanon that would render the South a useful security buffer, and at the same time the active Syrian military presence in Lebanon would be eliminated. If the agreement failed to be implemented, it would still relieve the pressure on Israel from its European friends and the United States.[14]

The Shi'a saw the agreement as a device whereby Israel would affect the political partition of Lebanon. Partial withdrawal of Israeli forces from the South was seen as a means for reducing the costs of occupying Lebanon, without eradicating the fact of occupation. This perspective is justified, in my view. In point of fact, the Israelis foreclosed a plenary withdrawal until January 1985, and even then it was clear that they intended to maintain a residual presence in south Lebanon through surrogate militia forces that were buttressed by hundreds of Israeli soldiers, military advisers, and intelligence agents.[15]

The agreement had two significant effects on Harakat Amal. First, it further pushed the movement into an alliance with Syria, an alliance that it had attempted to draw away from in the summer and fall of 1982. Second, it tarnished the neutrality and appeal of the good diplomatic offices of the United States and raised serious questions about U.S. motives in Lebanon. Although the diplomatic record indicates that U.S. envoys urged President al-Jumayyil to reach an accommodation with the Shi'a, particularly after mid-1983, the May 17 agreement gave the Shi'a reason to doubt the sincerity behind the Americans' entreaties.

By the second half of 1983, the tightly wound hopes of the previous autumn were unraveling with destabilizing speed. Not only was the implementation of the May 17 agreement in serious doubt, but so was the future of Amin al-Jumayyil, who achieved the feat of being discredited in the eyes of his own Maronite community as well as among the Sunni, Druze, and Shi'i communities. Israel's plans for a Maronite-dominated Lebanon were jettisoned; in early September, the IDF deployed southward, leaving behind the flaming Shuf, where fighting between Druze and Maronite militias had persisted since the previous fall.

Later in September, a fateful decision was made by the United States to provide naval gunfire support for the Lebanese army forces defending Suq al-Gharb (in Aley district). The U.S. engagement at Suq al-Gharb was another major turning point. Many observers believe that, through its action, the United States succeeded in becoming just another militia, in a situation where there was already no dearth of armed partisan formations.[16] In fairness to the United States, it should be noted that while the U.S. action was viewed by many Lebanese—Christian and Muslim alike—as a desertion of neutrality, there was a strong sense among U.S. policymakers that it was acting in support of the legitimate authorities. A good case may be made that the United States was lured into supporting Suq al-Gharb by the Lebanese army command precisely to force the United States to choose sides. During this period, the Lebanese army was seen by the Shi‘a and the Druze as merely a surrogate for the Lebanese Forces, a view not entirely unjustified, given the biographies of many of the officers in senior positions, and the fact that the first action undertaken by the reconstituted army had been a harsh campaign of demolishing illegally constructed homes in the southern suburbs (especially in Ouza’i). Whatever the truth of the plots-within-plots conspiracy theories, the U.S. action at Suq al-Gharb—which had little direct effect on the battle it was intended to influence—helped to exacerbate the communal polarization that was proceeding at an increasing pace.

Just prior to the new U.S. entanglement in the Shuf, the Lebanese army had mounted a grand-scale incursion, involving 10,000 Lebanese troops, on August 31, into the Muslim districts of Beirut following a period of unrest and turmoil. According to published—but hardly impartial—accounts, U.S. military officers actively encouraged and assisted in planning the move into West Beirut.[17] (The U.S. role—if any—in the August 31 incursion is not clearly discernible from objective published accounts.) In short, the Shi‘a came to see the United States as the consort of its oppressors, Israel and the Lebanese Forces. The friend of the enemies of the Shi‘a also came to be an enemy.[18]

Still, significant evidence of Amal's forebearance remained. Despite the army's assault and takeover of Ras Beirut, the movement continued to express support for the army as a national institution that had to be preserved. When the Druze leader Walid Jumblatt, former president Sulaiman Franjiya, and former prime minister Rashid Karami, acting with Syrian support if not under Syrian instructions, formed the National Salvation Front (NSF) in July 1983 to oppose President al-Jumayyil and the May 17 agreement, Harakat Amal declared its support for the front, but never joined it. It was interesting to observe, for some months afterward, Walid Jumblatt noting frequently that "Nabih is with us," while Nabih remained silent. Nabih Berri was cautious about standing too close to the NSF and proved to be a bit shy about voicing support. For example, in July 1983, Berri was asked about his relationship with the NSF. He replied: "I agree with them, and we are working jointly, but I do not want to leave Beirut. I have been invited several times to visit Zgharta [the home village of former president Sulaiman Franjiya] but I refused because I did not want anyone to be able to say that my decisions could in any way be influenced by Syria."[19]

The Challenge of the Radicals

But moderation has its limits, especially moderation without political recompense. As its centrist leadership failed to deliver, Amal was coming to be seen as increasingly ineffectual. In the latter half of 1983, frustration was rising in the Shiʿi-populated areas, and Harakat Amal seemed to be in danger of losing its grip on the population. Berri worried aloud, on several occasions, that he feared the moderates would each be pushed aside, only to be replaced by extremists, and he admitted that he was losing control in the streets.[20]

From within the community, a number of small groups dedicated to terror and violence sprang up or, more accurately, reemerged. One can only guess to what extent organizations like the al-Sadr Brigade and the Husain Suicide Commandos were autonomous of external control or succor, but whatever the case may be, it is plain that such groups represented a further fragmentation of Amal's waning authority. A more important and related development was the growing activism of Shiʿi clerics throughout the country. The events of the preceding year had exacerbated sectarian cleavages in Lebanon and helped to create a climate in which those who could evoke religious symbolism could generate a following. A number of clerics came to the fore, each claiming a slice of Amal's following. It soon became clear that this competition was of much greater significance than that between Berri and Shams al-Din.

Despite the intensity of their personal competition for ultimate communal authority, Shams al-Din and his associates, on the one hand, and Berri and his colleagues, on the other hand, share a conception of Lebanon as a multiconfessional society whose characteristic diversity is a given and a virtue. For both sides in this struggle, political and social justice is to be attained within the context of a reformed Lebanese state. None of the centrist contenders for power— admittedly taking some liberty with the word "centrist"—has proposed that the Shiʿa of Lebanon emulate their Iranian co-religionists by creating an Islamic republic. Indeed, Shams al-Din, ʿAkif Haidar, Berri, and other representative centrist figures have explicitly spurned such a solution for Lebanon. In their view, Lebanon's cultural heterogeneity, tradition of intercultural toleration (however much the tradition may have been abused and assaulted in recent years), and the political preferences of the majority of the Shiʿa preclude such a design.

Certainly, the Islamic Revolution was profoundly felt within Lebanon, but, as chapter 3 shows, after the period of ecstatic exuberance following the fall of the shah, the events in Iran proved to be more important as a spur to action than as a model for precise emulation. This is not to argue that the proponents of Islamic rule for Lebanon were absent from the scene, but their voices were drowned out by the centrist Shiʿi leaders whose promotion of the deconfessionalization of Lebanese politics found a rapt constituency. Their point was precisely *not* to stress religion as a political criterion, but to call for the abolishment of a system of politics based upon particularism. (In doing so, of course, they were proposing changes that would redound to the long-term benefit of the community with the plurality of votes, namely, the Shiʿa.) If, following the Israeli invasion, meaningful steps had been taken to reform Lebanon's problematic political system, the centrists might have carried the day. As the sad record shows so clearly, that was not the case.

As the events following the 1982 invasion unfolded, the centrists had only empty hands to show for their blandishments. Amal, seemingly on its way to becoming the nearly undisputed custodian of the political soul of the Shiʿa, found itself under serious challenge. Concurrently, the Supreme Shiʿi Council was becoming increasingly peripheral to the mass of politicized Shiʿa who experienced only further frustration and suffering. Propelled by despair, abetted by a strange objective alliance between Israel and Syria, and helped materially by Iran, a number of radical Shiʿi groups came to the forefront.

In the South, as we shall see in the following chapter, Israel's policies as well as the very logic of an underground resistance (i.e., secrecy and organizational decentralization) progressively radicalized the population. Syria, which in the hope-filled days of 1982 feared Amal might be overfriendly to a *pax* Americana in Lebanon, fostered the development of radical Shiʿi groups in order to counterbalance Amal and remind its straying leaders of their vulnerabilities. In July 1982, Syria permitted the establishment of a 1,000-man Iranian Pasdaran (Revolutionary Guard) contingent in Baʿalbak and the simultaneous fixing of a Pasdaran headquarters in the Syrian border town of al-Zabadani. Baʿalbak, and the surrounding area, came to be the locus of action for Husain Musawi's nefarious Islamic Amal, as well as for a number of radical clerics. Most significant, it was in the Biqaʿ that Hizb Allah (the party of God) seemed to enjoy the greatest freedom of movement. Not coincidentally, Baʿalbak, and especially the adjoining Shaikh ʿAbd Allah army barracks—appropriated by the militants—would come to be seen as at least one of the critical junctures in the terror network that appeared so sensationally in 1983. It is also noteworthy that as events began to follow a Syrian script, in 1984, the enthusiasm of Damascus for the Biqaʿ radicals seems to have cooled.[21]

The ethnocentric penchant of some western observers to impose order and structure on the disorderly and the unstructured is nowhere more clearly revealed than with reference to the Shiʿa of Lebanon. In a community long bereft of political organizations, it seems hardly a revelation to disclose that what we in fact find are weak and rudimentary organizational structures. Membership is all too frequently a political state of mind—a sense of affiliation—rather than a statement of formal affiliation. The newly politicized—angry, frustrated, and discontented with their circumstances—shift from one movement to another, blown by the winds of rhetoric and demagoguery. Shiʿi politics are fluid and loosely articulated, and the movements competing for Shiʿi members constitute a cabalistic collection that is as hard to penetrate analytically as it is to describe. These characteristics are no less true of Amal than of its rivals. Hizb Allah is a case in point. It brings together all of those fledgling groups that see Iran as their model and Khomeini as their leader. On the one hand, Hizb Allah is a palpable organization that receives orders and directions from Iran; yet, on the other, it is a fluid collection of groups over which Iran's real influence may be only nominal. It is certainly true that the Islamic Republic has been warmly supportive of Hizb Allah, since it serves as a potent antidote to the reputed equivocation of Berri and, at times, Shams al-Din.[22]

Founded in 1978, Hizb Allah reemerged in 1982 with cells in the Beirut area and its headquarters in the Biqaʿ Valley. While numerically inferior to Amal (in Beirut, the ratio may be about 5 : 1 in Amal's favor), Hizb Allah has proven to be a potent rival.

Whereas nonclerics dominate Amal, Hizb Allah's cadre consists in large part of firebrand clerics who seek to foment an Islamic revolution, in cooperation with some radical extremists, as well as those who simply believe that Islamic militance is the answer. Many of Hizb Allah's leaders are young clerics in their twenties and thirties. The leadership includes Shaikh Subhi Tufaili, thirty-nine years old—usually considered outspoken and radical, he has been referred to by some observers as the political leader of Hizb Allah; Shaikh ʿAbbas Musawi, thirty-seven years old—director of the religious school in Baʿalbak, he is responsible for military affairs and internal security;

Shaikh Ibrahim Amin, thirty-two years old—scion of an important family of clerics in the South, he was to be the ambassador to Iran of the Islamic Republic of Lebanon (which never came into existence); and Shaikh Hasan Nasr Allah, twenty-eight years old—also from the South, he apparently serves as the liaison with Iran and its forces in Lebanon.

Reportedly, the relationship between Iran and Hizb Allah is maintained through the Islamic Republic's Higher Defense Council, the vehicle through which Ayatollah Khomeini transmits his orders and guidance to Hizb Allah. The council consists of President al-Sayyid ʿAli Khamenei, Speaker ʿAli Akhbar Hashemi Rafsanjani, and Revolutionary Guards (Pasdaran) chief al-Sayyid Muhsin Rafaʾi. The Higher Defense Council is the central decision-making body of the Iranian military-security establishment.[23]

Iran has also sponsored the creation of a Majlis al-Shura (Consultative Council) for Lebanon. The council supervises the work of Hizb Allah within Lebanon and serves as the nodal connection between Iran and Lebanon. It consists of twelve men, most of whom are clerics, the remainder being military officials. The council subsumes seven committees named as follows: intellectual, financial, political, information, military, social, and legal. The entire operation appears to be well financed from Iran; not only are operating expenses provided, but there is also an extensive system for the payment of pensions to the families of individuals martyred in the cause of Hizb Allah (about $225,000 is distributed monthly to martyrs' families).[24]

Although the details of the relationship are not known, it is clear that the Islamic Amal organization of Husain Musawi is closely linked to Hizb Allah. In Musawi's terms, any Muslim who works for Islam and the Islamic Revolution and accepts the principle of the *wilayat al-faqih* (guardianship of the jurisconsult) is a member of Hizb Allah.[25] It should be noted, however, that Musawi also denies that Hizb Allah is an organization per se; he claims the party lacks offices, a formal membership, and other organizational characteristics.

In addition to Islamic Amal, the Hizb al-Daʿwa (party of the [Islamic] Call), originally created in Iraq in 1959, also appears to be a component part of Hizb Allah, having ceased to exist as a separate party in Lebanon as early as 1980.[26]

It is less clear what precise role al-Sayyid Muhammad Husain Fadl Allah, of the Bir al-ʿAbd Beirut suburb, plays in Hizb Allah. The son of the late Ayatollah ʿAbd al-Raʾuf Fadl Allah from the southern Lebanese village of ʿAinata, Shaikh Fadl Allah was born in the Iraqi city of Najaf in 1935 or 1936. He later studied under Ayatollah Abu al-Qasim Khu'i, an Iraqi who is one of the leading Shi'i clerics in the world. Fadl Allah arrived in Lebanon in 1966 and took up residence in the Nab'a quarter of East Beirut. In 1976, he was appointed as Khu'i's *wakil* (personal representative) in Lebanon. He resided in Nab'a—where he preached and wrote—until it was seized by the Phalangists in 1976. He then fled, as did all of the Shi'i residents of the quarter.[27]

Since the fall of 1983, Fadl Allah has emerged as one of the most influential clerics in Lebanon. Unlike his mentor, Ayatollah Khu'i, who has spurned involvement in politics, Fadl Allah has actively involved himself in the political arena and has frequently seemed positively to enjoy his status as a political celebrity.

He became known to the rest of the world in 1983, when some correspondents, apparently drawing on Israeli and hostile Lebanese sources, reported that Fadl Allah was centrally involved in at least some of the anti-American terror bombings of the last few years.[28] He is also widely mentioned as the leader or spiritual guide of Hizb Allah. Frankly, ferreting out the truth is not easy, and Fadl Allah has as much—or more—incentive to deceive as his adversaries do, but the following facts are well established.

Fadl Allah has consistently claimed that he is not the leader of any party or movement, though he acknowledges his own influence among the Shi'a. Plainly, it is unimportant whether he is or is not the leader (or guide, for that matter) of Hizb Allah. The most important point is that his message resonates throughout the Shi'i community. Additionally, it should be noted that his message is one that combines a call for the adherence of Muslims to Islamic law with a plea for intercommunal toleration (in sharp contrast to the venomous intolerance of many of those clerics who acknowledge a role in Hizb Allah). There is reason to believe that during one visit to Iran, in February 1985, Fadl Allah's refusal to demand the immediate establishment of an Islamic state led to a cold reception. While he does not deny that he would like to live in an Islamic state, he does not think that the conditions in Lebanon are appropriate for the establishment of such a state, and he has said so explicitly and frequently: "At this point we must make a distinction between the state of one religious party or the state with a vast majority of one view, in which religion is the state, and the situation like Lebanon, which is one of diversity."[29]

For Fadl Allah, the establishment of the Islamic state is a slow process that must be built on dialogue, education, and mutual understanding. He presumes, or purports to presume, that as the process proceeds, and when "an overwhelming majority of the people convert to Islam, and when we have favorable political conditions, then we could bring about an Islamic republic."[30] Shaikh Fadl Allah's patience should not be mistaken for equivocation. He often notes that in whatever state Muslims live, they must live according to the precepts of Islam. Furthermore, his view of the psychological dilemma of Muslims, in contrast to that of Christians, is decidedly asymmetrical. For Christians, in his view, there is no canon law requirement to live in a state governed by the precepts of their religion, given the clear separation of the temporal from the spiritual in Christianity. But for Muslims, there is a clear imperative to avoid such dualism: "The problem of the Muslim is the dualism arising from the difference between what is lawful on the level of the state and what is lawful on the level of faith. The problem of Islam is that it does not have a legal vacuum. Consequently, when a Muslim lives in a state that does not adopt Islam, his life remains confused because of the dualism he is living under."[31]

Much piffle has been written about Fadl Allah's views; but, in comparison to many of his brother clerics, he does not come off as a fanatic. Indeed, his interviews are lucid, substantive, and detailed expositions, which leave at least a margin for compromise. For many, Fadl Allah's views are just too moderate, but, significantly, some at the center of Shiʻi politics believe that he has a crucial role to play in consolidating the leadership of the community. Like Shams al-Din, whom he seems to have surpassed in influence—at least in the streets—his rivalry with Berri seems to be a personal one, not readily diminished.

As to the allegation that Fadl Allah has played a role in spawning or facilitating terror attacks, the simple fact is that it is doubtful that anyone in the West really knows. There is no denying that Fadl Allah's message has inspired opposition to the United States and Israel—he concedes as much—but whether he has taken a more direct role is at least unproven. Fadl Allah has his share of enemies, quite independent of his role in any particular incident, and one should presume that there is much disinformation available (from all sides). The March 1985 car-bombing at the hands of the shaikh's Maronite enemies, which took eighty lives but spared Fadl Allah, was a terrible reminder that, whatever his organizational role, Fadl Allah is not likely to fade into obscurity.

In contrast to Fadl Allah's relative public moderation, Hizb Allah has adopted an uncompromising and coldly militant stance. Hizb Allah represents a contending vision of society, a vision explicitly outlined in vituperative prose in an open letter published by Hizb

Allah in February 1985. Unlike Amal, which finds programmatic ambiguity a useful device with which to avoid opening the latent fissures in its following, Hizb Allah forthrightly declares its aim: the establishment of Islamic rule in Lebanon. In the complexity and confusion of contemporary Lebanon, Hizb Allah offers a simple and comfortable message, which is both accessible and intuitively pleasing to those who have heard more than their share of empty promises from ambitious politicians. The answer is found in the distinctive culture of the Shiʿa, the "main sources" of which "are the venerable Quran, the infallible Sunna, and the decisions and religious opinions made by the jurisprudent [Khomeini], who is the authority on tradition among us. These sources are clear, uncomplicated, and accessible to all without exception and they need no theorization or philosophy. All they need is abidance and application."[32]

The undisputed authoritative leader is Khomeini, who is viewed as the embodiment of the Islamic Revolution. The open letter declares clearly that Hizb Allah stands ready to follow Khomeini's dictates: "We . . . abide by the orders of a single wise and just command currently embodied in the supreme Ayatollah Ruhollah al-Musavi al-Khomeini, the rightly guided imam who combines all the qualities of the total imam, who has detonated the Muslims' revolution, and who is bringing about the glorious Islamic renaissance."[33]

In the perspective of Hizb Allah, the Shiʿa are under siege and facing a panoply of treacherous enemies, including the Maronite Phalange, Israel, France, the Soviet Union, and Iraq. But it is the United States that is the fundamental source of the troubles of the Shiʿa; "America is the reason for all our catastrophes," the open letter asserts. Everything is marginal to the imperative to confront the United States.

In a line reminiscent of Frantz Fanon, Hizb Allah notes that sacrifice is tantamount to liberation: "Thus, we have seen that aggression can be repelled only with sacrifices and dignity gained with the sacrifice of blood, and that freedom is not given but regained with sacrifice of both heart and soul."[34]

There is no mistaking the enmity of Hizb Allah for Nabih Berri and the political perspective he represents. For the proponents of Hizb Allah, there is no room for compromise with the enemy, whether the enemy appears in the form of Amin al-Jumayyil, the United States, or Israel. Thus, Berri's service on the ineffectual National Salvation Committee of 1982, viewed as "no more than an American-Israeli bridge over which the Phalange crossed to oppress the downtrodden,"[35] is a sufficient justification to anathematize him. Moreover, Berri's subsequent acceptance of a ministerial role in the government formed under Prime Minister Rashid Karami in May 1984 merely serves as further evidence of his connivance with the enemy. For the neo-Manichaeans of Hizb Allah, it could not be otherwise.

In the current depressed economic environment, it is hardly insignificant that Hizb Allah can offer not only the virtue of ideological simplicity and authenticity, but the rewards of hard cash as well. Whatever the individual's stake in the outcome of the political struggle for the soul of the Shi'a, the body must also be fed. The simple fact of the matter is that Hizb Allah seems not to suffer from a paucity of working capital. Fighters are paid relatively well; and while a regular salary may not buy enduring loyalty, it certainly helps to accumulate manpower at critical moments. In contrast to its radical foe, which seems to enjoy generous funding from Iran, Amal is basically dependent on the Shi'a of Lebanon for its funds. In the horrendous economic climate of mid-1986, when a militiaman's salary might be a family's only available source of income, the fact that Hizb Allah can afford full-time gunmen, while many of Amal's are part-timers or volunteers, is not at all a trivial matter. In addition, Hizb Allah has accumulated enough weaponry and war materiel to have to be considered a reasonably formidable militia, by Lebanese standards.[36]

The rise of the radicals has had profound effects on Amal. Although Amal still manages to hold its leading position, in the process of responding to its extremist competitors, it, too, has adopted more extreme positions. Amal remains at the center of Shi'i politics, but the center is nowhere near where it was in 1982. The radicalization of the Shi'a in general, and Amal in particular, is evident in the South, discussed in chapter 7, where the Israeli occupation has been an important prod to the community's increasing radicalism.

Muhammad Husain Fadl Allah. (Used by permission of George A. Nader.)

7. Making Enemies in South Lebanon

No other facet of Israel's misadventure in Lebanon is a clearer case of bad judgment and self-defeating policy than Israel's mishandling of the Shiʿi population of south Lebanon. This verdict is not a product of the smug comfort of writing retrospectively, for the denouement was clear almost from the onset of the occupation.[1] Israeli policymakers failed to understand the meaning of transparent sociopolitical developments among the Shiʿa of south Lebanon, and it seems they ignored the warnings of Israeli Arabists who did understand.[2] Of all the blunders committed by Israel in Lebanon, those committed in south Lebanon were the most unnecessary, the least easily excused by the dumb luck of history, and, perhaps, the most far-ranging in effect. For the first time in the history of the Arab-Israeli conflict, the IDF was defeated, and not by a standing army, but by a loosely organized, poorly equipped resistance force.

It is no small irony that it was the Shiʿa who so complicated Israel's predicament in Lebanon. The Shiʿi community had no place in Ariel Sharon's blueprint for a Maronite-dominated Lebanon; when the Maronites proved a weak and unsteady ally, it was the Lebanese Druze card that was played. Yet, the Shiʿa, especially the half million or so living in the South, were in many ways the objective allies of Israel. Living in a border region contiguous to northern Israel, the Shiʿa, like their Druze and Christian compatriots in the South, recognized a sound pragmatic rationale for maintaining peaceful relations with their militarily superior neighbor.

Although the Shiʿa had earlier lent their manpower to the Palestinian resistance forces based in Lebanon, well before the 1982 invasion, the Shiʿi community had tired of paying the cost—in blood, sorrow, and wealth—of the armed guerrilla presence in their midst. As we have seen, by 1981 and early 1982, the Shiʿa were actively fighting the *fidaʾiyin* and were doing so with at least modest success. Indeed, it is not at all farfetched to argue that, had the Israelis not invaded in 1982, a very serious Shiʿa-Palestinian conflict would have erupted in Lebanon; such was the expectation of the leaders of Amal in the South, and the steadily escalating clashes of 1981 and 1982 pointed in the same direction. Later, when it was clear that Israel had outstayed its welcome in south Lebanon and when the resistance to Israel's occupation of the South gained momentum, it would be instructive to note that many of the Shiʿi villages that were most steadfast in confronting the PLO prior to the June invasion also proved to be among the important centers of anti-Israeli resistance. This latter fact serves as verification of the unwillingness of the politically awakened Shiʿi community to tolerate domination by any foreign power, whether Arab or Israeli. Having begun to throw off the shackles of the PLO presence, the Shiʿi community was not about to wrap itself in the chains of Israel's occupation.

It is important to emphasize that there was nothing predetermined about the hostility that came to describe Israeli-Shiʿa relations. It was the errors produced by several years of clumsy occupation by Israel that alienated the Shiʿa. It need not have been so. This judgment is corroborated by Israeli Arabists who served as Arab affairs officers in south Lebanon (and whose advice seems to have been categorically rejected by Israeli policymakers). One such individual, Moshe Sharon, a widely respected scholar who teaches Islamic history at the Hebrew University, makes the point quite directly: "The present poor state of Shiʿa-Israeli relations did not exist immediately after Israel's drive into Lebanon in 1982, nor has its development been inevitable. On the contrary, most of the Shiʿis in South Lebanon were, in fact, prepared to cultivate peaceful, if not actually friendly, relations with Israel."[3]

Since the establishment of Israel, there had been remarkably few incidents of violence between the Lebanese of the South and Israel; while the Shiʿa felt no particular affection toward Israel, they felt no particular enmity either. Indeed, one of the remarkable aspects of the deteriorating relationship between the Shiʿa and the PLO was that the PLO earned demerits for its own misdeeds as well as for Israeli retaliation (whether the retaliation was proximate to the provoking act or not). Prior to the June 1982 invasion, there was good reason to believe that Israel might arrive at a modus vivendi with Harakat Amal in the South. Moreover, most of the southern-based Amal leadership expected such an arrangement to emerge. Both sides shared the goal of preventing the reestablishment of the Palestinian statelet in the South, and both had a serious stake in the restoration of civility and order in the area. But military success sometimes breeds hubris; and when hubris is tempered by insecurity, the combination can lead to disastrous results. This has clearly been the case in south Lebanon, where Israel's actions from 1982 to 1985 succeeded in spawning an effective resistance force manned by legions of new enemies.

Misreading Shiʿi Hostility toward the PLO

Buoyed by its cordial reception in June 1982, Israel set about attempting to enlist the existing Amal organization in the South as an adjunct to, or even substitute for, Saʿad Haddad's ragtag militia, particularly in areas where Haddad's militia had little influence and few supporters. In what can only be described as a supreme miscalculation, the IDF and the Israeli security services operating in the South (principally the Shin Beth) mistook the alienation of the Shiʿa from the Palestinians as positive evidence for the possibility of establishing close *formal* ties between Israel and the Shiʿi community. In fact, most of the Shiʿi population had no desire to trade one foreign overlord for another. Such wishful thinking on the part of Israel is not altogether surprising, however. The flush of victory did color the reasoning of Israeli policymakers, but there seems to have been no lack of an appreciation for the limited utility of Saʿad Haddad as an authentic leader in south Lebanon. Notwithstanding some one-sided reporting in the United States and Israel, Israeli officials seem to have clearly understood that Haddad and his weak militia were, as one IDF adviser put it, "unacceptable" to the majority of the population, which is to say, the Shiʿa.[4] As Clinton Bailey, an Israeli academic who served as an Arab affairs adviser in south Lebanon, observed in December 1982, the Shiʿi members of Haddad's militia were "looked upon as the dregs of Shiʿa society" by their co-religionists.[5]

Clumsy efforts to co-opt Amal during June and July 1982 failed. While the southern leadership of Amal did not eschew a quiet dialogue with Israeli personnel, they were both unwilling and unable to allow themselves to follow the Haddad prototype of open clientship. Referring to the Shiʿa, Fouad Ajami observes that "like Caesar's wife, they had to be above suspicion. They were sure that they would not be forgiven a close relationship with Israel."[6] Nonetheless, there were no outward displays of belligerence during the summer of 1982, and there were a number of cases of small-scale collaboration and co-operation. For instance, one on-the-scene observer reports that local Amal leaders assisted in identifying leaders of opposing factions, as well as arms caches belonging to the PLO and its allies in the Quwat Mushtarika.[7] This first phase was short-lived; the Israelis lost their patience with the Amal leaders and arrested thirteen of them during the summer of 1982. Thus began a process of polarization that continued well into 1985.

Israeli officials have subsequently admitted, both in private interviews with me and in public interviews, that they recognize that they could have done more to reach a working arrangement with the Shi'a (and with Amal in particular), but they remain skeptical that even a more enlightened approach to the Shi'a would have produced a more congenial relationship. In a limited sense, the skepticism is justified. So long as Israel was wedded to the establishment of an infrastructure of control in south Lebanon, an infrastructure that would render Israel the dominant power in the South (to the disadvantage of both the Beirut government and Damascus), a deal with the Shi'a was hardly possible. It was only if Israel was willing to change its objectives that a deal was possible, and even then it would have to be a quiet and tacit one. But Israeli decisionmakers, especially those who had a hand in approving and applauding the invasion, found the word "tacit" an unpalatable one. They wanted much more than the silent partnership many of the Amal leaders and rank and file were willing to concede.

Constructing an Infrastructure

The initial phase was soon followed by an Israeli campaign to emasculate Amal as a movement and to recruit individual Amal members and other Shi'is into a network of village militias that would operate under Israel's tutelage and direction. Simultaneously, the IDF sponsored the return of several long-absent Shi'i *zu'ama* in order further to undercut Amal's influence in the area. For example, after an absence of seven years, Kazim al-Khalil, a political affiliate of Camille Chamoun's National Liberal party, returned to Tyre. When al-Khalil first returned in July 1982, he attempted to reach a rapprochement with Amal; but, as one Amal leader told me, the *sulha* (reconciliation) quickly evaporated after a few acts of violent intimidation authored by al-Khalil's son.[8] With IDF assistance, al-Khalil did establish a small (forty-man) militia that was armed and uniformed by the Israelis. But al-Khalil has lost much of his political influence; indeed, few southerners believe that he could retain his parliamentary seat in anything approaching a fair election. Nonetheless, his presence in Tyre served modestly to undercut Amal, and it was part of the whole cloth of Israel's campaign to fragment a Shi'i community it could not control *qua* community.

Ironically, what Israel seemed to be doing was attempting to reverse the forces of modernization that had propelled the Shiʿa to break the bonds of their social isolation and begin to find a communal identity. Later, Yitzhak Rabin, the Israeli defense minister since 1984, observed that Israel's presence in Lebanon had "let the Shiʿi genie out of the bottle," but it is more apt to observe that socioeconomic change had done so. Israel's program would probably have worked at an earlier historical stage, but that stage was now only a memory, and one that few of the Shiʿis cared to relive.

Faced with an uncooperative Amal leadership, the Israelis created an organization purportedly independent of Haddad's force. The organization, the Haras al-Watani li-Quraʾ al-Janub (National Guard for the Villages of the South), was intended to unite village militias created under Israeli pressure. While there were some temporary local successes, the attempt ultimately failed. The principal cause of failure was the inability of Israel's and Haddad's agents to recruit locally respected leaders. Even if they wanted to deal with Israel for the sake of restoring civility to their homeland, popular local leaders were keenly aware of the dangers and disincentives for doing so. Moreover, Israel's preferential treatment of the Haddad militia signaled its unwillingness to give fair weight to the claims of the Shiʿa. Even where the militias were relatively active for a time, as in Jwayya, Majdal Silm, and Sarafand, the groups remained transparent implantations led by men far removed from the political mainstream.

Recognizing their failure, the Israelis renovated the militia plan and, in January 1983, created the Organization for a United South, subsequently—and sardonically—renamed the USA (or United South Assembly). The USA, apparently based on the West Bank Village League prototype, was to be comprised of village committees of from five to eight men, and each village was to be expected to mount a sixty-man militia. While the USA was not enthusiastically received, the skillful use of coercion helped to create about thirty village militias. In Sarafand, for example, a local Amal leader was arrested and the village notables were told that the price of his release was the formation of a militia.[9] In many cases, the only leaders available were those who were, for one reason or another, held in disrepute by their fellow villagers. Many residents of the South noted the irony that, in many cases, the very men who were recruited to serve in the militias were the social misfits and toughs who had been terrorizing the South for years.[10] Israel came to be judged by the company it chose to keep.

The militias served two complementary Israeli interests. First, they provided a justification for Israeli involvement in south Lebanon, and a façade behind which Israeli agents and forces could operate. From the beginning of the occupation, it was clear that Israel had decided to establish an infrastructure of control that would allow it to dominate south Lebanon at minimal cost in terms of Israeli manpower. (This is not to argue that Israel sought the annexation of the South; merely that it intended to be the dominant force in the region, and the cheaper the price of domination the better.) Second, and this may well explain the morphology of the Israeli-created militias, although spawned of coercion, it was hoped that the militias would be converted into nominal instruments of the Beirut government while remaining loyal and responsive to Israel. The partisan forces (al-Ansar) that were to be established under the terms of a Lebanese-Israeli peace treaty would have been no more than Israeli-created militias that had been relabeled.[11] Thus, Israel's surrogate forces were to be given an imprimatur of legitimacy. Along these lines, it is interesting to note that the Haras al-Watani were renamed, in May 1983, Ansar Jaysh Lubnan al-Hurr (Partisans of the Army of Free Lebanon) or briefly al-Ansar, thus corresponding in title to the militia created (on paper, for the most part) by the Lebanese government a decade before—a shrewd psychological gambit.[12] However, without close Israeli shepherding, it remained doubtful that any militia would ever attain any significant role in the security of the South. These alien implantations were—for most Shi'is—merely a symbol of Israel's continuing occupation. As the resistance gained strength, the surrogate forces became prime targets for attack.

Although there were minor and relatively infrequent guerrilla attacks on the Israeli forces in late 1982, the South was more or less peaceful until the spring of 1983. By that time, it was becoming clear that the Israeli occupation would be of long duration—a judgment reinforced by the May agreement, which was widely interpreted as amounting to the ceding of the South to Israeli control. Yet, during this period, the leaders of Harakat Amal continued to sit on their hands, preferring to wait out the Israelis. In doing so, they conceded the initiative to their political adversaries: The reorganized left—the Lebanese Community party and, especially, Munazzamat al-ʿAmal al-Shiyuʿi (Communist Action Organization)—which took a leading role in the National Resistance Front that had been formed shortly after the evacuation of the *fidaʾiyin* in August 1982;[13] and a number of local religious leaders who formed small, hard to penetrate, locally based cells of militant youths. Shaikhs like Raghib Harb (assassinated in February 1984) of Jibshit, ʿAbd al-Karim Shams al-Din of ʿArab Salim, and Saʿid ʿAli Mahdi Ibrahim of Adlun proved vehement opponents of the Israeli occupation, and in the process siphoned off a number of Amal members and sympathizers.

Meanwhile, the Beirut leadership of Amal, concerned that the radicals were attracting their supporters, both in Beirut and in the South, began adopting a much more militant line vis-à-vis the IDF presence. In the process, pressure on the southern leadership grew. The crucial turning point, in more than one respect, was October 1983, when the IDF committed a major blunder. On October 16, 1983, the Shi'a were celebrating 'Ashura, the tenth day of the Muslim month of Muharram. 'Ashura commemorates the A.D. 680 martyrdom of Husain, the grandson of Muhammad, and it is the most important holy day of the year for Shi'i Muslims. It is a day of great emotion, a day on which the Shi'a share the suffering and the bravery of Husain's struggle against injustice and superior forces. In Lebanon, the most important locale for the remembrance of 'Ashura is Nabatiya, an important town in the South and the religious center of Jabal 'Amil. On this day of great spiritual significance, an Israeli military convoy tried to make its way through the streets of Nabatiya, which were crowded with as many as 60,000 celebrants. The result was predictable. The Shi'a saw the IDF trucks as a degradation of 'Ashura and reacted with great hostility. The convoy was stoned, trucks were overturned, and the Israeli soldiers became frightened and began firing their weapons. At least two Shi'is were killed and a number of others were wounded.

In a country that had already lost 19,000 at the hands of the Israeli invaders, the incident in Nabatiya might seem trivial, but it has taken on enormous significance. The incident is widely viewed by the Shi'a of Lebanon as a great sacrilege, and it has become a rallying cry against the Israeli occupation of Lebanon. The Israeli Arabist Moshe Sharon has noted that a Lebanese Shi'i friend warned him that Israel must not become the enemy of the Shi'a, it must not join the slayers of Husain: "Do not join those who murdered Husain, because if you bring the Shi'is to identify you with the history of [their] suffering, the enmity that will be directed at you will have no bounds and no limits. You will have created for yourselves a foe whose hostility will have a mystical nature and a momentum which you will be unable to arrest."[14] Yet the Nabatiya incident dripped with evocative symbolism, and the obvious connections between the commemoration of Husain's martyrdom and the Israeli transgression were quickly noted by Shi'i religious leaders. Mufti Muhammad Mahdi Shams al-Din issued a *fatwa* (an authoritative interpretation of religious responsibility) on October 17, 1983, calling on all Shi'a to conduct "comprehensive civil opposition" against the Israeli forces. The Shi'a were warned that those who trafficked with the Israelis would go to hell. Shams al-Din's *fatwa*, as well as contemporaneous ones rendered by the *ulama* of Jabal ʿAmil and religious authorities in Sidon, seems to have sealed the Israeli failure in Lebanon.[15] Relatively insignificant in scale and casualties, the Nabatiya incident joined the pantheon of historical accidents that provide the grist for revolutionary slogans and battle cries. Much like the 1906 Denshawi incident in Egypt and the battle of Bunker Hill in America, Nabatiya crystallized the resentments and the anger that were building in south Lebanon.

On the Friday following the incident, October 21, Muslim clerics condemned the Israelis in mosques throughout the country. One of the most rousing Friday sermons was given by Shaikh ʿAbd al-Amir Qabalan. Qabalan, noteworthy for his moderate politics, his close relations with Amal, and his instinct for the vernacular of populism, ensured that even the dimwitted would understand the meaning of the ʿAshura confrontation.

> If we turn all our rifles, abilities, and potential against the Israeli enemy, we will be victorious. All of you know what happened on Sunday at Lebanon's Karbala, the Karbala of Jabal ʿAmil. You all know of the disturbances on ʿAshura, the tenth day of Muharram.
>
> [The] sword [of the Shiʿa] has not taken into account the fact that there are hot air balloons, gravity, and armored machines. It has transcended all military plans and considerations. The sword, the shroud, and naked flesh say no to the occupation. They repeat once again the saying of the Imam Musa al-Sadr: "Israel is an absolute evil." The disturbance of Nabatiya confirmed once again that there is no power but God's power and no will but God's will. There are no protectors and no proselytizers except those who are obedient to God. It is incumbent on us all to make the day of Nabatiya a lesson for all Lebanese. We must cooperate anew in order to renew the kinship between us [meaning between Muslims and Christians].[16]

Before the ʿAshura incident, many of the attacks on the Israelis were carried out by splinter groups, but the incident served as a call to arms for many who had heretofore avoided active resistance. Pushed by the looming fragmentation of their movement and pulled by the *fatwa*, many Amal leaders found that they had no choice but to act more aggressively against the IDF. The result was a marked increase in resistance activities. By 1984, an authoritative estimate indicated that, on the average, one Israeli soldier was being killed or wounded every day in the South. A United Nations estimate indicates that the Israelis were facing two armed attacks a day, as of early 1984, and the rate increased throughout the year.[17]

By November 1983, the breadth of the Israeli failure was demonstrated when the Shi'i who had been designated the commander of the Israeli-groomed Shi'i Brigade held a press conference in a Beirut suburb to announce that he had been misled by the Israelis and that he would now seek to join Harakat Amal.[18] One month before, on October 5, 1983, the previous commander of the brigade (which was reported to number 270 men), Husain Wahbi, was killed by a car bomb in the southern village of Adlun.[19] Then, in January 1984, Sa'ad Haddad, the commander of the Israeli-equipped, -directed, and -trained militia, died of cancer. Lacking a successor of any real stature from the South, Shi'i or non-Shi'i, the Israeli coordinator for Lebanese affairs, Uri Lubrani, apparently arranged with the cooperation of senior Lebanese military officials for a retired Lebanese general, Antoine Lahad (a Christian), to replace Haddad.[20] Lahad, a 1952 graduate of the Lebanese Military Academy, served in the South prior to the beginning of the civil war in 1975, but his home was outside of the South in Dair al-Qamar. Lahad is a Chamounist; in fact, Camille's son Dany (a close personal friend of Lahad's), who has been quite active in the South since 1983, may have played a crucial role in placing him in command of the force that has since been renamed the South Lebanon Army (SLA). It may also be noteworthy that Lahad is a business partner of Ibrahim Tannus, the Maronite commander of the Lebanese Armed Forces until early 1984.

While Israeli officials pinned great hopes, publicly at least, on the prospect for the SLA taking over many of the security tasks of the IDF, it was clear that such a success was most unlikely. The SLA, comprised at most of some 2,000 men—of whom 80 percent are Maronites, with the remainder roughly split between Shi'a and Druze—is hardly a formidable force. Few of the militia are well-trained, and many are not trained at all. In many places the members are men who are either too old or too young to seek gainful employment away from their home villages. As it was under Haddad, the militia is heavily dependent upon Israeli support and is in fact quietly controlled by Israeli intelligence agents, who are careful to stay in the background.

Significantly, the core of the Haddad militia consisted of regular army Christians who had been stationed in the South prior to the 1978 Israeli invasion. These men had a reasonably enlightened understanding of the need for intercommunal concord and seldom trampled on the Shi'i sensitivities. However, few of this cadre remain with Lahad. Instead, Lahad's force is composed, in large part, of Maronite Lebanese Forces fighters from the South, reinforced by some from Mount Lebanon who moved south in the wake of Israel's invasion.[21] In 1982 and during part of 1983, the Lebanese Forces operated as a competitor to Saʿad Haddad, wreaking vengeance on the Palestinians of the Sidon area in particular. The unsavory activities of the Lebanese Forces militia in the Palestinian camps and against Amal members were serious enough to cause concern both in the Beirut government and among Israeli security officials. Robin Wright, a particularly knowledgeable journalist in matters pertaining to south Lebanon, reported that a secret Lebanese government report warned presciently that the provocations of the Lebanese Forces had helped to make a Shiʿa-Maronite conflict the most serious potential flashpoint.[22] Expressing similar concern, Israel ordered the Christian units to leave the South in July 1983; according to a Lebanese Forces spokesperson, Israel gave the militiamen twenty-four hours to clear out.[23] No doubt, the Israeli decision was made easier by the fact that the Lebanese Forces had refused to cooperate with Saʿad Haddad, preferring to spread their own writ rather than supporting Haddad's. However, while the militia organizational offices were closed, many of the individual members stayed on as members of the Israeli-dominated militia, or as freelancers.

Lahad's prospects for success have not been improved by the integration of elements of the Lebanese Forces into the SLA. It is important to note that Shiʿi-Maronite relations in the South seriously deteriorated largely as a result of the excesses committed by "imported" Maronite militiamen; this has further reinforced the hostility of the Shiʿa toward Israel. Historically, the Maronite villagers of the South have lived in peace with their more numerous Shiʿi neighbors, but the failed attempt of the Lebanese Forces to extend its influence to the South has helped to accelerate the retreat of both the Shiʿa and Maronites of the South into their respective sectarian identities and has created an enmity that simply did not exist before 1982. As a result of these developments, if peace should ever come to the South, one of the most important peacekeeping responsibilities may be the protection of Maronite villages from Shiʿis seeking revenge.

Given the deteriorating circumstances faced by the Israeli forces and surrogates, the following comments by an Israeli journalist are a fitting epitaph for the Israeli effort in the South: "It is a fact that with the conquest of the villages and hamlets of southern Lebanon, we were received with rice and flowers. Now we are received with grenades and explosives. Something has happened to the Shiʿa sect. Our tanks and armored personnel carriers have not left them indifferent and smiling. The joy about our arrival as people liberating them from the terrorists' burden has changed with time into burning hatred. This is not something to be surprised about: We have behaved as a military government, with all that involves, and caused much suffering to the population."[24]

As the Israeli stay in Lebanon lengthened from months into years, the process of extrication became ever more difficult. Ironically, by forcing the Amal leadership to become more militant, Israel helped to resuscitate it. Even after the Nabatiya incident, moderate leaders like Dawud Sulaiman Dawud of ʿAbbassiya attempted to stand above the fray. But as the violence accelerated, and as it became clear that Harakat Amal was playing an ever-increasing role, the Israelis even began to pursue the moderates. As men like Dawud were pushed underground, they were consecrated as resistance leaders, and as a result they recaptured the control of the movement. Thus, a campaign to fragment and emasculate Amal has instead made it a deadly and unremitting foe.

Recognizing the Morass

Almost from the beginning, the year 1984 was one in which policies based on illusion and self-delusion were shattered by the cold reality of on-the-ground developments in Lebanon. In only the first few months of the year, the crash of faulty policies was nearly deafening. January brought the death of Saʿad Haddad, whose departure from the scene left a vacuum that could not be easily filled. In February, the Amal movement and its Druze allies reacted to the government's shelling of Shiʿi neighborhoods in the Beirut environs by taking over West Beirut, thereby fatally undermining Amin al-Jumayyil's pretensions of being something other than a narrowly based political leader. In conjunction with the seizure of West Beirut, Nabih Berri called with profound effect upon Shiʿi soldiers to lay down their arms rather than fight their co-religionists. In the process, the predominantly Shiʿi units of the army became little more than uniformed formations subordinate to Amal. By mid-month, the Multinational Force, which had suffered punishing blows during the previous fall at the hands of suicide drivers, was being withdrawn from Lebanon with little more than bitter memories of the deaths it had suffered.

As the international contingents sailed from Lebanon, Syria's resuscitation as the dominant power in Lebanon was plain to see; in March, the controversial May 17 agreement of the previous year was abrogated by a much weakened Lebanese government that scurried to adjust to the new realities of power distribution in Lebanon. Two months later, Nabih Berri, once the spurned leader of a spurned sect, was courted to become a minister in a government of national unity. Significantly, Berri's price for participation in the new government was the creation of a Ministry for the South that he would head, thus pitting him dead against Israel's occupation of south Lebanon.

Spurred by the events in Nabatiya the previous fall, as well as the activism of their political opponents in fighting Israel, Amal began to play an active role fighting the Israeli presence in the South. Throughout 1984, resentment toward Israel grew almost geometrically. As Israel implemented security measures to enhance the safety of its forces, it created even greater economic hardship and societal disruption. After the car-bombing of its intelligence facility in Tyre during the previous November, Israel began to isolate the South from the rest of Lebanon, making crossing into the Israeli-controlled sector an arduous and time-consuming process that fed resentment and seriously impeded commerce. Meanwhile, Israel continued dumping agricultural produce in south Lebanon at prices that made even locally produced fruits and vegetables uncompetitive.[25]

At mid-year, the dangerous dynamics of the situation in the South were easy to read. As the occupation of the South wore on, with debilitating effects for the economy and political stability of the area, moderation was discredited and extremism was validated. Any party attempting to work for law and order in the South was merely seen as a complement to the Israeli presence. The imperatives of political and physical survival pushed responsible, centrist leaders into the resistance. As a result, Israeli officials found that no significant Shi'i leader was even willing to respond to their quiet advances. By August, Amal was proving itself a formidable enemy,[26] capable of taking a heavy toll of Israeli soldiers, as well as Lebanese collaborators. (Rabin remarked in December 1984 that Amal was responsible for 80 percent of the attacks in the South.) From August 1983 to August 1984, 72 Israeli soldiers were killed in Lebanon, and most of the deaths occurred at the hands of the resistance in the South.

As the resistance became ever more punishing, Israel stepped up its countermeasures and loosened controls over Shin Beth agents operating in the area. Suspected resistance members were targets for Shin Beth arrests and, many would allege, even executions. While most of the political killings left only a web of suspicions, a few were handled clumsily and exposed the hands of the Shin Beth. For example, on June 14, 1984, Murshid Muhammad Nahas (who had been wounded several years before in a clash with the PLO) was gunned down—reportedly in cold blood—by Israeli Shin Beth agents in the southern village of Bidyas. Unlike other incidents, the Nahas killing held no mystery. It was widely covered by the press and substantiated by UNIFIL soldiers who monitored the movement of three carloads of Shin Beth agents into Bidyas.[27] The death of Nahas, like the murder of Hasan Sahli (whose family had played an active role in resisting the PLO) on June 11, 1984, was counterproductive in the extreme, since it provided further evidence of Israel's apparent goal of destroying precisely the elements that sought to create a south Lebanon freed of foreign influence. The tendency of the IDF to respond to armed attacks by coming down hard on villagers living in the vicinity has been skillfully used by the resistance forces to provoke Israeli attacks on villages not previously known for participating in the resistance.

Following the July elections that brought Shimon Peres to the prime ministership and Yitzhak Rabin to the Defense Ministry, there were significant changes in Israel's stated goals in Lebanon, the most important one being that Peres and Rabin seemed intent on withdrawing from Lebanon. But it was many months before the goals of the new government were reflected on the ground. So while Israeli goals in Lebanon shrank immensely throughout 1984, especially after the abrogation of the May 17 agreement and the July elections, it was not until the end of 1984 that the seriousness of the Israeli predicament became clear to Peres and Rabin. After trying unsuccessfully to come to a working arrangement with Amal—including the proposal of a truce in November 1984[28]—it became clear that there would be little respite except by getting out of the swamp that south Lebanon was in danger of becoming. In effect, the Israeli calculus changed significantly. Until late 1984, the dilemma was framed as follows: we want to get out, but how can we afford to, given the security risks? But in late 1984, the question became: given the risks of staying, how can we afford to stay? The Shiʿis were becoming increasingly radicalized and susceptible to the appeal of extremist Shiʿi leaders far to the flanks of Amal. Moreover, centrist leaders were of necessity being pulled by the political mood of their constituents to adopt a much more militant stance vis-à-vis Israel. In short, the prospects were only for the situation on the ground to continue to deteriorate, and the dreaded possibility of attacks into Israel seemed more real than ever.

On January 18, 1985, Peres succeeded in getting the cabinet to approve a staged withdrawal from Lebanon, premised in part on the notion that the vast majority of the Shiʿis were the enemies of *Israel in Lebanon*, rather than Israel per se.[29] Throughout the three stages of withdrawal, Israeli officials—and most notably Uri Lubrani, the Israeli coordinator of policy for Lebanon—attempted to come to an agreement with Amal. As Lubrani told me in December 1984, Israel simply wanted Amal to accept responsibility for the security of the South. As he put it, he wanted someone to hand the keys to. However, Amal's competition on the Lebanese stage with radical Shiʿi parties as well as a deep residual suspicion of Israel made any arrangement unacceptable, indeed impossible.

With Amal's demurral, frustration rose in Israel, with disastrous effect for some of the southern Lebanese who felt the brunt of the Israeli object lesson called the "iron fist" policy. With little subtlety, Israel embarked on a stern and spiteful campaign to demonstrate to the people how the South would suffer if used as a launching ground for forays into Israel. For those who might have missed the point, Rabin made it explicit many times, as in an interview published in March: "We will emphasize to [the Shiʿi leadership] that they only have two options: Either there is calm on both sides, or, if they attack us, their lives will be disrupted in such a manner that they will be ready to coexist by default, just as the PLO arrived at the same conclusion, to a certain extent, in 1981 [a reference to the cease-fire observed by the PLO from July 1981 to May 1982].[30] Simultaneously, and with a ration of exasperation, Israel still pursued a deal with Amal. The impatience felt in Tel Aviv was exemplified by Lubrani's call for a secret agreement between Israel and Amal. The forum for his proposal was the Op-Ed page of the *New York Times*, an unconventional forum for secret negotiations.[31]

On the Amal side, there was more than a little signaling going on. Consistent with past statements, Amal officials went out of their way throughout the spring to declare their opposition to attacks upon Israel from south Lebanon. Dawud Sulaiman Dawud, since at least 1980 a staunch opponent of the PLO's military presence in south Lebanon, spoke for many of his co-religionists when he declared that the *fidaʾiyin* were free to pursue their claims for Palestine in Palestine, but not in or from south Lebanon: "If they want, they can organize resistance cells in the West Bank and Gaza Strip, but not in south Lebanon. Our people in the south, the majority of whom are Shiite Muslims, have suffered enough as a result of the Israeli-Palestinian war."[32] Dawud, a widely respected leader of Amal whose popularity stems not only from his role as an early companion and aide to Musa al-Sadr but from his selflessness and honesty, made it quite clear that Amal would not stop attacking the IDF or its surrogates in Lebanon; however, he went to lengths to emphasize that he would not allow attacks upon Israeli territory or, for that matter, the use of indirect fire weapons (especially Katyusha rockets) against the Israeli security zone. His reasoning seems to be that the introduction of such weapons into the South could easily provoke Israel, which associates such weapons with past attacks on its border towns and settlements: "I am against any shelling from the liberated territory to the occupied territory. I told my men to go into the occupied areas and meet the Israelis face-to-face and shoot at them with pistols. It is much more effective than firing rockets from outside."[33]

Amal's refusal to sanction the reestablishment of the PLO in Lebanon is not only based upon the enmity produced by more than a decade of suffering from the PLO's heavy hand, but a pragmatic calculus to the effect that Israel means business and that the Lebanese Shiʿa would be the ones to pay the price of Israeli military action. ʿAkif Haidar has made the point more than once:

> Neither Lebanon nor the Amal movement now has enough strength to take a position concerning the problems dividing the Palestinians. We have always favored the unity of the Palestinian resistance and we will defend the Palestinian cause to the very end! *Their presence on Lebanese territory is something else. There is no longer any place for armed Palestinians in Lebanon.* The liberation of Lebanon is a Lebanese problem. We thank everyone for their help, but we are able to do it ourselves! We welcome a civilian Palestinian presence, as long as their problem has not been resolved. We offer them the possibility of carrying on political and diplomatic activity. However, in the refugee camps our Palestinian brothers must not carry arms. [emphasis added][34]

The bloody fighting in and around the Palestinian camps in the Beirut environs during 1985 and 1986 served as a stern reminder that Haidar's comments were more than an empty threat. While Amal took heavy casualties during the fighting, there was no mistaking the meaning of the battles—namely, Amal did not intend to permit the deleterious reestablishment of the PLO's military role, which not only might be used to weigh in against Amal in its campaign to subdue Sunni opponents in Beirut, but might also be transferred to the South. Nahib Berri summed up the operative fear very succinctly: "What the Palestinians are trying to do is set the stage for a return to the south and frankly, we will not allow that to happen."[35]

In the South, Amal backed up its rhetoric by delivering a clear message to the Palestinians in the area.[36] In short, no armed presence will be tolerated. To back up its words, Amal gunmen regulated traf-

fic in and out of the camps, and on at least one occasion ostenta-
tiously surrounded the Bas camp near Tyre to ensure that its inhabitants got the message. To the same end, Amal reacted to Hizb Allah
activities by disarming radicals and interdicting arms shipments intended for the South. (This interdiction spurred Hizb Allah to call
for a united resistance front that would exclude Amal.) Even before
the bulk of Israel's forces were withdrawn in early June 1985, senior
Israeli officers commented that Amal was taking an active part
against extremists intent on attacking Israel.[37] Yet, despite the clear
signals from Amal as well as the demonstration of its intent to keep
the peace, Israel was unwilling to leave its security in the hands of
others. Thus, instead of a complete withdrawal, Israel maintained
control of a border strip, somewhat larger than that under its control
from 1978 until the 1982 invasion.

Throughout 1985, the Lahad militia was plagued by wholesale
desertions of its members, while it simultaneously endured an average of more than 100 attacks—ranging from sniper incidents to
remote-controlled mines and roadside ambushes—per month (in
March 1985, the total exceeded 200). By June, it was clear that Lahad
would not be able to hold the border strip with his own assets, so
Israel buttressed his force with as many as 400 "advisers," who constituted as much as 25 percent of the militia. (In addition, from one
to two Israeli mechanized battalions, with supporting artillery, were
deployed in the eastern segment of the security zone, where they remained at the end of 1985.) One veteran observer, after encountering
some of Lahad's new "Shi'i recruits," noted: "It's the first time anyone has ever seen a Shi'i wearing a yarmulke."[38]

The Trap

On the face of it, Amal and Israel have a number of shared interests
in south Lebanon. Certainly, Amal is as desirous of restoring civility
in south Lebanon as Israel is intent upon ensuring the tranquillity of
its northern border. Neither side is interested in even contemplating
the reestablishment of an effective PLO military presence in south
Lebanon. And both Israel and Amal are intent on preventing a radical
Shi'i victory in the area or, for that matter, in Lebanon as a whole.
The challenge of Hizb Allah is felt keenly on both sides of the
border.

Israel recognized—albeit belatedly—that the mainline Amal organization is a centrist political force that does not wish to provoke
Israeli attacks upon Lebanon. And for Amal, as for all of the Lebanese of the South, the lessons of the occupation have been tough

ones. However cruel the "iron fist" policy may have been, it certainly succeeded in demonstrating that Israel is as capable of a ruthless policy of self-defense as any other Middle Eastern state.

It is clear that both Amal and Israel are caught in a viselike trap from which neither side can, of its own volition, extricate itself. Both parties are captured by the social forces that define their respective constituencies and their freedom of action. Israel's price for its full departure from Lebanon is a currency that Amal does not trade in, which is to say, a deal with Israel. If Amal provided the overt security assurances sought by Israel, it would jeopardize its competitive position vis-à-vis Hizb Allah, with which Amal competes for the political heart of the Shiʿi community. Moreover, if the ruthlessness of the "iron fist" has made its point, so has the established ruthlessness of Hafiz al-Asad, who has shown himself quite capable of calibrating his support for various Shiʿi groups in order to reward those who toe the Syrian line and provide an object lesson to those who do not. Given the requirements of its political milieu, Amal's dilemma is transparent: it must not be seen as abetting Israel's interests, but instead must present itself as the prime force responsible for expelling Israel from Lebanon.

A pervasive sense of insecurity makes it hard for embattled Israel to gamble on an incipient political organization whose leadership and membership are unstable and somewhat unpredictable. In addition, several of the engineers of the 1982 invasion remain ensconced in a jerry-rigged cabinet and are not about to support gleefully a unilateral withdrawal from Lebanon that would serve as a damning final indictment of the invasion they promoted, defended, and, in the case of Sharon, planned and led. Even after the January 1985 withdrawal decision was made, and despite the overwhelming sentiment of Israelis who wanted out of Lebanon, men like Moshe Arens and Ariel Sharon continued to attempt to derail the ongoing troop withdrawal.[39]

Thus, both sides are trapped in a potentially deadly embrace in south Lebanon. Neither side can escape of its own volition, and the truly tragic element is that both sides know they are trapped. In private, very senior Amal officials have poignantly acknowledged their dilemma, as have Israeli officials. It is possible that a modus vivendi will emerge as the pattern of actions clearly demonstrates intent, but it is also possible that one or both parties will misstep and thereby reinitiate the process of alienation and radicalization that marked the South in 1984 and early 1985. The dangers are well stated by the Israeli journalist Hirsh Goodman: "The danger with [the Israeli policy of automatic retaliation] is that the IDF could find

itself retaliating against precisely the people we want to be our allies
in the southern security zone, and more often than not for actions
over which they have no control."[40]

If Israel avoids overreaction and if Amal can continue to exercise
effective leadership, the outcome need not be disastrous, but the
chemistry of a modus vivendi is a delicate one that would be easily
upset by an overreaction by Israel or an underreaction by Amal.
Under the best of circumstances, Israel will be wise enough gradu-
ally to allow its support for the Lahad militia to taper off until the
surrogate force's deployment is constricted to its natural realm of action, which is to say, the Christian villages along the Lebanese-
Israeli border, while Amal simultaneously expands its control to the
areas evacuated by the Lahad forces. That we shall witness the best
of circumstances is at best a risky bet. The possibility of a reeruption
of violence in the South lurks like a phantom.

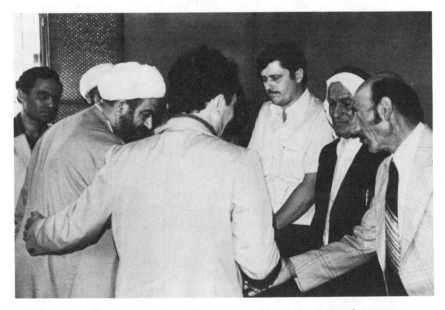

Shaikh ʿAbd al-Amir Qabalan *(fifth from right)* greeting Amal supporters
in a southern village in 1982. The author is the third person from the right.

8. Sectarian Estrangement and Social Fragmentation

The history of Lebanese politics is the history of factional politics. Political factions are nothing new, and it is the skillful balancing of one faction against another that has frequently been the defining characteristic of Lebanon's most distinguished and most successful political leaders. But, while a plethora of factions, militias, and parties may not be a particularly novel feature of the Lebanese scene, the present situation—in which the contending factions find themselves in an environment of seemingly endemic violent conflict—is certainly novel in both its duration and its complexity. For many young Lebanese in their teens and their twenties, violence is the only way of life they have known. The young men (and in some cases, young women) who populate the militias have no memory of a political system that functions except through the allocation of bloodshed.

The old men of Lebanese politics survive, but their influence is restricted and incomplete. War is a young man's game, and within each of Lebanon's sects it is the brash, militant, and war-hardened young bloods who call many of the shots. The militant Shiʿi clerics are almost all in their thirties, the commanders of the largely Maronite Lebanese Forces are in their late twenties and thirties, the Druze leadership is not much older, and, at forty-five, Nabih Berri, the leader of the Shiʿi Amal movement, is nearly an old man. The titles and respected offices may still be in the possession of the graybeards, but titles mean little without a corresponding militia, and respect is hard to come by in any case. The sense of futility shared by many of the older generation is poignantly expressed by the senior Sunni Muslim religious leader, the Mufti Hasan Khalid:

> When spiritual leaders have a meeting, they make one statement after another, but no one listens to them. . . . it is arms-carrying

gunmen who make things happen, not lawmakers and men of thought who develop plans, programs, and courses of action. Those people no longer have significant influence in Lebanon. That is why we find that those who can make things happen in Lebanon are gunmen acting for limited interests. I do not wish to put down those people; they may be better than us. But they don't know as much as those eminent people know about legislation and the law.[1]

In an important sense, Lebanese politics have long resembled international balance of power politics, with shifting alliance patterns and a grudging collective acceptance of each actor's existence, but no more. The formula that ended the comparatively minor civil war in 1958—"no victor, no vanquished"—is now frequently rejected.[2] A sect must dominate or be dominated, or withdraw from the game, as the Druze seem to have done, and as the Maronites appear prepared to do.

The Lebanese have been widely admired for their vitality, resilience, and optimism, and with good reason. For instance, Lebanese business owners have been known to rebuild their shops and offices two, three, even five or six times. In the face of widespread destruction, and political and moral aimlessness, the Lebanese have still managed to see a glass half full and have pointed with almost childlike hope to the future. One long bloody year after another, the Lebanese waited for the last battle, the last death, the last car bomb, the last atrocity that would mark the end of their shared travail. The hopefulness that sprang up following the Israeli invasion of 1982 is largely explained by the generally held view that the last shot had finally been fired. But the period since 1982 has held only disappointment.

Today a malaise hangs over Lebanon, a sense of hopelessness that is reflected in people's faces, in a heavy pessimism, and in a ruined economy; perhaps it is in economic terms that Lebanon's sad state is most starkly illustrated. Throughout the turmoil of the past decade, which included two invasions and three foreign interventions, not to mention general chaos, the sturdy Lebanese currency had held its ground. Buoyed, admittedly, by the plentiful remittances received by the PLO, the Lebanese pound (lire; L£) still served to illustrate the resiliency of the Lebanese and their laissez-faire economy. From the time the fighting began in 1975 until the Israeli invasion of 1982, the L£ faltered only slightly, and in the autumn following the invasion— when many thought the country was on the threshold of rebirth— the L£ traded at just over 3L£:$1. But the high hopes of 1982 vanished, and the once durable, even awesome L£ opened 1985 by trading at 12L£:$1 and ended the year at an abysmal 18L£:$1; 1986 was even worse, as the L£ fell to nearly sixty to a dollar.

The sectors of the economy have suffered incredible damage. One study found that 40 percent of the agricultural machinery had been destroyed, agricultural production had dropped by 30 percent, agricultural exports had fallen 80 percent, industrial production had dropped 60 percent, and the all-important services sector had ceased to function. All indications are that the situation is only becoming worse.[3]

Thwarted hopes, impoverishment, and continuing violence have pushed many Lebanese back into the familiar comfort of their sectarian identities. More than at any time during the past decade of slaughter and mayhem, the hyphenated identity of the Lebanese as Lebanese-Maronites, Lebanese-Shiʿa, Lebanese-Druze, and Lebanese-Sunnis has come to demarcate the political scene. The retreat into familiar communal identities has been spawned by the widespread recognition that the retention of privileges by one sect necessitates the denial of those privileges to another sect. In short, politics in Lebanon have more than ever become a zero-sum game, and the costs of losing the game are perceived as severe. This is not to assert that heightened sectarianism has engendered sectarian unity, for that has not been the case. Driven by intergenerational competition, contending regional interests, personal rivalries, the resentment of the poor, and the selfishness of the rich, as well as contradictory conceptions of the role of religion in defining society, rampant factionalism has become a defining characteristic of Lebanese politics.

Aspiring sectarian leaders face challenges both across the barricades and behind the barricades. The processes of modernization, education, labor migration, and improved access to the media and to the metropolis, to name a few decisive factors, have fed the politicization of the lower and lower-middle classes. Old style politics, built on political bosses and charismatic leadership, have been rejected without being replaced by an effective substitute. Awash in relatively sophisticated weaponry, Lebanon is a country in which the instruments of violence have been democratized. The ultimate expression of the cruelly indiscriminate, but hardly random, violence that marks the situation is the continuous use of car and truck bombs that kill and maim innocents more frequently than they kill belligerents. In three 1985 incidents alone—in Tripoli, Bir al-ʿAbd, and Sinn al-Fil—over 205 human beings died as victims of this blatant form of terrorism, and the gruesome statistics continued to accumulate in 1986. Militias dominate the landscape, yet it is the weakness of the militias that is apparent rather than their strength. No single militia is capable of imposing its will upon contentious Lebanon, yet each possesses the capacity to subvert stability and deny peace.

Of Lebanon's seventeen sects, three, in addition to the Shiʿa, are playing particularly important if very different roles in the continuing imbroglio. Two of the three, the Maronites and the Sunnis, are fractionized politically and dispersed geographically. In the following sections, a snapshot of each sect is presented in order to give the reader a sense of the political scene in mid-1986.

The Maronites

As the reader will recall, the Maronite Christians were accorded a monopoly on the presidency in the 1943 National Pact (*al-Mithaq al-Watani*) that distributed the three major political offices—of president, prime minister, and Speaker of the parliament—to the Maronites, Sunnis, and Shiʿa, respectively, on the basis of supposed population shares. In addition, the National Pact divided the seats in the Chamber of Deputies (or parliament) between the Christian and Muslim sects (with proportionate shares for each sect) on the basis of six Christian seats to every five Muslim seats. (In the current 99-seat chamber, elected in 1972, the allocation is 30 Maronite, 20 Sunni, 19 Shiʿi, 11 Greek Orthodox, 6 Druze, 5 Armenian, 6 Greek Catholic, and 2 Protestant seats.)

As we saw in chapter 2, differential population growth between the sects has invalidated the demographic assumptions that helped to justify the original formula, and the widespread modernization that has characterized Lebanon since the end of World War II has thrust forward ranks of newly politicized citizens who see themselves as having been shortchanged in the political bargain. Thus, Maronite (and Christian) dominance has come increasingly under challenge; as early as 1976, the Lebanese president, Sulaiman Franjiya, accepted a "Constitutional Document" negotiated in Damascus that would provide for the Muslims and Christians evenly sharing seats in the parliament, as well as modestly limiting the rather considerable powers of the president. Unfortunately, the agreement came to naught, in large measure because of the disruptive measures of Kamal Jumblatt, the father of the current Druze leader.

During the two-year civil war of 1975–1976, a number of largely Maronite militias were fielded. Some were directly linked to the established political parties associated with the community—notably, the National Liberal party of Camille Chamoun and the Kata'ib or Phalange party of Pierre al-Jumayyil—but others were products of the conflict. Of the latter type were the Lebanese Forces (al-Quwat al-Lubnaniya), which evolved from a command structure intended, in 1976, to coordinate the activities of an array of disparate forces to the predominant Maronite political organization, by 1980. The Lebanese Forces drew into its ranks many lower- and lower-middle-class Maronites (as well as a good number of Greek Catholics and some Armenians) who felt that the traditional parties were unrepresentative and staid.[4] It was the Lebanese Forces that served as the vehicle for the rise of the son of Pierre al-Jumayyil, Bashir, whose reputation for military brashness and bravery combined with a charismatic if authoritarian style that brought him to the forefront of Maronite politics.

The Lebanese Forces—co-conspirators in Israel's 1982 invasion—was, or so it was thought at the time, the vicarious victor in the Lebanese civil war. The assassination of Bashir in September 1982 brought the victory celebrations to an end, but not the ambitions of his heirs. The election of Bashir's brother Amin to the presidency was a bitter pill for the Lebanese Forces to swallow, and in many Maronite circles Amin was seen as little more than a usurper of the role that rightfully belonged to the martyred Bashir. From the first days of his tenure in office, it was clear that Amin did not have the support of his own community, and it was only the considerable presence of the respected Pierre (who died in September 1984) that kept his Maronite adversaries at bay. Amin is deeply conscious of his problems with the Lebanese Forces, and he has spent much of his presidency casting worried glances over his shoulder.

Amin's failure to move purposefully toward intercommunal reconciliation, when he had a real chance to do so in 1982 and early 1983, was in no small part due to his personal commitment to restore the old Lebanon rather than build a new one. It also stemmed from his need to satisfy the young leaders of the Lebanese Forces, who sought to consolidate the victory that they thought Israeli arms had purchased for them in 1982.

From 1982 to 1985, the Lebanese Forces suffered one defeat after another. In attempting to subdue the Druze-populated regions of Aley and the Shuf, it was soundly defeated by the Druze militia, which once again demonstrated a military prowess that has long distinguished the sect. Arguably, it was the Lebanese Forces' adventure in the Druze region that most profoundly contributed to the thwarting of the hopes that blossomed in 1982. In the South of Lebanon as well as in Beirut, the Lebanese Forces also attempted to expand its domain, and in both cases failed. For instance, when it attempted to exploit the Israeli withdrawal from Sidon in March and April 1985, it was vanquished by a Syrian-encouraged coalition of Druze, Sunni, and Shiʿi fighters, leaving behind thousands of Christians who were displaced from their villages as a result of the fighting.[5]

As early as 1984, it was becoming evident that the Lebanese Forces was playing a weak hand. After a particularly senseless episode of shelling by the Lebanese army, apparently acting in league with the Lebanese Forces, the Shiʿi Muslims rebelled and, on February 6, 1984, seized West Beirut.[6] It was this development that precipitated the hasty "redeployment" of the Multinational Force that had been sent to Lebanon, in a fit of moral embarrassment over the slaughter in the Sabra and Shatila camps (which had occurred shortly after the MNF had been withdrawn from Lebanon the first time). With the withdrawal of the international forces, and the earlier retreat of the IDF to southern Lebanon, it was patent that Lebanon was destined to move into the Syrians' waiting arms.

Pressured by both the Druze and the Shiʿa, and faced with rapidly waning U.S. military support, Amin al-Jumayyil was increasingly susceptible to Syrian influence. This was well demonstrated in the formation of the National Unity cabinet in April 1984, which brought Amin's arch-enemies Walid Jumblatt and Nabih Berri into the government. In March 1984, the problematic May 17 agreement between Lebanon and Israel, a prime irritant to Syria, was annulled. In October, the leading Shiʿi ally of the Maronite community, Kamil al-Asʿad, was replaced by Husain al-Husaini, who is on friendly terms with Damascus and who certainly does not generate the same visceral enmity that his predecessor did within the Shiʿi community. By the end of 1984, the momentum was clearly running with the opponents of the Lebanese Forces.

Nonetheless, the Lebanese Forces has stubbornly resisted recognizing its diminished power. In early 1985, Damascus attempted to secure its gains by beginning a process of negotiations between its allies and friends in Lebanon. Quite naturally, the Lebanese Forces was not included and watched with great anxiety as the discussion proceeded in the Syrian capital. Rather than capitulate to Syrian influence, the thirty-three-year-old Samir Jaʿjaʿ, a seasoned veteran of nine years of front-line fighting, seized control of the Lebanese Forces and declared in no uncertain terms that his organization rejected any sort of security pact or customs union with Syria and that he would stand against the mounting political claims of the Sunnis, Shiʿa, and Druze. Jaʿjaʿ's *coup de main* seemed to be short-lived.

On April 1, 1985, President Hafiz al-Asad dispatched General

Muhammad al-Khulil to Amin al-Jumayyil with a clear and tough message: either bring the uprising (*intifadah*) under control or else.[7] Amin, who is not exactly noted for his decisiveness, was aided by the shrewd ex-president Camille Chamoun, who organized a conference in Bkirki on April 9, which was attended by many major Christian politicians and religious leaders. The predictable outcome of the conference was a statement intended to assuage the Syrian president. In the statement the conference attendees committed themselves to the unity of Lebanon, its Arab identity, and a special relationship with Syria. The Bkirki conferees denounced the partition or cantonization of Lebanon and thereby allayed Syria's suspicions that the Maronite community would promote the dismantlement of Lebanon. Simultaneously, a strong message was quietly conveyed by the U.S. embassy in Beirut indicating that the United States would not support the uprising and viewed it as harmful to the interests of Lebanon and to those of the Christians. The Bkirki conference, buttressed by the position of the United States and with the defeats that Ja'ja''s forces were suffering in south Lebanon, ensured that the uprising would end, at least for the moment.

On May 9, Ja'ja' was replaced by Elie Hubaika (who had earlier commanded the forces that carried out the carnage in the Palestinian camps in September 1982). Hubaika was appointed the chief of a newly formed executive committee of the Lebanese Forces, and he wasted little time in voicing his support for Syria and cutting the ties to Israel. On May 18, the Lebanese Forces office that had been opened in Jerusalem in 1982 was closed, and the head of the office, Pierre Yazbak, voiced the compelling calculus that had clearly motivated Hubaika and his colleagues: "We have no option but to reach an understanding with Syria. Our strategy now is simply survival. Anything else would be sheer suicide."[8]

Hubaika has showed himself to be pragmatic and resourceful. On July 31, he met with Sulaiman Franjiya, former president, friend of Hafiz al-Asad, and warlord in Zgharta (in northern Lebanon). Franjiya's son Tony and his son's family were murdered at the hands of the Lebanese Forces in 1978, and the old man is known to harbor a keen sense of revenge (upon Bashir's slaying in September 1982, he noted that he regretted that he could not take credit for the deed), so the meeting surprised many observers; however, it is not clear that it produced more than interesting news copy. Notwithstanding his ties to Syria, Franjiya has refused to go along with any reform in which the presidency would be shared with non-Maronites. He attended the reconciliation conferences held in Geneva and Lausanne in 1983 and 1984 (both boycotted by the Lebanese Forces), and it was he who spelled defeat for the 1984 meeting in Lausanne by insisting that the Maronites cling to the presidency.

Hubaika moved in a very different direction. Faced by a compelling sense of the inevitable, he inched toward a Syrian-engineered solution that would seek to redistribute parliamentary seats evenly between Muslims and Christians, abolish the sectarian allocation of political offices, including the presidency, and, naturally, recognize Lebanon's "special" relationship with Syria. On September 9, 1985, Hubaika became the first Lebanese Forces leader to visit Damascus and, like a prodigal son, was warmly received by Hafiz al-Asad. From Hubaika's standpoint, the lure seems to have been a Syrian guarantee to the Lebanese Christians, which has been described by Jim Muir, one of the most astute and most dogged journalists on the Lebanese scene, as follows: "The unwritten deal, if it is concluded, will be that Syria will guarantee the security of Lebanon's Christians, in exchange for assurances that their community will no longer provide a springboard for Syria's enemies."[9] Approaching Lebanon realistically, Syria opted to deal with those who actually wielded power, the leaders of the major militias. Beginning in the fall of 1985, Damascus was the scene for a series of tripartite negotiations with the principal Druze, Shiʿi, and Maronite leaders, which is to say, Jumblatt, Berri, and Hubaika. The result was the frequently postponed agreement that was finally signed on December 28, 1985.

But, from the moment of signing, Hubaika's ability to deliver the Maronite community was very much in question. His grip on the Lebanese Forces was tenuous at best, and he certainly lacked the ability to impose his will on an unreceptive community. Significantly, Hubaika's efforts were opposed by three former presidents— Charles Hilu, Camille Chamoun, and Sulaiman Franjiya—as well as Franjiya's son Robert and Chamoun's son Dany, both of whom have displayed no inclination to turn away from politics.[10] Although the Lebanese Forces under Hubaika's command could take tough steps selectively, as when confronting elements loyal to Samir Jaʿjaʿ in East Beirut on October 14, it was doubtful in the extreme that the young Hubaika (he was twenty-nine years old when he signed the tripartite agreement) could deliver the Maronite community, and, in fact, he failed to do so.

The agreement did succeed in one unintended respect: opposition to it served as a unifying cry within the Maronite community. On January 15, Samir Jaʿjaʿ, acting in league with the Kataʾib party, now led by President Amin al-Jumayyil, stormed Hubaika's strongholds and after serious fighting expelled Hubaika from Beirut. Ironically, Syria's attempt to reconcile the Lebanese only succeeded in reconciling the president with his own community, a significant feat given Amin's lack of popularity.

Since the second uprising of Ja'ja', Syria has applied heavy direct and indirect pressure on those who thwarted the tripartite agreement. The president's village, Bikfaya, has been heavily shelled and is nearly in ruins. Maronite-populated areas have been subjected to severe artillery and rocket fire, which has only fed the obduracy and sense of unity under siege that is now deeply shared among the Maronite Christians.

The Druze

Throughout much of their history in Lebanon, the leadership of the Druze has been contested by two clans, the Jumblatts and the Yazbaks. Walid Jumblatt has, however, enjoyed a historic opportunity due to the failure of the Arslan family (representing the Yazbak clan) to produce a powerful successor to the now deceased Majid Arslan, who was for many years the political foe of Kamal Jumblatt (Walid's father, who was murdered in 1977; it is widely believed, at Syrian hands). Majid's son, Faisal, made the politically fatal mistake of aligning with Bashir al-Jumayyil's Lebanese Forces and thereby discrediting himself.[11] Walid's remaining challengers are narrowly based and lack his formidable hereditary claim to leadership in what is very clearly the most insular sect in Lebanon, if not in Islam.

The Druze, constituting as little as 6 or 7 percent of Lebanon's population, historically have been one of the most powerful sects in the country. The fortunes of geopolitical factors have given the Druze a mountainous redoubt that is not easily held by an invader, as the Lebanese Forces discovered. It is fair to assert that it has been Druze-Maronite agreement that has made periods of stability possible, but the past also includes a litany of excesses by one community against the other.[12]

Walid is the president of the Progressive Socialist party (al-Hizb al-Taqadami al-Ishtaraki), which is purportedly secular; but its membership is almost entirely Druze, and it serves, in effect, as the Druze militia. Walid, long dismissed as immature, self-indulgent, erratic, and uncourageous, has surprised many of his most severe critics (and even a fair number of his supporters). He may well prove to be the most clever and effective player on the Lebanese political scene. As the Israeli forces made their way past Walid's palatial residence in Mukhtara, he was quick to recognize that the day of *fida'i* supremacy in Lebanon had passed. (It is noteworthy that—although Walid was the head of the Lebanese National Movement, the admixture of left-wing, reformist, and revolutionary parties that stood with the PLO—no significant Palestinian presence had ever been allowed in the Druze homeland in the Aley and Shuf districts.)

As the Lebanese Forces entered his barony, Walid cut a deal with Israel, which was finding the Maronite militia a weak ally in its plan for reshaping Lebanon. The parameters of the bargain were that the Druze would guarantee to keep the *fida'iyin* out of their areas in re-turn for an Israeli withdrawal. Even while the Israelis occupied the Druze mountains until August 1983, there were odd tacit alliances at work that included Israeli soldiers looking the other way while Syrian-supplied military materiel flowed to the Druze and the Israe-lis themselves (in part responding to pressures from their own small but influential Druze community) supplied the Druze with weapons even as they were continuing to provision the Lebanese Forces. Al-though it is little talked about in public, in private senior Israeli offi-cials see their arrangements with the Druze as a great success (and one they wish they were able to emulate with the Shi'a of the South). It is perhaps significant that the portion of southern Lebanon where the IDF remains most active is in the vicinity of the Druze towns of the eastern region, towns that conceivably afford Israel con-tinuing access to the Shuf.

Taking support where he could find it, Walid discovered a useful ally in the Amal movement and its leader, Nabih Berri. But this is hardly a marriage made in heaven; rather, it is a form of political co-habitation that is likely to come to a stormy end. The Druze pro-vided key support to Amal in its takeover of West Beirut in Febru-ary 1984, but even then there were significant tensions in the relationship.

In April and May 1985, when Amal struck against the Sunni Murabitun militia in West Beirut, Druze support proved important and crucially timed; however, when, in May, Amal began its bloody campaigns against the Palestinian camps south of Beirut, the Druze not only refused to join in, but allowed elements of the anti-Arafat Palestine National Salvation Front units positioned in the Shuf to provide artillery fire against Amal positions.

It is widely felt that the failure of the Druze to support the drive against the camps made Walid and the Progressive Socialist party many enemies in Amal, and among the Shi'a in general, but in fact there were many enemies already. The PSP and Amal have clashed repeatedly in West Beirut, most seriously in November 1985, and there is good reason to doubt that the Amal-PSP alliance will long persist, despite the creation of ephemeral organizations joining the two militias.

On August 6, 1985, Jumblatt and Berri met in Shutara formally to announce the creation of a National Union Front (Jabhat al-Ittihad al-Qawmi), yet another in a series of similar groupings that have proven perishable. The front also includes a number of small pro-Syrian parties, such as the Arab Democratic party and the Lebanese Communist party. The program of the front calls for the creation of a new constitution, the abolishment of sectarianism in politics, the promulgation of a new electoral law that would make Lebanon a single electoral district, and the strengthening of the parliament at the expense of the presidency.[13]

The National Union Front program, if implemented, would result in a significant diminishment of the political power of both the Sunni and the Maronite communities, since they would lose their rights to the presidency and the prime ministership, respectively. Moreover, if the multiple electoral districts were abolished in favor of a single national district, traditional political leaders would find that their locally based patronage networks might no longer serve as a guarantee to elected office. Therefore, it is hardly unexpected that the program has been widely condemned by Maronite and Sunni politicians, as well as by a number of Shiʿi competitors to the Amal movement who see in the program the enhancement of Amal at their expense. Finally, it is at least odd that a nonsectarian outcome would be expected to result from a gathering of organizations that are sectarian in their essence.

The Druze, though they may be militarily adept, hardly command a large enough share of the general population to have reasonable expectations of a controlling role in Lebanese politics. In contrast, the Shiʿa transparently see themselves as the ascending force in Lebanese politics, and for the Druze (like all other non-Shiʿi Lebanese) the prospect of living in a Shiʿi-dominated Lebanon is hardly an appealing one.

Walid's strategy seems to be two-pronged. First, he will do nothing to alienate Hafiz al-Asad, but he will do his best to keep his distance whenever possible. In this regard, his good relations with both Libya and the Soviet Union serve to counterbalance Syrian influence, as does the quiet working arrangement with Israel. Second, he will focus on buttressing his political stronghold by continuing to maintain his autonomy from the Beirut government. He has been operating a port at Khalda since 1984, thus providing his community with a crucial outlet to the Mediterranean Sea. His public statements, typically dripping with cynicism, clearly indicate his aspirations for a Lebanon that he can dominate, or no Lebanon at all, and he is enough of a realist to understand that the former possibility is not a serious one. In an August 1985 interview, he stated it all most clearly: "I want a Lebanon according to my way and not theirs. . . . We are not a reformist movement. If the war is for this purpose we do not want it. I have said: Either kill or be killed. I still mean that and that is it. We want to change the entire system."[14]

Walid Jumblatt tramped docilely off to Damascus to participate in the Syrian-dominated tripartite negotiations aimed at producing a settlement, but few believed that he placed much stock in the prospects for success. Jumblatt clearly recognizes that any political solution can only diminish the power of the Druze, and therefore his power as well.

The Sunnis

The Sunni community, urbane, well-educated, and the traditional trustee for the premiership, is clearly the most fragmented politically. Unlike Lebanon's other sects, which are minorities both in Lebanon and in the larger Arab world, the Sunnis suffer from no such insecurity. Their sect dominates the Arab world, and for that matter the Islamic *umma* (community). The Sunni militia was the PLO, and as the fortunes of the PLO have waned in Lebanon, so have those of the Sunni community. Now they find themselves exposed and vulnerable in Lebanon, where they lack powerful militias, and they are sensitive to the danger that the Syrian regime will sacrifice their interests in order to strike a deal with the Maronite, Shi'i, and Druze militias.

In West Beirut, where Shi'i control has been consolidated since February 1984, the Sunnis find themselves in the unaccustomed role of the dominated. The Amal assault on the Palestinian camps in May and June of 1985 had a traumatic effect on the Sunnis, who were probably correct in concluding that, by reducing the power of the predominantly Sunni Palestinians, the Shi'a sought further to emasculate the Lebanese Sunnis.

The small Murabitun militia—whose perilous situation is well illustrated by the fact that its leader, Ibrahim Qulailat, resides in Paris—has been the frequent target for Amal attacks, most seriously on May 16 and 17, 1985, when Amal fighters, with Druze support, attacked Murabitun offices and positions. Clashes between Murabitun fighters and Amal have continued, but there is little prospect that the militia will pose a threat to the numerically superior Amal. Other Sunni militias have emerged to challenge Shi'i suzerainty in West Beirut; none has fared well. Most recently, the Sixth of February movement, led by Shakir Birjawi, was crushed by Amal on June 2 and

3, 1986. The decimation of these militias has left many Sunnis with the conclusion that an armed Palestinian presence in Lebanon is their only hope for countering the Shi'i ambitions.

An important phenomenon, although not widely noticed outside of Lebanon, is the recruitment of Sunnis to populist religious movements that extol Sunnism vis-à-vis Shi'ism. Several Beirut-based Sunni Muslim organizations have capitalized on the Shi'i-Sunni tensions to recruit followings along sectarian lines. As with the Shi'i community, these organizations tend to be loosely structured associations that are neighborhood based. 'Abd al-Hafiz Qasim, the head of the Muslim 'Ulama Association, leads one of the most important such movements, the Islamic Military Council, which is straightforwardly oriented to asserting an independent Sunni identity. One Sunni cleric has gone so far as to state that it is legal (from the standpoint of Islamic law) to spill the blood of a Shi'i.[15]

In Sidon, the two most important Sunni leaders are Nazih al-Bizri, who earned significant local support by his staunch opposition to the Israeli occupation, and Mustafa Sa'ad, the leader of the locally based Popular Nasirist Organization (al-Tanzim al-Sha'bi al-Nasiri). Both Bizri and Sa'ad have developed an uneasy relationship with the Shi'i Amal movement. Since Mustafa Sa'ad was blinded in a January 1985 car-bombing attack that also took the life of his daughter, his brother Usamah has assumed day-to-day leadership of the Popular Nasirist Organization. Mustafa has remained the overall leader. A militia grouping created by Sa'ad played an important role in defeating the Lebanese Forces in the villages east of Sidon in April 1985.

The traditional Sunni political leadership has been decidedly ineffectual in representing Sunni interests in the tumultuous conditions existing in Lebanon. Nonetheless, Sunni notables have been reasonably outspoken in criticizing the Shi'i-Druze partnership. Tamam Salam, the president of the Sunni charitable foundation al-Maqasid, has characterized the program of the National Union Front as no more than a new derivative of the discredited National Movement.[16] Sunni notables, such as Rashid Karami, the present prime minister, and former prime ministers Rashid al-Sulh, Sa'ib Salam, and Salim al-Huss, have made the required pilgrimages to Damascus and wrung their hands over the reign of chaos in West Beirut, but with little effect. In September 1985, after fighting erupted yet again around the Palestinian camps, and in the midst of heavy shelling between East and West Beirut, Prime Minister Karami sent Salim al-Huss to Damascus to request Syrian military intervention to put an end to the fighting. The Syrians took their time in responding; it was not until some nine months later that Hafiz al-Asad felt compelled to act.

In Lebanon's second largest city, Tripoli, Shaikh Saʿid Shaʿban leads the Tawhid or Islamic Unity Movement, which he founded in 1982. Shaʿban is widely believed to receive financial support from Iran, and his relations with the Islamic Republic are excellent. The fiery Shaʿban calls for an Islamic state, for in his view the only alternative to Islamic rule is pagan rule.[17] It is important to note, though, that Shaʿban does not accept the Iranian model for Islamic rule; instead of duplicating Shiʿi Iran's guardianship of the jurisconsult, he seeks the reestablishment of the Sunni caliphate, which would institutionalize authority rather than leaving it in one man's hands, as it does in the case of Ayatollah Khomeini. Noted for his anti-Christian views, Shaʿban is quite explicit in expounding his solution to the Lebanese dilemma: "I can see no other solution to the Lebanese crisis than the takeover of Lebanese politics, administration and bureaucracy by Muslims. If the Muslims rule, they will be fair, but if the others rule, they will strangle other sects."[18]

Tawhid and several allied groups have sought to control Tripoli. Tawhid controlled the city's port (worth at least $80,000 per month in customs receipts) until October 1985. It has acted ruthlessly against leftists and secularists, and one author reports that, in 1983, the movement massacred Communists and their families, and then discarded their corpses in the sea to rid the earth of their bad influence.[19] The forces opposing Shaʿban's movement included the Arab Democratic party, which has been heavily backed by Syria and whose ranks include a number of imported ʿAlawis. Serious fighting occurred in 1984, and, despite Syria's September 1984 efforts to reach an agreement that Tripoli would be policed by Syrian and Lebanese forces, fighting continued throughout 1985.

The most recent heavy fighting in Tripoli occurred in September 1985, when Syrian artillery supported Lebanese militiamen attacking the Tawhid positions. Press reports indicated that over 200,000 were forced to flee the city to escape the heavy shelling. Outgunned and suffering heavy casualties, the Tawhid appeared to be heading toward decisive defeat, but two apparently interrelated developments intervened to bring the fighting to an uneasy end. On September 30, four Soviet embassy employees were kidnapped in Beirut by the Islamic Liberation Organization, which subsequently demanded that Syria stop the fighting in the northern city if it wished to see the hostages released. Then, following an October 1 diplomatic intervention by Iran, an Iranian delegation proceeded to Tripoli for the purpose of escorting Shaʿban to Damascus.

On October 3, an agreement between President al-Asad and Shaʿban was reached whereby all the Tawhid heavy and medium weapons would be turned over to the Syrians, and the secular allies of Damascus would once again be allowed to establish offices in Tripoli. The agreement was a bitter one for Shaʿban; he had rejected similar terms a month before, but he had little choice but to agree. At the end of October, three of the four Soviet hostages were released (one had been killed shortly after being abducted), and the Syrians set about enforcing the agreement with at least temporary success.

If the situation in Tripoli holds, the Syrians will have succeeded in bringing a modicum of peace to two Lebanese cities. On September 7, 1985, the Syrians engineered a security plan for the Greek Catholic city of Zahle that provided for a Syrian contingent of 100 soldiers and 20 intelligence agents to work in cooperation with local police to establish law and order. Meanwhile, the intrepid Shaikh Shaʿban, who can hardly be accused of diffidence, may well attempt, as he has in the past, to extend his influence to Beirut, where Sunni-Shiʿi tensions may provide him a receptive audience.

The Shiʿa

The Shiʿa are fractiously riven; as the situation in Lebanon has deteriorated, leaders such as Nabih Berri have found themselves under serious challenge, and not just from outside of the Amal movement.

Berri's delicate situation was well illustrated during the TWA hijacking incident of June and July 1985. Although Amal was not involved in planning or carrying out the hijacking, Berri quickly found himself in a situation where his more extreme competitors in Hizb Allah (who may themselves have co-opted the hijackers) were stealing his limelight and undercutting his authority among the Shiʿis. Accordingly, Berri acted by taking custody of the hostages, much as he had acted in February 1984 when his move into West Beirut was in part calibrated to arrest the erosion of his following. But the very limitations of his action serve to illustrate his dilemma and the dynamics of the political environment in which he operates. We are dealing with political movements, not well-defined political parties in the western sense. Followers are more easily swayed, cajoled, or enlisted than directed. Suasion is the technique of a man in Nabih Berri's situation. He can do no more than the political mood of his constituency permits; if he forgets this norm, he risks finding himself without a following. In the case of the ill-fated TWA flight, Berri could secure the hostages, but their release had to await the intervention of far more powerful actors, Syria and Iran. At best, Berri managed to keep the lid on the pot. He denied his competitors a clear-cut victory, but they succeeded in demonstrating his lack of clear-cut authority. In short, Berri gained a temporary stalemate, but the internecine competition continues.

Within Amal, he faces a phalanx of competitors, but to date he has skillfully countered the challenges. After postponements for two consecutive years, Amal held its sixth congress on April 4, 1986. The one-day meeting proved to be a skillful exercise by Berri in solidifying his control over the movement. Not only was he reelected as the chief of Amal, but he assumed the chairmanship of the political bureau from his nominal deputy ʿAkif Haidar, who was made the head of the newly established research bureau.

Berri's principal rival within Amal, Hasan Hashim, boycotted the session, as did several important leaders from the South. Exploiting Hashim's absence, Berri was able to replace him with one of his supporters, ʿAtif ʿAun, as the chair of the executive committee. Hashim's departure may be a mixed blessing. He retains an important following in southern Lebanon, good relations with Speaker Husain al-Husaini, and friendly ties to a number of pro–Hizb Allah clergy. In short, he could develop into an even more potent rival outside of Amal than he has been within it. The leading cleric in Amal remains Shaikh ʿAbd al-Amir Qabalan, who heads the Shariʿa (religious law) department of the movement. As before, the movement's leadership includes several personalities who are known to be much more supportive of the Hizb Allah line than Berri. Important among these individuals are Mustafa Durani, the chief of central security, and Zakaria Hamza, member of the political bureau.

Despite Berri's apparent success in consolidating his own position—some observers expected the congress to mark his downfall—there has been a marked fragmentation in authority throughout the Shiʿi community. Local opportunists, thugs, and strongmen have proliferated madly, feeding on the rampant insecurity that marks many of the Shiʿi-controlled areas. Whether inhabiting storefronts in West Beirut or villages in the South, local leaders, more noteworthy for their rapacity than their capacity, have diluted the effective control of both Amal and Hizb Allah. Imposing order in the anarchic circumstances of mid-1986 will be no easy task. One thing is certain: the longer the fragmentation process continues, the more awesome the task of imposing order becomes.

Adding to the problems is the fact that, within Lebanon, there are widespread apprehensions about the ascendant Shiʿi community. For many non-Shiʿi Lebanese, the Shiʿa appear as a behemoth threatening to dominate Lebanon culturally, socially, and politically. Thus, all manner of novel realignments among Lebanon's other sects are possible. Nonetheless, while some have predicted that the Shiʿa will

dominate the state, there is, in fact, little of the state left to dominate. The Shiʿa have a compelling interest in the territorial integrity
and independence of Lebanon, and they may—after a time—provide
the glue for putting Lebanon back together (in whatever form), but
even the most optimistic Shiʿi politicians see a long and hard road
awaiting them.[20]

Conclusions

The two communities that have a unique stake in the reconstruction of Lebanon are the Shiʿa and the Maronites, and the possibility
that the two communities will act on their shared stake in Lebanon should not be summarily dismissed. As minority sects in a predominantly Sunni Arab world, neither the Maronites nor the Shiʿa
stand to benefit from the dismantlement of Lebanon. Unlike the
Sunnis, who enjoy the security that comes from belonging to the regional majority, the Shiʿa and the Maronites can find only insecurity
outside of Lebanon. The Druze are far too small in numbers reasonably to expect much more than they have accomplished, which is to
say, autonomy in the Shuf region where they predominate. Moreover, the Druze have proven quite capable of doing what is necessary
to dissipate the power of their Lebanese rivals, a category that clearly
includes both the Shiʿa and the Maronites.

The sporadic clashes that have marked the relationship between
the Shiʿa and the Druze stem from a conflict of interests; while they
remain united in principle, there is justification to wonder how long
the Berri-Jumblatt partnership will endure. The Shiʿi campaign
against the armed Palestinian presence that punctuated 1985 and
1986 has already brought the contradictions in the Druze-Shiʿa relationship into the open. It will continue to do so.

Meanwhile, external powers will continue to exert considerable
influence over events within Lebanon. Israel, despite—some might
say, because of—its failures in Lebanon, maintains an understanding
with the Druze, as well as contacts with the Maronites; it is by no
means clear that Israel will promote the reconstitution of Lebanon,
if the alternative is a conflictual environment that will promote the
debility of several of its adversaries.

Iran continues its support for Lebanese clients, and there are growing signs that Hizb Allah has very broad links to Iran. Amal's relatively moderate political program and its nonclerical leadership have
not played well in Tehran for several years, and Iran is likely to continue to lend support to Amal's adversaries.[21]

But it is Syria's hand that is the strongest. Syria's policy seems to be based on clearheaded realism. Syria has no illusions; it treats Lebanon as it is. Rather than going out on the same limb that it did in 1976 when it intervened en masse, Damascus has clearly sought to bolster those Lebanese elements that serve its interests and have the power to exercise effective control over parts of Lebanon. And, as the daunting failure of the December 28 agreement demonstrates, even Hafiz al-Asad cannot always be sure about where power actually resides in Lebanon.

After six months of sulking over the failed attempt to engineer a settlement in Lebanon, during which Vice-President ʿAbd al-Halim Khaddam spurned numerous entreaties from Lebanese Sunnis to help bring an end to the mayhem, the Syrians acted on a modest scale. On July 4, a contingent of soldiers and *mukhabarat* (security agents), numbering about 800 by mid-month, was sent to West Beirut to support the meager government forces in yet another effort to impose law and order in West Beirut.

Despite their apprehensions about again becoming embroiled in Beirut, it was hard for the Syrians to avoid acting. May and June had seen Amal initiate a fierce but largely unsuccessful campaign against the Palestinian camps. Rather than subduing the *fidaʾiyin*, the battles seemed only to be reunifying the disparate *fidaʾi* factions, an outcome that would undercut Syrian ambitions, to be sure. The battle of the camps also threatened to enliven Sunni anger in Syria, always a matter of concern in the ʿAlawi-dominated regime. Syria's Iranian ally applied some heavy diplomatic pressure and also may have offered to ease up on its demands that Syria pay its overdue bills for Iranian oil. Moreover, there is no reason to doubt that al-Asad would like Syria to be seen as a regional power that can bring stability (if not reform) to Lebanon and that must be taken seriously by the United States in the context of any peace process. However, the new Syrian intervention brought only a respite. Although the presence of Syrian forces did prompt the militias to withdraw from the streets, within days a new campaign of car-bombings ricocheted back and forth across the Green Line separating East from West Beirut.

Even with the healthy cynicism that is an occupational hazard of following Lebanese events, it is overly skeptical to claim that the Lebanese do not want peace. Indeed, the day before the most recent Syrian initiative, Lebanese Christians and Muslims alike participated in a general strike to voice their despair at the continuing conflict. If such fundamental and profoundly important intersectarian unity could be sustained, the self-destruction of Lebanon just might be brought to an end. Unfortunately, while it is undeniable that the

Lebanese yearn dearly for peace, they all want it on their own terms. It seems all too likely that the struggles within—and among—the Sunni, Shi'i, Druze, and Maronite communities will continue and that there will not be an early halt to the fighting that springs from irreconcilable visions of what Lebanon should become.

While most sectarian leaders ceremonially condemn partition, it is plain that partition is emerging nonetheless. Lebanon is destined to be a state-in-fragments for years to come. This is not to imply that Lebanon will disappear in the process, for it is likely that the fiction of a state will be maintained, perhaps to be brought back to real life as the barons, princes, and warlords of its fragments discover that they can offer no viable substitute. And Lebanon will probably continue to survive the intrigues and ambitions of its more powerful neighbors to the east and the south, just as it has survived foreign interlopers for centuries, because the one thing going for Lebanon, in addition to the incredible vitality and durability of the Lebanese people, is its indigestibility.

But, sadly, peace in Lebanon seems no more than a fondly remembered dream. It is certainly not soon to be experienced by the Shi'is and their fellow Lebanese.[22]

Author's photo of Lebanese villagers with ruined village in background, UN jeep in foreground.

Appendix A. The Charter of the Amal Movement

Translated by Barbara Parmenter

In the Name of God, the Compassionate, the Merciful

The Amal Movement in Lebanon is an extension of a timeless human movement, an expression of man's hopes for a better life, which drive him to resist all that undermines his life, dulls his talents, or threatens his future.

It is a link in the universal movement of man in history, a movement led by prophets, holy men, and pious defenders, and propelled and enriched by immortal martyrs.

By this strong historical bond and worldwide accompaniment, the Mahrumin Movement [the original name of the Amal Movement, meaning the "movement of the deprived"] in Lebanon is reinforced, its path cleared, and its continuation and success assured.

When we attempt to outline the features of this movement, we find:

First—This movement emanates from belief in God, in its true meaning rather than its abstract understanding. This is the basis of all our daily activities and of our human relationships, and it is what continually renews our faith and determination, increases our hope, and guides every aspect of our behavior.

This movement is founded on belief in man, his freedom, dignity, and nobility, and in his life's mission, which is the aim of his creation.

The truth is that belief in man is the earthly dimension of belief in God, an inseparable dimension consistently affirmed by authentic religious sources.

Second—Our lofty heritage in Lebanon, so full of trials and tribulations, shining with acts of heroism and sacrifice, abounding in values and cultures, outlines our path and confirms our genius and our share in civilization.

At the same time, the benefit we gain from the experiences of others around the world, on the condition that our original character is maintained, attests to our earnest desire for progress and perfection. We believe in the unity of the human family, and that the gains made by any of her children are the property of all and in the service of all.

Third—The Amal Movement believes in the citizen's complete freedom and relentlessly combats despotism, feudalism, authoritarianism, and all forms of discrimination.

Political sectarianism in the Lebanese system prevents political development, divides citizens, and upsets national unity. For that reason, our movement rejects it and considers it a manifestation of political backwardness in our country.

Fourth—The movement opposes economic injustice in all its forms, including the formation of monopolies and the exploitation of the individual by which he is transformed into a mere consumer and society into a market of consumption. The movement likewise opposes the restriction of economic activities to financial ventures and usury.

Fifth—The movement believes that the provision of equal opportunities for all citizens is their most basic right, and that the primary duty of the state is to ensure the advancement of social justice.

Sixth—The Amal Movement is a patriotic movement adhering to the principles of national sovereignty, the indivisibility of the motherland, and the integrity of her soil. For that reason, it resists imperialism and combats the aggressions and covetous schemes to which Lebanon is exposed.

The movement considers adherence to national [pan-Arab] interests, to the liberation of Arab lands, and to freedom for all the Arab people to be one of its patriotic obligations that it will not shirk.

It goes without saying that the safeguarding of southern Lebanon, its defense and development, forms the basis and substance of patriotism. The motherland cannot exist without the South, and there can be no patriotism without fidelity to this beloved region of Lebanon.

On the international side, the movement rejects on principle the division of the world into two camps that discounts the will of other peoples, shatters the unity of the human family, and dissipates its energies. The movement is a part of the pageant of humanity striving toward emancipation from oppression, and therefore supports all international cooperation toward this end.

Seventh—Palestine, the holy land, which has been and continues to be subject to all kinds of injustice, Palestine and her people are in the heart and mind of our movement. The struggle for her liberation is our prime duty, and the honor and faith of our movement lies in our solidarity with her people and in our defense and support of their resistance.

This is especially necessary because it is Zionism that poses the real and continuing danger to Lebanon, to the values in which we believe, to the entire region, and to the whole of humanity, which it subjects to division and discrimination. In Lebanon, Zionism sees the peaceful coexistence of factions as a constant challenge and a living condemnation of its existence.

Eighth—The Amal Movement is a movement of the people, not an organization with special interests and privileges; indeed, it is in the forefront of the fight against privilege and discrimination between citizens.

The movement does not oppose cooperation with honorable individuals and groups who desire to build a better Lebanon. It does not monopolize for itself the honor of this struggle; rather, it gains inspiration from others and inspires others to act.

The Amal Movement is not a sectarian movement, nor a charity organization, nor a religious guide. It is a movement of all the deprived to meet urgent and pressing needs, to define and work toward the realization of basic general goals, and to fight on the side of the oppressed to the end.

It is a movement of those who feel frustration in their daily lives, of those who are anxious for their future, and of those who shoulder their responsibility toward the deprived and the anxious with honor and enthusiasm.

It is a Lebanese movement toward a better [world].

The Amal Movement member must:

1. Believe in the Amal Charter, work to implement its principles, and acquire necessary discipline to respect and carry out the decisions of the leadership.

2. Be mature and rational.

3. Not belong to any other party, organization, or political force. If the applicant is a member of a political party, or militia and ends such activities, he must give evidence of his withdrawal from the party in question by actively putting into practice the precepts and basic principles of our movement. The probation period will last a period of six months.

4. Merge heart and soul with the principles and aims of the movement and become a model of these for the people.

5. Undergo training when he is physically fit.

6. Be endowed with the proper moral, educational, and social qualities.

7. Swear the Amal Movement's oath, the text of which follows, in front of the commander or whomever the commander designates.

"I swear by Almighty God that I believe in the words of the Amal Movement's Charter, which I have studied; that I shall exert all my powers to implement it in accordance with the decisions of the movement's organization; that I shall serve the organization and put its interests ahead of my own; that I shall consider its members as my brothers and guard my knowledge of them as a trust never to be divulged to anyone other than the organization; and that I shall be a sound model in my personal behavior, in my sacrifices and exertions, in my adherence to values, and in my love for the people. This I swear by God; may the prophets, holy men, martyrs, and pious people witness what I say."

8. Have this membership accepted by the organization bureau, and register his name with this bureau after submitting a handwritten and signed application.

Insights into the Charter

Introduction to the Charter

1. Our movement is not a temporary historical phenomenon isolated by complex social conditions. Rather, it lies in the heart of every person who believes that there are certain just laws that must govern the relationships between people. These are divine laws, and they follow two parallel lines:

—The fixed line unites the laws of life and the bases of its preservation, in harmony with the fundamental principles by which the universe, human beings, and all life was created. These are considered to be constant and enduring truths, such as faith in God, the creator of time, belief in the limitations of man and his needs, and belief in the rights and responsibilities of every member of a society toward his fellows.

—The evolving line encompasses all the variables in life, and depends on the types of methods employed to produce the daily necessities of food, clothing, and shelter; to divide roles and tasks among a society's members; and to create infrastructures that are in keeping with the progressive development of a society: centralization, decentralization, a system of movement.

2. Our movement emanates from the spiritual hunger people feel for wholeness—a hunger that supplies the source of effective revolutionary energy—and is founded on the rules of reason, the free expression of the spirit, and the feelings of the heart.

3. It is part of a human movement toward justice, freedom, and equality, and is thus a natural extension of the movement of the prophets, peace be upon them, who called for an end to the tyranny of rulers and their decrees, a tyranny that enslaved humanity with earthly laws and human systems of rule. The movement is nourished by the struggle of freedom fighters whose martyrdom has lit the way of truth.

4. This profound bond across the ages gives us courage and confidence that we shall be victorious just as our predecessors were victorious in achieving the goals of humanity in solidarity with divine principles and laws.

"If you assist God, God will aid you and ensure your steps."

The First Principle

I. THE EXISTENCE OF GOD

If we examine the universe and all that it contains, life and its significance, the relationship of humans, animals, and plants with nature, and the details of our creation, we find clear signs of the precise organization of the cosmos. For example:

—the rotation of the earth about its axis to produce night and day; the revolution of the earth around the sun to produce the four seasons; and the orbit of the moon around the earth by means of the latter's gravitational pull.

—the presence of the atmosphere enveloping the earth, which prevents the escape of gases such as oxygen and carbon dioxide, and which protects us from falling meteors by breaking them up upon contact with the atmosphere. The atmosphere also protects living organisms and ensures their survival by deflecting large amounts of solar radiation, particularly ultraviolet light.

—the relation among humans, animals, and plants, in which the first two inhale oxygen and exhale carbon dioxide, a dynamic equilibrium that maintains the amount of oxygen in the air at 21 percent and the amount of carbon dioxide at .03 percent.

—the sun's evaporation of a portion of the earth's surface water to form clouds in the upper atmosphere and produce rain, which supplies drink and other needs to human beings and needed water to the land. The rainwater finds its way to rivers, which then flow to the sea, and the hydrologic cycle repeats itself, making possible the continuation of life.

—the role of plants as an important basis of life, supplying food for herbivores, which in turn are the source of food for carnivores, while humans consume both plants and animals. How do plants grow? They grow in the ground with the help of inorganic materials produced from organic materials by the action of decomposers, microscopic organisms that feed on the corpses of humans, animals, and plants, reducing them to their primary organic elements. In this way, the life cycle is maintained.

—when we examine the creation of man, we discover that he himself is a miracle: the operation of the eyes and vision; the role of oxygen in oxidizing food inside the body and transforming it into energy; the digestion of food through secretions from the mouth, stomach, bile, and pancreas, turning it into liquid that capillaries on the sides of the small intestines can then absorb and transfer to the blood; the actions of the heart, which circulates these nutrients to all parts of the body; the action of the liver, which maintains the level of blood sugar; and the links between the brain and the rest of the body to transmit images and sensations, and to issue commands.

These examples and many others could fill volumes. A journey out to the edges of the cosmos and within the soul of man brings us to a single truth: that the most simple elements of human life and the physical world are brought into being by some efficient cause. The table is hewn by the carpenter, the shirt sewn by the tailor, the shoe cut by the shoemaker. Everything has a maker, every event a cause, and every being a creator, and the vast, well-ordered universe and all its elements follow stable and enduring laws. Thus, there can be no doubt in the existence of the Almighty God.

2. THE ATTRIBUTES OF GOD

He is absolute in everything; no place or time confines Him for He is the creator of place and time. There is nothing like Him; He is the One without any associate.

"Say He is the one God, the steadfast God; He neither begets nor is begotten; He has no equal."

He knows all the secrets of existence, the nature and needs of men, and their relation with creation.

"We created man and we know how his soul tempts him."

No matter how much physicists claim to know and understand, God is the creator of the physical world. No matter what the claims of psychologists, He is the creator of the psyche and understands its workings. No matter what claims people make with their modern techniques and understanding, God is the creator of the ages and all that passes. God is able to mark the days of man and his life,

His knowledge is higher than all the sciences and is their perfection. The journey that follows His course and His law will arrive at the proper path.

He is omnipotent and does whatever He desires in whatever way He pleases. He created man from a drop of sperm and determines the span of his life, at the end of which man dies to be resurrected on the Day of Reckoning—to enter Paradise if he was obedient or the fire of Hell if he was sinful. Of this there is no doubt so long as we believe in the absolute power and permanence of God, against Whom no one can compete.

He is righteous and does not create life in vain, for the unbeliever to enjoy his godlessness while the believer toils wearily in a world of vice. Rather, He does justice to the oppressed, rewards the faithful, and raises the believer to the highest rank.

3. THE ABSTRACT CONCEPT OF FAITH IN GOD

The abstract concept of faith represents a distorted understanding not rooted in the proper foundations of dynamic interaction with life. It is a passive, stultified faith reflecting the decay and backwardness of a society. Godless imperialism, by its devices and enticements, has contributed to implanting this false belief out of fear for its own international interests and hegemony.

The manifestations of this abstract, unsound understanding of faith take four forms:

The first form: faith based on rituals.   This is faith that confines worship to practices empty of revolutionary substance, and aimed at external appearances, forgetting that the scope of psychological integration includes the social domain and that the *Jihad* works in two directions—toward the self and toward the society. This faith withdraws into itself, and shuts the door of the soul in ritual worship that has no meaning.

The second form: sectarian faith.   Sectarian fanaticism endangers true faith and is a tool of feudalism, monopolies, profiteers, and self-proclaimed leaders. There is a fundamental division between true faith and the faith of those who conceal themselves behind slogans and rituals.

This type of faith reveals a narrow mind, a dull intellect, and a false ideology. It is the root of chaos and dissension, and represents the basic factor in the disintegration of Islamic unity, a unity affirmed in God's message, may He be praised: "Hold fast to the reins of God, all of you; do not become separated and do not struggle among yourselves, for you shall surely go down in defeat and be scattered to the wind."

The third form: faith based on ethnicity. Some people understand faith not as a property of the soul expressed through behavior in harmony with the divine plan, but on the basis of what they inherited from their fathers, of a name written on their identity cards, regardless of ensuing contradictions in behavior and belief, and of inconsistencies with ideal standards of action. Their faith becomes an element of social identity rather than a true characteristic of the soul.

The fourth form: faith detached from life. This faith results automatically from European understandings of religion and belief, which revolve around the principle that religion is separate from life, politics, and society. This so-called faith thus becomes a few prayer rituals and fasting on certain days. An escapist mentality among those who pretend to be religious distinguishes this type of faith. They refuse to interact with people on the pretext that it is forbidden, and take no interest in social matters, claiming that there is no link between religion and politics.

4. THE TRUE MEANING OF FAITH IN GOD

(A) Faith in God means to submit to and to obey the Creator in all matters, in thought and in deed, to implement His commands and steer clear of His prohibitions, and not to act licentiously or make false claims for ourselves, for we are neither more knowledgeable than God nor more compassionate. The Most High says: "This is my straight path; follow it and do not follow others, for they shall cut you off from His path."

This bond with God leads to human happiness because God's commandments harmonize with human nature.

(B) [Faith in God also means] strengthening self-control and self-examination in order to consolidate the relations between people and to maintain their proper behavior.

(C) [Faith in God] denies the separation between social issues and the relation of the individual to himself and to his Lord, for each of these completes the other.

"You believe in part of the Book and do not believe in other parts of it; but there is no recompense for those who act in this way except ignominy in this life and a worse torture on the Day of Reckoning."

Faith in God therefore requires, for example, that family laws should follow the revealed law of God, and likewise with other social, political, and economic matters.

(D) We should attach ourselves to this world only to the degree that it does not enslave us, and in a way in which the lawful things are encouraged and the forbidden are avoided, so that the world becomes a way station in our lives rather than a permanent abode.

"For the life of this world is but a temporary delight."

(E) We must look to more distant goals (the Hereafter) that encourage work and devotion without developing a bond to earthly life, which drives man to give up hope for happiness in the Hereafter.

"Seek the life hereafter that God grants to you."

5. MAN IN THE MEASURE OF LAW

The principal standard for divine law is concern for man and his affairs. This means that divine law circumscribes man's relation with God, with himself, and with others, in order to achieve his spiritual tranquillity, to assure his successful journey in this life, and to make him happy with his fate on the Day of Reckoning.

The divine plan's concern for man is emphasized by its encouragement of good deeds that influence the acceptance of all a man's actions.

For it was revealed in the Quran:

"You see that he who lies about his religion is also the one who rebuffs the orphan and does not feed the poor."

And in the Hadith:

"All beings are the children of God, and the dearest to Him is the one who serves His children most."

Faith in human existence, freedom, and dignity is a prerequisite for faith in God, which means to acquire His perfect attributes and be free of their contraries.

The Second Principle

"Maintaining our heritage and deriving benefit from the experiences of others throughout the world."

To speak of our heritage does not mean simply to extol the radiant history of the Islamic community, but to make the past serve the present and the future and an inspiration for reshaping the community's existence. A community cut off from its heritage resembles a tree without roots. We therefore would like to analyze and explain the reasons for, and benefits of, using our heritage as a guide by which we can build a glorious present rather than loitering amidst the tattered and obsolete ruins of the past.

Research clearly shows that the Arabs enjoyed an advanced civilization before the rise of Islam, but that it had degenerated and come to a halt in the darkness of the *Jahiliyyah* [*Jahiliyyah* is derived from the word for ignorance and refers to pre-Islamic times]. Islam raised the spirit of civilization to lofty heights encompassing the various spheres of the intellect, economy, society, and ethics. Within the growing diversity and complexity of this culture, civilization rapidly advanced as religious doctrines, philosophies, and sciences cross-pollinated in the mind of the community. Armies went forth to spread the message of monotheism and the liberation of all peoples, and a theocratic state was established in Medina under the leadership of Muhammad (God bless him and grant him salvation). This was the seed for that vast empire that would one day grow to twice the size of that of the Romans.

The most important elements in the success of this human experiment for the Islamic community were:

(A) A special way of looking at life, based on certain goals, strategies, and tactics (the divine plan).

(B) Undertaking the responsibilities of faithfulness, as a result of being conscious of the message and working on its behalf.

(C) Obedience to upright leadership: "Obey God, the Prophet, and your rulers."

(D) Overcoming self-interest, that is, putting the interest of the community ahead of private interests, for in that lies the favor of God.

I. OUR CULTURAL, INTELLECTUAL, LITERARY, AND SCIENTIFIC HERITAGE

(A) In the intellectual sphere:

—The holy Quran offers a solid intellectual basis for the development of civilization, a model of eloquence, the confirmation and consummation of the messages of Judaism and Christianity, and the primary source for a well-ordered set of laws regarding social life.

—The Sunna incorporates the words, deeds, and judgments of the Prophet (may God bless him and grant him salvation), explains and elaborates on the Quran, and completes our understanding of the message.

—Philosophy and thought handed down through the generations are an intellectual aid to believers for understanding their heritage.

(B) In the literary sphere:

—The emergence of master poets during the *Jahiliyyah* and in the Islamic period, and the establishment of grammatical and linguistic foundations by people such as Abu al-Aswad al-Du'li (who laid down the principles of grammar under the instructions of the Imam 'Ali), Hassan al-Basri, al-Kissa'i, Sibawayh, and Naftuwiyyah.

—The appearance of great works of prose such as *Nahj al-Balagha* by the Imam 'Ali, *Kalila wa Dimna, al-Aghani, al-Bukhala', al-Biyan wa al-Tabyin,* and *al-Hayawan* by al-Jahiz.

(C) In history and geography:

—The emergence of al-Waqidi, al-Ya'qubi, al-Baghdadi, al-Balathiri, Ibn Khaldun, al-Mas'udi, Yaqut, and Ibn Batutah.

(D) In science and mathematics:

—The emergence of Ibn Sina, al-Razi, Usama ibn Munqad (in medicine), Jabir ibn Hayyan (in chemistry, who learned from the true imam), ibn Jabir, al-Khawarizmi, and ibn Haytham (in mathematics)—they likewise discovered microbes, invented the compass, paper, glass, and gunpowder, and extracted sugar. . . .

"The works and travels that the learned men of Islam contributed to the world, encompassing all the various arts and sciences, and which the Crusades carried back to the countries of the West, combined with the previous contact between Arabs and Europeans in Spain, filled the bare and impoverished libraries of Europe with an inexhaustible supply of treasures produced by Muslim genius. This resulted in the spread of civilization and a scientific renaissance throughout Europe and the lifting of her peoples to the level of civilization that we see today."

2. OUR LEGACY OF VALUES

Our heritage is rich in values based on heavenly prophecies and a divine plan abounding in high spiritual, social, intellectual, and humanitarian standards.

(A) Spiritual values:

—faith in God, His prophets, messages, angels, and books.

—the call to worship God alone and obedience to Him.

—belief in fate and divine decree (not predestined fate nor free will, but something between the two).

—the renunciation of pleasure in worldly things (not renunciation in the sense of not owning things but of things not owning you).

(B) Social and educational values:

—the performance of educational rites such as prayer, pilgrimage, and almsgiving.

—the invocation of God (the invocation of God is the weapon of the believer and the light of heaven and earth).

—to work for truth and justice (to plunge into the floods for justice wherever need be).

—the self as the standard in relationships (wish for others what you wish for yourself, and consider hateful for them what is hateful to yourself).

—keeping company only with good people (associate with the good people and separate yourself from the bad).

—steadfastness and patience (throw off your cares with resolutions of patience and conviction).

—obedience to parents—respect for people—avoidance of sins—the reform of women's rights.

(C) Intellectual values:

—the fight against magic, astrology, and fortunetelling (the magician among the Muslims should be killed).

—the rational contemplation of God's creation.

"In the creation of the heavens and earth and of night and day are signs for those with minds."

—the human being is the deputy of God on earth.

"I appoint for earth a deputy."

—the mind is the judge.

"Say 'Bring us your proof if you are honest.'"

—the call to science.

—the use of independent judgment in Islamic law.

(D) Humanitarian values:

—devotion to freedom, dignity, and human rights.

—"For we respect the sons of Adam."

—devotion to freedom of belief (there can be no coercion in religion).

—the call to peace (You who believe, join the religion of peace, all of you).

3. OUR LEGACY OF HEROIC ACTS AND SACRIFICES

Our heritage is laden with heroic acts and noble sacrifices, both for the sake of defending our advancement and for correcting mistakes.

Because European culture is on the march to devour our civilization and principles, bold and organized action is needed to resist this aggression through faith, confidence, and sacrifice for our just cause. If we are resolved to advance against the enemy, then our incentive and standard must be the path taken by our noble martyrs and heroes.

Our discussion of our heroes thus offers a living model for the community to emulate in its struggle: Moses, Jesus, and Muhammad in their fight against the enemies of truth, and the examples of Hamza, Salman al-Farisi, Bilal, al-Miqdad, 'Amar ibn Yasir, Hujjur ibn 'Addi, Maythim al-Tamar, and Rashid al-Hijri.

4. DERIVING BENEFIT FROM THE EXPERIENCES OF OTHERS WHILE PRESERVING OUR ORIGINAL CHARACTER

We know that the community's customs and traditions derive directly or indirectly from its heritage, and that the purity of character in our heritage guarantees its continuity through the generations, but to stop short at the external manifestations of our heritage is disastrous, for it misses its essence and truth. It is therefore incumbent that:

(A) We restore to our traditional customs and expressions their true contents by drawing upon our spiritual and intellectual resources. We must bring back to our remembrance of 'Ashura its revolutionary opposition to falsehood and injustice, and restore true meaning to the manifestations of faith (the veil, the pilgrimage, etc.) by educating religiously aware young veiled women and performing the pilgrimage in accordance with the precepts of God. We must replace symbols and appearances with truths and substance that reflect our original character and repudiate false pride.

(B) Each of our members must be an example, and not claim with his tongue what he cannot translate into practice with his limbs, for "God will not help a people until they are willing to help themselves."

(Faith is not simply adornment and good intentions, rather it is that which abides permanently in the heart and is confirmed by action.)

In this way, a new and aware generation will come into being, a generation that will shake off the dust of backwardness and cease striving after the dregs of other cultures. This generation will create a new renaissance emanating from:

—the divine plan as a standard for judgment; what accords with it we shall accept in our thought, and what contradicts it we shall reject.

—learning—this is knowledge that informs human belief and behavior, such as philosophy, economics, and jurisprudence. Such learning derives from the plan of God and is handed down through the generations. It does not include sciences such as medicine, engineering, and chemistry. This does not imply a rejection of others; indeed, we may benefit from their experiences while preserving our own heritage. We can borrow from them:

—any respectable means that we deem appropriate to reach our humanitarian goals.

—their scientific expertise and their achievements in legal analysis and understanding.

The Third Principle

1. BELIEF IN THE COMPLETE FREEDOM OF CITIZENS

Freedom is rooted deep in human nature and is essential to human dignity. Religions therefore forbid for man any actions that are incompatible with the loftiness of his soul, oppose discrimination between men and women, and call for freedom as an innate right.

"Why do you enslave the people when they were born free?"

The meaning of freedom, for us, is a person's right to undertake any activity provided that it does not infringe on the rights of others or harm himself. This freedom is thus restricted by law and is known as responsible freedom.

Since the word "freedom" is synonymous with the word "right" (because the attainment of a person's just right is the essence of his freedom), it is necessary to distinguish among a number of rights and freedoms:

(A) Private and personal freedom, the branches of which are as follows:

—the right to life: the unjust killing of a person is not allowed, nor are assaults on the physical well-being of people; it is forbidden to torture or enslave a person; a person's means for survival must be safeguarded.

—the right to personal dignity: the preservation of the inviolability of the house and family, and protection from unfounded accusation and slander.

—the freedom to work: the right of the individual to choose his job, and his right to refuse to work when his rights are not guaranteed.

—freedom of thought: the right to express an opinion; freedom of belief, learning, and teaching.

(B) Collective freedom:

—political rights.

—vocational freedom (unions).

—religious freedom (organizations).

(C) Conditional economic freedom:

This type of freedom must be restricted by laws that preserve the rights of people as a collective.

In order to secure complete freedom for citizens, it is necessary to combat all injustice in the form of despotism, authoritarianism, feudalism, and discrimination between citizens.

Our charter therefore condemns above all else injustice and aggression.

"Do not think that God is not cognizant of what the tyrants are doing."

The Imam 'Ali said:

"I swear if I were offered the seven heavens and everything beneath them as a bribe to disobey God by stealing one grain of barley from an ant, I would not do it."

If this is the case, then what of the man who sheds human blood as if it were of less value than water, or he who disdains honor and dignity?

Our charter does not allow leniency for oppressors and tyrants or for their supporters. The Most High said:

"Do not place your trust in those who are unjust, for you will be burned by the hellfire; without God you have no guardian, and you will not be rendered victorious."

The free person does not accept the world as it is and attempt to justify it; rather, he rebels against its iniquity and rejects worldly idols to find true freedom in the worship of God. . . . He is revolutionary in his faith, in his philosophy, and in his political leadership, and a denouncer of tyrants and false leaders (the greatest act of courage is to speak the truth before an unjust ruler).

2. THE DUTY TO COMBAT FEUDALISM AND POLITICAL FEUDALISM

In a feudal system, a small proportion of the people own most of the land, usually illegally. Some feudal laws prohibited the peasant from leaving the landowner without paying his debts that he had incurred to the landowner. This was impossible since his annual income hardly sufficed to feed his children. Thus, he was forced to borrow money from interest-charging moneylenders simply to secure his daily needs. This combined with the experience of dispossession, poverty, hunger, and disease forced the peasant to remain under the yoke of feudalism.

The descendants of the feudal overlords have inherited the political leadership of the Lebanese state, and political feudalism still plays its influential role in appropriating government positions, usurping public profits for private accounts, and maintaining its dominance over the people. The movement shall therefore exert every effort to expose and depose this feudal leadership.

3. THE FIGHT AGAINST THE SYSTEM OF POLITICAL SECTARIANISM

The existence of sects in Lebanon has turned into a political phenomenon that has taken over the helm of government and appropriates public profit for the interests of the sectarian party. A bitter struggle has ensued between the different parties, each vying for its own interests and privileges. Political blocs have formed around the leadership of each sect as they gasp for air groping in the darkness in their effort to glean the crumbs of state offices to feed their followers and so maintain their power. The system of political feudalism has exploited this phenomenon and sees in it an ideal mechanism for controlling the commercial market; it has therefore grabbed for every opportunity to promote it. This has impelled our movement to seek the elimination of the reactionary system of political sectarianism, because this system prevents political development, causes the stagnation of national institutions, discriminates between citizens, and disrupts national unity.

The Fourth Principle

The state has not seriously considered a development plan, nor the implementation of economic projects that would enable citizens to feel safe and secure and that would reinforce their patriotic spirit. This is due to blind discrimination between different regions of the country and to the selfish and profiteering practices of the people's representatives. Poverty has thus spread to engulf the majority of the population, for whom the state has become an institution to steal from the people. Unemployment runs rampant among the youth, and these armies of unemployed provide an accurate picture of real deprivation in a country that should be just and free.

When the citizen was deprived of his right to work and produce, he was transformed into a mere consumer, and society in general became a collective of consumers, without factories or productive projects. All concern became focused on the services sector, which plunged the Lebanese economy into crisis, a crisis reflected in the general condition of the Lebanese people. The ensuing anxiety and lack of stability led to the disintegration of society and to violent outbreaks, as seen in recent events.

The country is in need of sound scientific and statistical studies on the basis of which the oppression and deprivation that encumber the Lebanese people can be lifted and the danger facing the community can be overcome. Criminal hands have toyed with this country and the fangs of profiteers among its leaders gouged it to pieces, tearing the substance of Lebanese existence and allowing deprivation to invade the spirit and soul of the people.

The cure for this deprivation lies in developing a practical plan for ensuring justice and providing sufficient opportunities in politics, social life, housing, education, and culture. Clearly, a raise in the standard of living of the deprived will not be achieved by charity, but it is possible through economic growth fueled by national and Arab loans that will be repaid from the returns of the projects established.

However, we must take care to combat two phenomena:

1. THE FIGHT AGAINST MONOPOLIES

A monopoly results when a person, group, or particular enterprise enjoys exclusive domain over a certain manufacture. This includes monopolies of selling and buying.

Monopolies are the primary feature of the Lebanese economy, due to its dependence on a corrupt free market system, to a lack of planning, and to the prevailing selfish and individualist spirit that impels the largest merchants to suppress a particular commodity in order to sell it at an exorbitant price after creating an artificial shortage. Is there any greater injustice than this?

The charter of the Mahrumin Movement therefore condemns monopolies and would make it incumbent on the state to control sales, weights, and measures, and to set the prices of goods and commodities, to prohibit fraudulent pricing and spare the poor working masses. This is in accordance with the divine message, which the Imam ʿAli reaffirmed in this principle:

"Let selling be magnanimous and openhanded, by a just measure, and at prices that are fair to both seller and buyer; he who involves himself in a monopoly, even after being warned against it, shall be made an example of and punished severely."

And the teacher of humanity, Muhammad, said:

"Every monopolizer is a sinner."

2. THE FIGHT AGAINST USURY

The Lebanese free market system allows the practice of usury among individuals and institutions in the belief that such practices stimulate the economy.

Because usury provides the best means for exploiting people and for reaping enormous profits with no effort, and because it is the basis for capitalist wealth, opposing usury means opposing capitalism and exploitation.

Since banks are the nerve center for economic life at the present time, and it is impossible for commercial, industrial, and agricultural institutions to continue without engaging in financial activities, an alternative to the system of usury must be found. This alternative exists in the system of silent partnership, which the divine plan offers as a solution to the financial problems induced by usury. A silent partnership is when one party or person provides another with capital to do business. The profits are divided between them and any loss is incurred by the party that provided the capital. If there is loss, the person carrying out the enterprise loses only his time and efforts.

Usury results in many serious social problems, among them the creation and deepening of hostility between people, the corruption of society, the destruction of morals, and the disruption of social cohesion.

The Fifth Principle

1. THE MAHRUMIN (AMAL) MOVEMENT IS A PATRIOTIC MOVEMENT

The preservation of national sovereignty and the integrity of the nation's land:

Our movement is completely devoted to national sovereignty and to independence in defining its own political course. It rejects any foreign mandate over the motherland, works toward preserving its territory and borders, and protects its dignity against subversion and slander. In this way, the nation will be able to determine its own fate without the intervention of malicious forces or special interests in any of its affairs.

The sovereignty of the motherland cannot be achieved without according sovereignty to its citizens and protecting them both from political convulsions and capers and from restrictions on their free will and thought. Such sovereignty must be accompanied by a fusing together of the people in the tolerant melting pot of patriotism to produce a strong and healthy Lebanon embracing all her different cultures.

National sovereignty is influenced directly or indirectly by the mutual attraction between the various civilizations that are founded on the cultural components of the divine messages. This reinforces Lebanon's status as a cultural window at which the West, with its practical experience, meets the East, with its faith and spiritualism. National sovereignty is therefore an essential requirement in preserving the motherland's special cultural role.

Following from the principle of national sovereignty, we see that the integrity of the motherland's soil is a keystone, indeed the primary foundation for the realization of national sovereignty.

2. THE FIGHT AGAINST IMPERIALISM, AGGRESSION, AND AMBITIOUS DESIGNS TO WHICH LEBANON IS EXPOSED

There can be no doubt that the integrity of the motherland is vulnerable to imperialist schemes to extend the tentacle of their power in order to stunt the nation's cultural mission and cripple the movement for Arab liberation.

The movement therefore affirms in its program for political action the necessity of continuing the struggle firmly to establish the unity of Lebanon's land and people, heedful of the dangers posed by imperialism in all its forms. Particularly intensive precautions must be taken in regard to Zionist designs in Lebanon, in order to thwart conspiracies aimed at annexing parts of Lebanon, particularly the South, to the Zionist state.

3. ADHERENCE TO [ARAB] NATIONAL INTERESTS, THE LIBERATION OF ARAB LANDS, AND FREEDOM FOR ALL THE NATION'S PEOPLES

The comprehensive political report prepared by the political office of the Mahrumin Movement found that the Arab world suffers from a variety of crises that contribute to the continuation of political, economic, and social backwardness. The problem of fragmentation stands at the forefront of these crises. Fragmentation is a natural and direct result of the long history of imperialist attempts to subjugate and gain control of the Arab world for its important strategic location and for its natural wealth and vast resources.

Imperialism aims at preventing the development of a unified national consciousness that would provide the necessary climate for a strong and advanced Arab society. It has succeeded in diluting national sentiment shared by the Arab masses, a sentiment nourished through the generations by a unity of language, civilization, culture, history, and religion. This unity has upheld the historic struggles for Arab liberation against the conspiracies of imperialist forces.

The movement therefore concluded that a continued holy war was necessary for the sake of:

(1) bringing an end to the imperialist presence in the Arab world (the Zionist entity), and turning our guns to the issue of liberation.

(2) not allowing the acceptance of capitulations that run contrary to the higher national interest of strengthening Arab solidarity.

4. THE ESSENCE AND BASIS OF PATRIOTISM: THE PROTECTION OF SOUTHERN LEBANON AND THE DEFENSE OF ITS GROWTH

Due to southern Lebanon's geographical position bordering the enemy, and to Zionist greed for its land and water, and based on the vital connection between the issue of southern Lebanon and the Palestinian question, the Mahrumin Movement shares in the demand for self-sufficiency, for the transformation of the South into an armed fortress, and for the pursuit of a popular armed struggle, united by strategy and fate with the Palestinian revolution, to confront our common Zionist enemy. The forces of the Lebanese resistance—Amal—are a direct expression of this course.

The movement believes that the means for the South's protection lie in its development. It is therefore necessary to initiate development projects, as the motherland cannot survive without the South, and there can be no true patriotism without fidelity to the South.

The Sixth Principle

1. WORLD ZIONISM

This is a political movement that seeks to establish a national homeland for the Jews in Palestine, and is called Zionism in reference to Mount Zion where Solomon's Temple was built.

The chief propagandist of Zionism was the Hungarian Herzl, who believed that the Jews should liquidate their property in all parts of the world in order to establish a modern state. The Englishman Chaim Weizmann continued these efforts and was able to obtain from Balfour, the British foreign secretary, a promise to establish a Jewish national homeland in Palestine.

The British Mandate opened the gates of unlimited immigration to Palestine, and the English aided the Jews in obtaining land by means of enticements and force. Jewish emigration to Palestine continued and the pressure on the Arabs intensified. The issue was brought to the United Nations, and Palestine was partitioned into an Arab state and a Jewish state, while Jerusalem was internationalized. The Arabs of Palestine rebelled against the partition plan and other Arab countries decided to assist them. The Jews launched vicious attacks on peaceful Palestinians and embarked on a war of nerves. The Arabs from Israel suffered expulsion, persecution, and continuous aggression. Inside Israel, nearly a quarter of a million Palestinians were subject to brutal treatment as Israel made everything Jewish and attempted to eliminate the Arab language and the Islamic religion, heritage, and values. The support of and solidarity with the

Palestinian resistance is therefore necessary for the strategic depth of our battle line, for only by truly embracing the Palestinian revolution can we root out the Zionist presence.

2. ISRAEL REPRESENTS A PRESENT AND FUTURE DANGER TO LEBANON AND THE ARAB WORLD

(A) The Zionist danger threatens Lebanon directly because the Zionists covet the Qasimiyyah [Litani] River and desire to occupy the South for its strategic importance. Israel likewise covets the springheads of the Jordan River and its tributary, the Hasbani River. It engages in widely disseminated propaganda to direct tourists to Israel, competes with Lebanese manufactures, and is bent on diverting international lines of communication and transport to Israel. Israelis wage war on Lebanese émigrés abroad by encouraging Zionists to gain control of Lebanese firms and turn world opinion against Lebanon.

(B) The Zionist danger to Arab states: the geographical position of Palestine bisects the Arab world and threatens Arab countries in peacetime and in time of war. Israel competes economically with the Arabs, to say nothing of its expulsion of the Palestinian people, its desecration of holy places, and its alliance with world imperialism, which considers Zionism as its bridgehead in the region, by which it can foment conflict, kindle the flame of war, and prevent the progress of the Arab people.

3. THE DANGER OF ZIONISM TO VALUES AND TO ALL OF HUMANITY

Israel is a society founded on sectarian bigotry and racist sentiment that provides fertile ground for oppression in all domains. The motive force behind human activity in such a society is materialism, and the concern of the people focuses increasingly on wealth. The growth and expansion of production leads to a preoccupation with foreign markets and the acquisition of more territory.

Values, all values, have been distorted in Israel. Coexistence has turned to segregation, love to hate, peace to war, security to fear, justice to oppression, and patriotism to bigotry, racism, aggression, and destruction. This state of Israel, despite its pretensions to piety, embraces racism, bigotry, and heretical secularism, in which relationships are not based on faith in God, nor on the recognition of values. Such distortions gravely endanger human values and ideals, a distortion toward which Zionism is striving in Lebanon because it sees that peaceful coexistence among sects challenges and condemns its racism and godlessness.

The Seventh Principle

1. THE MOVEMENT DOES NOT DISCRIMINATE BETWEEN CITIZENS AND COOPERATES WITH HONORABLE PEOPLE

In view of the inherent and natural equality between people by birth and lineage, the movement adheres to the principle of nondiscrimination between citizens in regard to social responsibilities, rights, and obligations.

The bonds of creation are deeply rooted and form the building blocks for more general bonds between people that emanate from the heart of a person and from his sense of participation with his countrymen in determining the progress of their lives. Hence, there should be no sectarian, regional, or racial discrimination (the Messiah was asked, "Which people are better?"; and he picked up two handfuls of dirt and said, "Which of these is better? All people were created from dust, so the most respected of them is he who is the most pious").

The movement is founded on a belief in national unity and equality among citizens and so extends its hand to all honorable individuals and parties that desire to build a better motherland and to cooperate in the shaping of its future. This offer springs from the movement's belief in the advantages of constructive cooperation and its appreciation of others's talents and abilities. The isolation of any party or person is unacceptable; indeed, all people must unite for the good of the nation.

2. THE MOVEMENT IS NOT SECTARIAN OR PARTISAN

The Mahrumin Movement does not work for the good of a particular sect or party. Its principles are the property of all people, and its battle is for the sake of all. It distinguishes between religious commitment and sectarian fanaticism that impedes the nation's path to progress.

It likewise sees in its progressive religious program the guarantee for eliminating the taint of fanatic sectarianism from religion. The true religious spirit is capable of hammering the first nail in the coffin of loathsome sectarianism and partisanship.

The movement does not preach from above, nor does it entice

with charity organizations; rather, it works to prepare a sound foundation for change and to set up the forces to aid in carrying out the process of enrichment in the intellectual, material, and social spheres.

And finally . . .

—the Mahrumin Movement is a movement of all the people

—it embraces their needs

—it devises solutions

—it acts quickly to implement these

—it fights on the side of the deprived to the end

—it is a movement of all honorable Lebanese

—those who feel presently deprived

—and those who are anxious for their future

—it is a Lebanese movement toward a better world.

An Amal membership card.

Appendix B. Nass al-risala al-maftuha allati wajjaha hizb allah ila al-mustad ʿafin fi lubnan wa al-ʿalam

Text of Open Letter Addressed by Hizb Allah to the Downtrodden in Lebanon and in the World

February 16, 1985

Text of open letter addressed by Hizb Allah to downtrodden in Lebanon and the world, pointing out in its projections and path on occasion of the first anniversary of the martyrdom of Raghib Harb, the symbol of Islamic resistance and the paramount martyr.

Dated February 15, 1985.

"In the name of God, the merciful and the compassionate: Those who put their trust in God, His prophet, and the faithful are God's party and they shall prevail. God almighty is always true."

Dedication

To the torch that burned bright, lit for the downtrodden in Lebanon the path to free and honorable life and burned with the blaze of his innocent blood the tyranny and myth of the Zionist entity;

To the pioneer who was faithful to his kinsmen, who offered them the model for *jihad* and who did not spare his own life until he died a martyr in supporting them and a witness to the injustice of world arrogance and its insolence;

To the symbol of the triumphant Islamic resistance and of the splendid uprising through which our kinsmen are still recording their most magnificent Husaini [Shiʿite] epics in the South and in Western al-Biqaʿ;

To him who scattered America's dreams in Lebanon and who resisted the Israeli occupation, carrying the banner of action under the patronage of 'Abd Allah Khomeini, the leader jurisprudent whom he always liked to describe as the amir [prince] of the Muslims;

To paramount martyr Raghib Harb, may God be pleased with him, on whose anniversary we present this open letter to the downtrodden in the world, including in its lines the revolutionary Islamic political line embodied by the happy martyr and his brothers so that it may act as a clear path and guide to all the strugglers in Lebanon. We beseech God, may He be praised, to grant us steadfastness, to strengthen us, and to give us victory over the tyrants.

God's peace, mercy, and blessings be with you.

Hizb Allah

In the name of God, the compassionate and the merciful:

Say, "the truth is from your Lord"; let him who will, believe and let him who will, reject [it]; for the wrongdoers we have prepared a fire whose [smoke and flames], like the walls and roof of a tent, will hem them in; if they implore relief, they will be granted water like melted brass that will scald their faces. How dreadful the drink! How uncomfortable a couch to recline on!

God is always true.

Who Are We and What Is Our Identity?

Free downtrodden men,

We are the sons of Hizb Allah's nation in Lebanon. We greet you and address the entire world through you: notables, institutions, parties, organizations and political, humanitarian, and information associations. We exclude nobody because we are eager for all to hear our voice, understand our word, comprehend our projections, and study our plan.

We, the sons of Hizb Allah's nation, consider ourself a part of the Islamic nation in the world, which is facing the most tyrannical arrogant assault from both the East and the West—an assault intended to deprive this nation of the content of the message with which God has blessed it so that it may be the best nation known to the world, a nation that encourages virtue and discourages vice and that believes in God. The assault is also aimed at usurping this nation's wealth and resources, at exploiting the capabilities and skills of its sons, and at controlling all its affairs.

We, the sons of Hizb Allah's nation, whose vanguard God has given victory in Iran and which has established the nucleus of the world's central Islamic state, abide by the orders of a single wise and just command currently embodied in the supreme Ayatollah Ruhollah al-Musavi al-Khomeini, the rightly guided imam who combines all the qualities of the total imam, who has detonated the Muslim's revolution, and who is bringing about the glorious Islamic renaissance.

Therefore, we in Lebanon are not a closed organizational party nor a narrow political framework. Rather, we are a nation tied to the Muslims in every part of the world by a strong ideological and political bond, namely Islam, whose message God completed at the hands of the last of His prophets, Muhammad, may God's peace and prayers be upon him and upon his kinsmen. God has established Islam as a religion for the world to follow, saying in the venerable Quran: "Today I have perfected your religion for you, and I have completed My blessing upon you, and I have approved Islam."

Therefore, what befalls the Muslims in Afganistan, Iraq, the Philippines, or elsewhere befalls the body of our Islamic nation of which we are an indivisible part and we move to confront it out of a religious duty primarily and in the light of a general political visualization decided by the leader jurisprudent.

The main sources of our culture are the venerable Quran, the infallible Sunna, and the decisions and religious opinions made by the jurisprudent, who is the authority on tradition among us. These sources are clear, uncomplicated, and accessible to all without exception and they need no theorization or philosophy. All they need is abidance and application.

As to our military power, nobody can imagine its dimensions because we do not have a military agency separate from the other parts of our body. Each of us is a combat soldier when the call of *jihad* demands it and each of us undertakes his task in the battle in accordance with his lawful assignment within the framework of action under the guardianship of the leader jurisprudent. God is behind us, supporting us with His care, putting fear in our enemies' hearts, and giving us His dear and resounding victory against them.

Arrogant World Is in Agreement on Fighting Us

Free downtrodden men,

The countries of the tyrannical arrogant world in the West and the East have agreed to fight us and have been instigating their agents against us, trying to distort our reputation and to fabricate lies against us in a malicious attempt to drive a wedge between us and good and downtrodden men and in an endeavor to dwarf and deface the important major accomplishments we have made at the level of our confrontation with the United States and its allies.

Through its local agents, the United States has tried to give people the impression that those who have put an end to its arrogance in Lebanon, who drove it out humiliated and frustrated, and who crushed its plot against the downtrodden in this country are no more than a handful of fanatics and terrorists who are only concerned with blowing up drinking, gambling, and entertainment spots and other such activities.

But we are confident that such insinuations will never deceive our nation because the entire world knows that whoever thinks of confronting the United States and world arrogance does not resort to such peripheral acts that preoccupy them with the tail and make them forget the head.

America behind All Our Catastrophes

We are moving in the direction of fighting the roots of vice and the first root of vice is America. All the endeavors to drag us into marginal action will be futile when compared with the confrontation with the United States.

Imam Khomeini, the leader, has repeatedly stressed that America is the reason for all our catastrophes and the source of all malice. By fighting it, we are only exercising our legitimate right to defend our Islam and the dignity of our nation.

We declare frankly and clearly that we are a nation that fears only God and that does not accept tyranny, aggression, and humiliation. America and its allies and the Zionist entity that has usurped the sacred Islamic land of Palestine have engaged and continue to engage in constant aggression against us and are working constantly to humiliate us. Therefore, we are in a state of constant and escalating preparedness to repel the aggression and to defend our religion, existence, and dignity.

They have attacked our country, destroyed our villages, massacred our children, violated our sanctities, and installed over our heads criminal henchmen who have perpetrated terrible massacres against our nation. They are still supporting these butchers who are Israel's allies and preventing us from determining our destiny with our free will.

Their bombs fell on our kinsmen like rain during the Zionist invasion of our country and the Beirut blockade. Their planes raided our civilians, children, women, and wounded day and night whereas the areas of the agent Phalangists remained safe from the enemy's bombardment and a center for directing and guiding the enemy forces.

We appealed to the world's conscience but heard nothing from it and found no trace of it.

This conscience that we missed in the days of tribulation is the same conscience that was mobilized and alerted when the criminal Phalangists were blockaded in the city of Zahle in al-Biqaᶜ and when the allies of Israel in Dair al-Qamar, in al-Shuf, were besieged. We were horrified and then realized that this world conscience stirs only at the request of the strong and in response to the interests of arrogance.

The Israelis and Phalangists massacred several thousands of our fathers, children, women, and brothers in Sabra and Chatila in a single night but no practical renunciation or condemnation was expressed by any international organization or authority against this heinous massacre that was perpetrated in coordination with the NATO forces, who, only a few days, rather hours, earlier, had departed from the camps that the defeated [Palestinians] agreed to put under the protection of the wolf in response to the maneuver of Philip Habib, the U.S. fox.

Those criminal attacks came only to reaffirm our firm belief that "you will find that those most hostile to the faithful are the Jew and the idolators."

We Have No Alternative to Confrontation

Thus, we have seen that aggression can be repelled only with sacrifices and dignity gained only with the sacrifice of blood, and that freedom is not given but regained with the sacrifice of both heart and soul.

We have opted for religion, freedom, and dignity over humiliation and constant submission to America and its allies and to Zionism and their Phalangist allies. We have risen to liberate our country, to drive the imperialists and the invaders out of it, and to determine our fate by our own hands.

We could not endure more than we have endured. Our tragedy is more than ten years old and all we have seen so far are the covetous, hypocritical, and incapable.

Zionist-Phalange Coordination

Nearly 100,000 is the number of the victims of the crimes perpetrated against us by America, Israel, and the Phalange.

Nearly one half million Muslims have been displaced and their quarters of al-Nabᶜa, Burj Hammud, al-Dikwana, Tall al-Zaᶜtar, Sibniya, al-Ghawarina and in Jabail have been almost totally destroyed. Our kinsmen staying in Jabail are still exposed to the tragedy without a single international organization moving to rescue them.

The Zionist occupation continues to usurp the lands of the Muslims, extending over more than one-third of Lebanon's area in prior coordination and full agreement with the Phalange, who have denounced the attempts to confront the invading forces and have taken part in implementing some of Israel's schemes so as to complete Israel's plan and to give it what it wishes in return for its leading them to power.

Thus, butcher Bashir al-Jumayyil had attained the presidency with the help of Israel, of the Arab oil countries, and of the Muslim deputies who are subservient to the Phalange. He gained this presidency in the wake of a skillful maneuver to beautify his image in a surgery room called the Salvation Committee—a committee that is no more than an American-Israeli bridge over which the Phalange crossed to oppress the downtrodden.

But our people were not willing to endure this humiliation and they wiped out the dreams of the Zionists and their allies. But America persisted in its rashness and brought Amin al-Jumayyil to succeed his buried brother. Amin's first accomplishment was to destroy the homes of the evacuees, to attack the Muslims' mosques, to order the army to demolish the quarters of the downtrodden on the heads of their occupants, to enlist the help of NATO forces against us, and to conclude the ill-fated May 17 accord that turned Lebanon into an Israeli protectorate and an American colony.

Our Basic Enemies

Our people could not withstand all this treason and decided to confront the imams of infidelity of America, France, and Israel. The first punishment against these forces was carried out on April 18 and the second on October 29, 1983. By that time, a real war had started against the Israeli occupation forces, rising to the level of destroying two main centers of the enemy's military rulers. Our people also escalated their popular and military Islamic resistance to the point where they forced the enemy to make its decision on phased withdrawal—a decision that Israel was compelled to adopt for the first time in the history of the so-called Arab-Israeli conflict.

For the sake of the truth, we declare that the sons of Hizb Allah's nation have come to know well their basic enemies in the area: Israel, America, France, and the Phalange.

Our Objectives in Lebanon

Our sons are now in a state of ever-escalating confrontation against these enemies until the following objectives are achieved:

Israel's final departure from Lebanon as a prelude to its final obliteration from existence and the liberation of venerable Jerusalem from the talons of occupation.

The final departure of America, France, and their allies from Lebanon and the termination of the influence of any imperialist power in the country.

Submission by the Phalange to just rule and their trial for the crimes they have committed against both Muslims and Christians with the encouragement of America and Israel.

Giving all our people the opportunity to determine their fate and to choose with full freedom the system of government they want, keeping in mind that we do not hide our commitment to the rule of Islam and that we urge to choose the Islamic system that alone guarantees justice and dignity for all and prevents any new imperialist attempt to infiltrate our country.

Friends

These are our objectives in Lebanon and these our enemies. As for our friends, they are all the world's downtrodden peoples and all those who fight our enemies and who are eager not to harm us, be they individuals, parties, or organizations. We especially address this letter to them to say:

O partisans and organized people, wherever you are in Lebanon and whatever your ideas, we agree with you on major and important goals embodied in the need to topple the American domination of the country, to expel the Zionist occupation that bears down heavily on the people's lives, and to strike all the Phalangist endeavors to control government and administrative affairs, even though we may disagree with you on the methods and level of confrontation.

Come, let us rise above quarreling over minor issues and let us open wide the doors of competition for achieving the major goals.

It is not important that a certain party control the street. What is important is that the masses interact with this party.

It is not important that many military parades be held for the citizens. What is important is to increase the operations against Israel.

It is not important that we draft statements and call for conferences. What is important is that we turn Lebanon into a graveyard for American schemes.

You carry ideas that do not stem from Islam. This should not prevent cooperation between us for these objectives, especially since we feel that the motives urging you to engage in the struggle are fundamentally Islamic motives emanating from the injustice inflicted upon you by tyranny and the oppression exercised against you by it. Though formed through non-Islamic ideas, these motives must inevitably revert to their essence when you find that revolutionary Islam is the force leading the struggle and confronting oppression and arrogance.

However, we shall accept no provocation, instigation, or aggression from you against our security or our dignity, we are obliged with you to deal with any problem with the good word first, and we are eager not to let you obstruct our movement toward our objectives.

You will find us eager to open up to you. You will also find that our relationship with you will grow stronger the closer our ideas move toward each other, the more we feel that your decisionmaking is independent, and the more the interest of Islam and the Muslims dictates that this relationship be bolstered and developed.

O downtrodden partisans,

You have sought what is right but have missed it, and those who seek what is right and miss it are not like those who seek what is false and hit it.

Therefore, we extend our hand to you and tell you sincerely: "O our people, answer God's summoner" and "Respond to God and the Messenger when He calls you unto that which will give you life."

We Are Committed to Islam But We Do Not Impose It by Force

O free, downtrodden people,

We are a nation committed to the message of Islam and a nation that wishes the downtrodden and all people to study this divine message because it will bring about justice, peace, and serenity in the world.

God, may He be praised, says: "Let there be no compulsion in religion; Right stands out clearly from wrong; whoever rejects evil and believes in God has grasped the most trustworthy handhold, that never breaks. And God hears and knows all things. God is the Protector of those who have faith; from the depths of darkness He will lead them forth into light. Of those who reject faith, the patrons are the evil ones; from light they will lead them forth into the depths of darkness. They will be companions of the fire, to dwell therein [forever]."

Therefore, we do not wish to impose Islam on anybody and we hate to see others impose on us their convictions and their systems. We do not want Islam to rule in Lebanon by force, as the political Maronism is ruling at present.

But we stress that we are convinced of Islam as a faith, system, thought, and rule and we urge all to recognize it and to resort to its law. We also urge them to adopt it and abide by its teachings at the individual, political, and social levels.

If our people get the opportunity to choose Lebanon's system of government freely, they will favor no alternative to Islam.

Therefore, we urge adoption of the Islamic system on the basis of free and direct selection by the people, not the basis of forceful imposition, as some people imagine.

We declare that we aspire to see Lebanon as an indivisible part of the political map opposed to America, world arrogance, and world Zionism and to see Lebanon ruled by Islam and its just leadership.

This is the aspiration of a nation, not of a party, and the choice of a people, not of a gang.

Our Minimum Aspiration in Lebanon

Therefore, the minimum we shall accept in terms of achieving this aspiration, which we are lawfully charged to achieve, is:

Rescuing Lebanon from subservience to either the West or the East, expelling the Zionist occupation from its territories finally and adopting a system that the people establish of their free will and choice.

Why Do We Confront the Existing Regime?

This is our visualization and these are our projections of what we want in Lebanon. In the light of this visualization and these projections, we confront the existing regime due to two main considerations:

1. Because it is a protégé of world arrogance and a part of the political map that is hostile to Islam.

2. Because it is a fundamentally oppressive structure that no reform or patchwork improvement would do any good and that must be changed from the roots "and whosoever judges not according to what God has sent down, they are the evildoers."

Our Position toward Opposition

We determine our stance vis-à-vis any opposition to the Lebanese regime in light of the two above-mentioned considerations.

We consider any opposition moving within red lines imposed by the arrogant forces a superficial opposition that will ultimately agree with the existing regime.

Any opposition moving within the sphere of protecting and safeguarding the constitution currently in force and not committed to making fundamental changes in the system's roots is also a superficial opposition that will not achieve the interests of the oppressed masses.

Moreover, any opposition moving within the positions where the regime wants it to move is an imaginary opposition that serves only the regime.

On the other hand, we are not at all interested in any projection for political reform within the framework of the rotten sectarian system, just exactly as we are not interested in the formation of any cabinet or the participation of any figure in any ministry representing a part of the oppressive regime.

Words to Christians in Lebanon

O honorable, downtrodden men,

We wish to address through you a few words to the Christians in Lebanon, especially to the Maronites:

The policy followed by the leaders of political Maronism through the "Lebanese Front" and the "Lebanese Forces" is incapable of achieving peace and stability for the Christians in Lebanon because it is a policy founded on bigotry, sectarian privileges, and alliance with imperialism and Israel.

The Lebanese tragedy has proven that the sectarian privileges are one of the main causes of the big explosion that has brought about the collapse of the country and that the alliance with America, France, and Israel did the Christians no good when they needed the support of these forces.

Moreover, the time has come for the fanatical Christians to come out of the tunnel of sectarian loyalty and of the illusions of monopolizing privileges at the expense of others. It is time for them to respond to the divine call and to resort to reason instead of arms and to conviction instead of sect.

We are confident that Christ, God's prophet, peace be upon him, is innocent of the massacres perpetrated by the Phalange in his name and yours and innocent of the stupid policy adopted by your leaders to oppress you and oppress us.

Muhammad, God's prophet, peace and mercy be upon him, is also innocent of those who are counted as Muslims and who do not observe God's law and who do not seek to apply God's rules to you and to us.

If you reconsider your calculations and you realize that your interest lies in what you decide with your own free will and not in what is imposed on you with iron and fire, then we will renew our call to you in response to God's words: "Say, 'O people of the Book! Come to common terms as between us and you; that we worship none but God; that we associate no partners with him; that we erect not, from among ourselves, lords and patrons other than God.' If then they turn back, say: 'Bear witness that we (at least) are Muslims.'"

O Christians of Lebanon,

If you find it too much for the Muslims to share with you some government affairs, then God also finds it an excess for us to do so because the Muslims would be taking part in a government that is unjust to you and to us and that is not founded on the basis of the Shariʿa that was completed by the last of the prophets.

If you want justice, then who is more just than God, who has revealed from heaven the message of Islam alongside the prophets so that they may rule among men justly and may give each his due right?

If somebody has misled you, exaggerated matters for you, and made you afraid of reactions on our part to the crimes the Phalange have committed against us, then this is completely unjustifiable because peaceful Christians are still living among us without being disturbed by anybody.

If we are fighting the Phalange, it is because they are blocking your view of the truth, they turn you away from the way of God, and they desire on the earth improper deviation and they have waxed proud with great insolence.

We wish you well and we call you to Islam so that you may enjoy this world and the hereafter. If you refuse, then all we want of you is to uphold your covenants with the Muslims and not to participate in aggression against them.

O Christians,

Free your thoughts of the residues of hateful sectarianism, liberate your minds from the shackle of fanaticism and insularity, and open your hearts to our invitation to you to join Islam because in it lies your salvation and happiness and your good in this world and in the hereafter.

We extend this invitation of ours to all the downtrodden non-Muslims. As for those who belong to Islam denominationally, we urge them to observe it practically and to rise above fanaticism that is hateful to the religion.

We assure all that this is the age of the victory of Islam and of right and of the defeat of infidelity and falsehood. Join with right before the day comes when the unjust bites his own hand and says: I wish I had followed the prophet's path and I wish I had not taken so and so for a companion because he has misled me, and the devil always lets man down.

Our Story with World Arrogance

Honorable, downtrodden men,

As for our story with world arrogance, we shall sum it up for you in these words: we believe that the struggle of principles between the United States and the Soviet Union ended forever a long time ago. The two sides have failed to achieve happiness for mankind because the idea they have offered mankind, though assuming the different forms of capitalism and communism, agrees in material content and fails to deal with the problems of mankind.

Neither western capitalism nor eastern socialism has succeeded in establishing the rules of the just and serene society, nor have they been able to establish a balance between the individual and society or between human nature and public interest.

The two sides have mutually recognized this fact and have realized that there is no more place for ideological struggle between the two camps. They have both turned to struggle for influence and interest, hiding from public opinion behind the mask of disagreement on principles.

In the light of this understanding, we believe that the ideological struggle between the two camps has been folded forever and been replaced by the struggle for influence and interests between the countries of the arrogant world that are led today by America and the Soviet Union.

Consequently, the oppressed countries have become the struggle's bone of contention and the oppressed peoples have become its fuel.

While we consider the struggle between the two superpowers a natural outcome of the material content that motivates each of them, we cannot agree to have this struggle conducted at the expense of the interests of the downtrodden and the expense of their wealth and rights.

Therefore, we stand against any western or eastern imperialist intervention in the affairs of the oppressed and of their countries and we confront every ambition and intervention in our affairs.

While denouncing America's crimes in Vietnam, Iran, Nicaragua, Grenada, Palestine, Lebanon, and other countries, we also denounce the Soviet invasion of Afghanistan, the intervention in Iran's affairs, the support for Iraqi aggression, and so forth.

In Lebanon and in the Palestine area, we are mainly concerned with confronting America because it is the party with the greatest influence among the countries of world arrogance, and also with confronting Israel, the ulcerous growth of world Zionism. Therefore, we are concerned with confronting America's allies in NATO who have gotten embroiled in helping America against the area's peoples. We warn the countries that have not gotten involved yet against being dragged into serving American interests at the expense of our nation's freedom and interests.

Israel Must Be Wiped Out of Existence

As for Israel, we consider it the American spearhead in our Islamic world. It is a usurping enemy that must be fought until the usurped right is returned to its owners.

This enemy poses a great danger to our future generations and to the destiny of our nation, especially since it embraces a settlement-oriented and expansionist idea that it has already begun to apply in occupied Palestine and it is extending and expanding to build Greater Israel, from the Euphrates to the Nile.

Our struggle with usurping Israel emanates from an ideological and historical awareness that this Zionist entity is aggressive in its origins and structure and is built on usurped land and at the expense of the rights of a Muslim people.

Therefore, our confrontation of this entity must end with its obliteration from existence. This is why we do not recognize any cease-fire agreement, any truce, or any separate or nonseparate peace treaty with it.

We condemn strongly all the plans for mediation between us and Israel and we consider the mediators a hostile party because their mediation will only serve to acknowledge the legitimacy of the Zionist occupation of Palestine.

Therefore, we reject the Camp David treaty, the [King] Fahd plan, the Fez plan, the Reagan plan, the Brezhnev plan, the French-Egyptian plan, and any plan including even tacit recognition of the Zionist entity.

We underline in this regard our condemnation of all the deviant countries and organizations that chase after capitulationist solutions with the enemy breathlessly and that agree to "barter land for peace." We consider this a betrayal of the Muslim Palestinian people's blood and of the sacred Palestinian cause.

On the other hand, we view the recently voiced Jewish call for settlement in south Lebanon and the immigration of the Ethiopian Jews and others to occupied Palestine as a part of the expansionist Israeli scheme in the Islamic world and as an actual indicator of the danger emanating from the recognition of or coexistence with this entity.

Escalating Islamic Resistance

When speaking of usurping Israel, we must pause before the phenomenon of Islamic resistance that sprang from the occupied Lebanese territories to impose a new historic and cultural turn on the course of the struggle against the Zionist enemy.

The honorable Islamic resistance that has inscribed and continues to inscribe the most magnificent sagas against the Zionist invasion forces, that has destroyed by the faith of its strugglers the myth of invincible Israel, that has been able to place the usurping entity into a real dilemma as a result of the daily military, economic, and human attrition it inflicts on this entity, forcing its leaders to acknowledge the severe resistance they face at the hands of the Muslims. . . .

This Islamic resistance must continue, grow, and escalate, with God's help, and must receive from all Muslims in all parts of the world utter support, aid, backing, and participation so that we may be able to uproot this cancerous germ and obliterate it from existence.

While underlining the Islamic character of this resistance, we do so out of compatibility with its reality, which is clearly Islamic in motive, objective, course, and depth of confrontation. This does not at all negate its patriotism, but confirms it. On the contrary, if this resistance's Islamic character were effaced, its patriotism would become extremely fragile.

Appeal for Broad Islamic Participation

We take this opportunity to address a warm appeal to all Muslims in the world, urging them to share with their brothers in Lebanon the honor of fighting the occupying Zionists, either directly or by supporting and assisting the strugglers, because fighting Israel is the responsibility of all Muslims in all parts of the world and not just the responsibility of the sons of Mount ʿAmil and Western al-Biqaʿ.

With the blood of its martyrs and the struggle of its heroes, the Islamic resistance has been able to force the enemy for the first time in the history of the conflict against it to make a decision to retreat and withdraw from Lebanon without any American or other influence. On the contrary, the Israeli withdrawal decision has revealed real American worry and has formed a historic turning point in the course of the struggle against the usurping Zionists.

Through their Islamic resistance, the strugglers—the women with rocks and boiling oil for their weapons, the children with their shouts and their bare fists for their weapons, the old men with their weak bodies and their thick sticks for their weapons, and the youth with their rifles and their firm and faithful will for their weapons— have all proven that if the nation is allowed to manage its affairs freely, it is capable of making miracles and of changing the imaginary fates.

Policy of Government Avariciousness and Treasonous Negotiation

Let us pause a little before the government parades that emerge seasonally in an attempt to mislead the people into believing that the government supports the resistance against the occupation to declare clearly:

Our people have come to loathe verbal and media support and to despise those who offer it. If some statements have been issued by some pillars of the existing regime, let nobody imagine that the masses are unaware of the fact that these statements do not represent the position of the entire regime, especially since the regime is not about to throw its army into the battle to share the honor of liberation.

As for the [regime's] financial support for the resistance, it is insignificant and it has not reached the strugglers in the form of weapons, munitions, combat costs, and so forth.

Our people reject the policy of avariciousness at the expense of the resistance. The day will come when all those who have traded in the blood of our heroic martyrs and who have glorified themselves at the expense of the strugglers' wounds will be judged.

We cannot but stress that the policy of negotiating with the enemy is high treason against the resistance that the regime claims to support and aid and that the regime's determination to enter into negotiations with the enemy was nothing but a plot aimed at recognizing the legitimacy of the Zionist occupation and giving it privileges for the crimes it has committed against the downtrodden in Lebanon.

We add that the Islamic resistance, which declared its refusal to abide by any results emanating from the negotiations, reaffirms that the struggle will continue until the Zionists withdraw from the occupied territories as a prelude to their obliteration from existence.

International Forces and Suspect Role

The international forces that world arrogance is trying to deploy in the Muslims' territories from which the enemy will withdraw so that they may form a security barrier obstructing the resistance movement and protecting the security of Israel and of its invasion forces are collusive and rejected forces. We may be forced to deal with them exactly as we deal with the Zionist invasion forces.

Let all know that the commitments of the imposed Phalangist regime are not in any way binding to the Islamic resistance strugglers. Other countries must think carefully before they get immersed in the swamp in which Israel has drowned.

Defeatist Arab Regimes

As for the Arab regimes falling over themselves for reconciliation with the Zionist enemy, they are decrepit regimes incapable of keeping up with the nation's ambitions and aspirations and they cannot think of confronting the Zionist entity usurping Palestine because these regimes came into existence under a colonialist guardianship that played the major role in the creation of these eroded regimes.

Some reactionary rulers, especially in the oil countries, are not reluctant to turn their countries into military bases for America and Britain and are not ashamed to rely on foreign experts, appointing them to top official positions. They are implementing the policies set for them by the White House circles to smuggle their countries' wealth and divide it among the imperialists by various means.

Some of them claim to be protectors of the Islamic Shariʿa so that they may cover up their treason and may justify their submission to America's will while at the same time considering the entry of a single revolutionary Islamic book into their country something banned and prohibited.

As a result of the defeatist policy followed by these reactionary regimes vis-à-vis Israel, the latter has been able to persuade many of them that it has become a fait accompli that cannot go unrecognized, not to mention the necessity of acknowledging the need to ensure its security.

This defeatist policy is what encouraged the buried al-Sadat to commit his high treason and proceed to conclude peace with Israel and sign the humiliation treaty with it.

The policy of defeatism is what is now governing the movement of the Gulf Cooperation Council, the Jordan-Egypt axis, Iraq, and the Arafat organization.

The defeatist policy toward America is what is directing the position of the reactionary rulers toward the war of aggression imposed on the Islamic Republic of Iran and is standing behind the boundless financial, economic, and military support for the agent Saddam out of the belief that the Zionized al-Tikriti regime can destroy the Islamic Revolution and can prevent the dissemination of its revolutionary blaze and concepts. This defeatist policy is what motivates the reactionary regimes to keep their peoples ignorant, to water down and dissolve their Islamic identity, and to suppress in their countries any Islamic movement opposed to America and its allies. It is also the policy that causes these regimes to fear the awakening of the downtrodden and to prevent their involvement in political affairs because of the big danger posed to the survival of these regimes by awareness on the part of peoples of the corruption of their governments and of their suspect ties and by sympathy from these peoples for the liberation movements in all parts of the Islamic world and of the world generally.

We find in the reactionary Arab regimes a barrier blocking the development of the awareness and unity of the Islamic peoples and we consider these regimes responsible for obstructing the attempts to keep the wound open and the struggle continued against the Zionist enemy.

We have great hope in the Muslim peoples that clearly have begun to complain in most of the Islamic countries and have been able to infiltrate into the world of revolutions to learn from its experiences, especially from the triumphant Islamic Revolution. The day will come when all these brittle regimes will collapse under the blows of the oppressed, as the throne of the tyrant in Iran has already collapsed.

While waging a ferocious battle against America and Israel and their schemes in the area, we cannot but warn these regimes of working against the nation's rising tide of resistance to imperialism and Zionism. These regimes must learn from the Islamic resistance in Lebanon great lessons in determination on fighting the enemy and on defeating it.

We also warn these regimes against getting involved in new capitulationist plans and in aggressive schemes aimed against the young Islamic Revolution because such involvement will lead the leaders of these regimes to the same fate faced by Anwar al-Sadat and by Nuri al-Saʿid [last Iraqi prime minister under the monarchy] and others before them.

International Front for Oppressed

We address all the Arab and Islamic peoples to declare to them that the Muslims' experience in Islamic Iran left no one any excuse since it proved beyond all doubt that bare chests motivated by faith are capable, with God's help, of breaking the iron and oppression of tyrannical regimes.

Therefore, we urge the peoples to unite their ranks, to chart their objectives, and to rise to break the shackle that curbs their will and to overthrow the agent governments that oppress them.

We strongly urge on all the oppressed of the world the need to form an international front that encompasses all their liberation movements so that they may establish full and comprehensive coordination among these movements in order to achieve effectiveness in their activity and to focus on their enemies' weak points.

Considering that the imperialist world with all its states and regimes is uniting today in fighting the oppressed, then the oppressed must get together to confront the plots of the forces of arrogance in the world.

All the oppressed peoples, especially the Arab and Muslim peoples, must realize that Islam alone is capable of being the idea to resist aggression, since experiences have proven that all the positive ideologies have been folded forever in the interest of American-Soviet détente and other forms of détente.

It is time for us to realize that all the western ideas concerning man's origin and nature cannot respond to man's aspirations or rescue him from the darkness of misguidedness and ignorance. Only Islam can bring about man's renaissance, progress, and creativity because "he lights with the oil of an olive tree that is neither eastern nor western, a tree whose oil burns, even if not touched by fire, to light the path. God leads to His light whomever He wishes."

God Is with Unity of Muslims

O Muslim peoples,

[Beware the malicious imperialist sedition that seeks to divide your unity, to sow division among you, and to arouse Sunni and Shiʿi sectarian fanaticism.]

Know that colonialism was able to control the wealth of the Muslims only after it divided and fragmented their ranks, instigating the Sunnis against the Shiʿa and the Shiʿa against the Sunnis, entrusting this task afterward to its agents among the mediators of the countries, to evil ʿulama at times, and to leaders that colonialism imposed on the people.

God is with the unity of the Muslims and this unity is the rock on which the schemes of the arrogant are smashed and the hammer that crushes the plots of the oppressors.

Do not allow the policy of "divide and rule" to be practiced in your countries and fight this policy by rallying behind the venerable Quran:

"Hold fast, all together, by the rope that God [stretches out for you], and be not divided."

"As for those who divide their religion and break up into sects . . ."

"Remember God's favor on you; for you were enemies and He joined your hearts in love, so that by His grace, you became brothers; and you were on the brink of the pit of fire, and He saved you from it."

O *'Ulama* of Islam

As for you, O *'ulama* of Islam, your responsibility is as big as the tragedies that have befallen the Muslims. You are best qualified to perform your duty of leading the nation toward Islam and of alerting it to the plots that its enemies are hatching in order to dominate this nation, plunder its wealth, and enslave it.

There is no doubt that you are aware that the Muslims look up to you in your capacity as bearers of the trust given by God's prophet, may God's peace and prayers be upon him, and as heirs of the prophets and the messengers. Be the hope and offer the good example by declaring what is right and by standing in the face of the oppressors and the tyrants. Be the model in rising above the frippery of this world's life ornaments and by yearning for paradise and martyrdom for the sake of God.

You have in God's prophet a good example of how he starved with the people and how he ate when they ate, of how he led the faithful in prayer, and how he led them in the arenas of the *jihad*.

He was their refuge in their hard times, he warmed their lives with his instructions and solutions, and they followed him with confidence and assurance.

O Muslim *'Ulama,*

Imam Khomeini, the leader, has stressed repeatedly the need to [rest of sentence indistinct]. If they find out that a shopowner is not upright, they say that so and so is not upright and if they find that a merchant cheats, they say that so and so is a cheat. But if they find, God forbid, that a religious *'alim* is not upright, then they will say that religion is not right.

O Muslim *'Ulama,*

Because of this and other things, your responsibility is very heavy. Ask for God's help to perform this duty and beseech God, may He be praised, with the invocation Imam 'Ali, may God be pleased with him: "God, we do not ask you for a light burden but for strong backs." You will then find out that the nation is most responsive to your appeals, instructions, and leadership.

Know that the imperialist is aware of the importance of your position in the nation and that this is why he has directed his strongest stabs to the hearts of the struggler *ulama*, hatching an infernal plot to conceal Imam Musa al-Sadr when this imperialist felt that the imam was an insurmountable obstacle in the face of his aggressive schemes, killing the Islamic philosopher Shaikh Murtada Mathari, and executing Ayatollah Muhammad Baqir al-Sadr, the great Islamic authority, when the imperialist felt the danger imam's stance posed— a danger embodied in Imam Baqir's words: "Fuse with Imam Khomeini as he has fused with Islam." The imperialist is lurking for every religious *alim* performing his Islamic duty in the best manner possible.

On the other hand, imperialism has been penetrating the Muslims with glib preachers who have no fear of God, who offer religious interpretation where there can be no interpretation, who sanction peace with Israel, prohibit fighting it, and justify the treason of the oppressive rulers.

The imperialist would not have done all this if it were not for the importance of the religious *ulama*'s influence over the people.

Therefore, one of your most important responsibilities, O Muslim *ulama*, is to educate the Muslims to abide by the dictates of Islam, to point out to them the political line they should follow, to lead them toward glory and honor, and to devote attention to the religious institutes so that they may graduate leaders faithful to God and eager to uphold religion and the nation.

Final Word Regarding International Organizations

Finally, a word must be said regarding international organizations and institutions, such as the United Nations, the Security Council, and others.

We note that these organizations are not podiums for the oppressed peoples generally and that they continue to be ineffective due to the domination of their decisions by the states of world arrogance, whether in terms of the implementation or the obstruction of such decisions.

The veto enjoyed by a number of states is nothing but a proof of the soundness of what we are saying.

Therefore, we do not expect anything to come out of these organizations would serve the interest of the oppressed and we urge all the self-respecting countries to adopt the plan to abolish the veto right enjoyed by the states of arrogance.

We also urge these countries to embrace the plan to expel Israel from the United Nations by virtue of its being a usurping and illegal entity, in addition to its being an entity hostile to mankind's inclinations.

Free, downtrodden people,

These are our visualizations and objectives and these are the rules that govern our course.

Those who accept us by accepting right, and God is the best friend of what is right. As for those who reject us, we will endure until God issues his judgment on us and on the oppressors.

God's peace, mercy, and blessings be upon you.

Hizb Allah

Notes

Preface

1. Transliteration from Arabic to English always presents some difficulty. In this work, I utilize the system of transliteration adopted by the *International Journal of Middle East Studies*, except that I omit diacritical marks and I do not generally distinguish between long and short vowels. Only the vowels *a*, *i*, and *u* are used except in quotations, where the original transliteration is preserved. In some instances involving proper names, I have preferred common usage to consistent transliteration (e.g., "Jumblatt" in preference to "Junbalat"). In general, I have tried to stick to a sensible system of transliteration that will not be overly offensive to Arabists or unduly confusing to the informed reader.

There are several commonly employed nouns and adjectives used to refer to the Shiʻi sect of Islam. In this work the following forms of reference are used: "Shiʻism" is a proper noun referring to the Shiʻi religion. "Shiʻi" is both a proper noun and an adjectival modifier. In the former usage, a "Shiʻi" is an adherent of Shiʻism; in the latter form, we would refer to the "Shiʻi religion." "Shiʻa" is a collective noun, as in the "Shiʻa of Lebanon." In references to a number of Shiʻi persons, I often prefer "Shiʻis" to "Shiʻa," both for the sake of readability and to stress that I am not referring to the entire community. Thus, references to the community as a whole use the word "Shiʻa." Variant forms of transliteration are sometimes found in quoted material from non-Arabic sources.

2. See "ʻUlama li-islam yuʻlanun al-mauqif al-sharʻi al-wajib ʻala al-muslimin ittikhadhihi bishan lubnan al-ghad" (The Lawful Necessary Position of the ʻUlama on Behalf of Islam, Taken for the Sake of the Future Lebanon, Is Announced to Muslims), a four-page document distributed in Lebanon in June 1986 (no other publication data are shown).

3. For a warts-and-all description of UNIFIL, see my paper "Observations on U.N. Peacekeeping in Lebanon," delivered at the 1983 International Conference of the Inter-University Seminar on Armed Forces and Society, October 21–23, 1983, at the Palmer House, Chicago, Illinois. See also my "UNIFIL and the Shiʻi Community," in *UNIFIL*, ed.

Kjell Skjelsbaek (Oslo: Norwegian Institute of International Affairs, in preparation).

1. Introduction

1. David R. Smock and Audrey C. Smock, *The Politics of Pluralism: A Comparative Study of Lebanon and Ghana*, p. ix.

2. Elie Adib Salem, *Modernization without Revolution: Lebanon's Experience*, p. xiii.

3. For a notable exception, see Iliya Harik, *Lebanon: Anatomy of Conflict*.

4. See my "Lebanon's Shifting Political Landscape," *New Leader* (March 8, 1982), 8–9.

5. Noteworthy titles include Walid Khalidi, *Conflict and Violence in Lebanon: Confrontation in the Middle East;* Marius Deeb, *The Lebanese Civil War;* and Kamal S. Salibi, *Crossroads to Civil War: Lebanon 1958–1976.*

6. John Kifner and Thomas Friedman of the *New York Times;* Trudy Rubin, John Cooley, and Robin Wright of the *Christian Science Monitor;* William Claiborne, Jonathan Randal, and David Ottoway of the *Washington Post;* and David Ignatius of the *Wall Street Journal* all set very high standards in their reporting from Lebanon. As a group, foreign correspondents represent an enormously talented, and generally unappreciated, selection of men and women. One is often led to suspect that if they were given a freer rein by their editors the quality of their reporting would be enhanced. To say that the correspondents often missed the "real story" in Lebanon is a commentary on the way most newspapers work, not a derogation of the seriousness of the correspondents.

7. This period is brilliantly treated by William R. Polk in *The Opening of South Lebanon, 1788–1840: A Study of the Impact of the West on the Middle East.*

8. For example, see Joseph Chamie, *Religion and Fertility: Arab Christian-Muslim Differentials.*

9. Ibid., p. 44.

10. Robert Melson and Howard Wolpe, "Modernization and the Politics of Communalism: A Theoretical Perspective," *American Political Science Review* 64 (December 1970): 1112–1130; reprinted in *Nigeria: Modernization and the Politics of Communalism,* by Melson and Wolpe; quotation at p. 16 in the latter volume.

11. It is significant that the major policy statement delivered by Prime Minister Rashid Karami on May 31, 1984, calls for the abolition of religious specification on identity cards, an important symbolic and practical step toward the abolishment of sectarianism. Unfortunately, this reform, like so many others, remains unimplemented.

12. Lewis W. Snider, "The Lebanese Forces: Their Origins and Role in Lebanon's Politics," *Middle East Journal* 38 (Winter 1984): 1–33, see 3.

13. See my chapter "Harakat Amal," in *Religion and Politics* (Political Anthropology, 3), pp. 105–131. On the general issue of political and social

change in Lebanon, see Paul A. Jureidini and Ronald D. McLaurin, "The Impact of Social and Generational Change on Lebanese Politics" (unpublished paper, March 1984); and Edward Azar et al., *The Emergence of a New Lebanon: Fantasy or Reality?*

2. The Sources and Meaning of Change among the Shi'a of Lebanon

1. One measure of the marginality of the Shi'a is the fact that most political studies written prior to the civil war almost totally ignore them. The following two books are notable exceptions: Michael C. Hudson, *The Precarious Republic: Political Modernization in Lebanon;* and David R. Smock and Audrey C. Smock, *The Politics of Pluralism: A Comparative Study of Lebanon and Ghana.*

2. David Urquhart, *The Lebanon: Mt. Souria, A History and a Diary,* 2 vols., 1: 223.

3. Albert H. Hourani, *Syria and Lebanon: A Political Essay,* p. 135

4. Leonard Binder, "Political Change in Lebanon," in *Politics in Lebanon,* ed. Leonard Binder, pp. 283–327.

5. Ibid., p. 301.

6. Useful population estimates may be found in the following two sources: Joseph Chamie, "The Lebanese Civil War: An Investigation into the Causes," *World Affairs* 139 (Winter 1976/1977): 171–188; and Riad B. Tabbarah, "Background to the Lebanese Conflict," *International Journal of Comparative Sociology* 20, nos. 1–2 (March 1979): 101–121. For a unique demographic study, see Joseph Chamie, *Religion and Fertility: Arab Christian-Muslim Differentials.*

7. In order of estimated magnitude, Lebanon's confessions include Shi'i Muslims, Maronite Christians, Sunni Muslims, Greek Orthodox, Druze, Greek Catholics, and Armenian Orthodox.

8. Chamie, "Lebanese Civil War," p. 179.

9. Hudson, *Precarious Republic,* p. 79.

10. Tabbarah, "Background to the Lebanese Conflict," p. 118.

11. Hasan Sharif, "South Lebanon: Its History and Geopolitics," in *South Lebanon,* ed. Elaine Hagopian and Samih Farsoun, pp. 10–11.

12. Ibid., p. 11.

13. See Lewis W. Snider, "The Lebanese Forces: Their Origins and Role in Lebanon's Politics," *Middle East Journal* 38 (Winter 1984): 1–33; and Snider, "Political Instability and Social Change in Lebanon" (unpublished, January 1984).

14. Augustus R. Norton, "Lebanon's Old Politics Must Yield to the New," *New York Times,* January 3, 1984.

15. Political change is most clearly ignored in Gabriel Almond and James S. Coleman, eds., *The Politics of the Developing Areas* (Princeton: Princeton University Press, 1960); but also consult Almond and G. Bingham Powell, Jr., *Comparative Politics: A Developmental Approach* (Boston: Little, Brown, 1966). For a useful discussion and critique of the literature in

the context of political change, see Samuel P. Huntington, "The Change to Change: Modernization, Development, and Politics," *Comparative Politics* 3 (April 1971): 283–322.

16. Emrys L. Peters, "Aspects of Rank and Status among Muslims in a Lebanese Village," in *Mediterranean Countrymen: Essays in the Social Anthropology of the Mediterranean*, ed. Julian Pitt-Rivers, pp. 159–200; and Peters, "Shifts of Power in a Lebanese Village," in *Rural Politics and Social Change in the Middle East*, ed. Richard Antoun and Iliya Harik, pp. 165–197.

17. Karl W. Deutsch, "Social Mobilization and Political Development," *American Political Science Review* 55 (September 1961): 493–514. One of the few detailed attempts to apply Deutsch's work in a Middle East setting is Farhad Kazemi, *Poverty and Revolution in Iran: The Urban Poor, Urban Marginality and Politics*, pp. 68ff.

18. Deutsch, "Social Mobilization," p. 493.

19. Ibid., pp. 497–498.

20. Ibid., p. 498.

21. William J. Foltz, "Modernization and Nation-Building: The Social Mobilization Model Reconsidered, in *From National Development to Global Community: Essays in Honor of Karl W. Deutsch*, ed. Richard L. Merritt and Bruce M. Russett, pp. 25–45; quotation at p. 26.

22. See Hudson, *Precarious Republic*, esp. pp. 53–86.

23. World Bank, *World Development Report*, p. 147. Also useful is Michael Johnson, "Popular Movements and Primordial Loyalties in Beirut," in *Sociology of "Developing Societies": The Middle East*, ed. Talal Asad and Roger Owen, pp. 178–194; in particular, see p. 178.

24. Salim Nasr, "Backdrop to Civil War: The Crisis of Lebanese Capitalism," *MERIP Reports* 73 (December 1978): 3–13.

25. Alan B. Mountjoy, "Migrant Workers in the Arab Middle East," *Third World Quarterly* 4 (July 1982): 530–531.

26. Nasr, "Backdrop to Civil War," p. 10.

27. Deutsch, "Social Mobilization," pp. 497–498.

28. Jerrold D. Green, *Revolution in Iran: The Politics of Countermobilization*, p. 2.

29. Ibid., p. 3.

30. Jorge Dominguez, "Political Participation and the Social Mobilization Hypothesis: Chile, Mexico, and Cuba, 1800–1825," *Journal of Interdisciplinary History* 5 (Autumn 1974): 237–266; quotation at p. 266.

31. David R. Cameron, "Toward a Theory of Political Mobilization," *Journal of Politics* 36 (February 1974): 138–171; quotation at p. 139.

32. Ibid., p. 140.

33. Gabriel A. Almond, "Approaches to Developmental Causation," in *Crisis, Choice and Change: Historical Studies of Political Development*, ed. Gabriel A. Almond, Scott C. Flanagan, and Robert J. Mundt, pp. 1–41; see also Augustus R. Norton, *External Intervention and the Politics of Lebanon*.

34. The primacy of politics is well argued in Seymour Martin Lipset, ed., *Politics and the Social Sciences*. Of particular interest is Lipset's introduction (pp. vii–xxii); and Giovanni Sartori, "From the Sociology of Politics to Political Sociology," pp. 65–100.

35. Leonard Binder, *In a Moment of Enthusiasm: Political Power and the Second Stratum in Egypt*, p. 27. As Binder notes: "Although the distinction between the types of mobilization is important, that distinction is often lost in much academic discourse."

36. For example, Clifford Geertz, *Old Societies and New States: The Quest for Modernity in Asia and Africa*.

37. Karl W. Deutsch, *Nationalism and Social Communication: An Inquiry into the Foundations of Nationality*.

38. For a lively critical discussion of Deutsch's position on assimilation versus dissimilation, see Walker Connor's important article, "Nation-Building or Nation-Destroying?" *World Politics* 24 (April 1972): 319–355, esp. 321–328.

39. Deutsch, "Social Mobilization," p. 501. See also Deutsch's *Politics and Government: How People Decide Their Fate*, 2d ed., p. 544, where he notes: "Social mobilization makes people more available for change. It does so by inducing them or teaching them to change their residence, their occupations, their communications, their associates, and their outlook and imagination. It gives rise to new needs, new aspirations, new demands and capabilities. *But all these patterns of behavior may disunite a population or unite it. They can make people more similar or more different. They may produce cooperation or strife, integration or succession* [emphasis added]."

40. To be "in politics" all too frequently means to be included in a clientelist system. Even the most secular-sounding party names are often no more than *au courant* labels for confessionally discrete political groupings with obscure or vaguely articulated political programs (e.g., the almost wholly Druze Progressive Socialist party): "Younger aspirants for public leadership, with rare exceptions, all seek to establish their political base not by articulating a programme or identifying critical issues or specific problems requiring reform but by building up a personal entourage of clients and followers" (Samir Khalaf, "Changing Forms of Political Patronage in Lebanon," in *Patrons and Clients in Mediterranean Societies*, ed. Ernest Gellner and John Waterbury, p. 195).

41. Fuad I. Khuri, *From Village to Suburb: Order and Change in Greater Beirut*, p. 211.

42. See Hudson, *Precarious Republic*, p. 21.

43. Iliya Harik, "The Political Elite as a Strategic Minority," in *Leadership and Development in Arab Society*, ed. Fuad I. Khuri, pp. 62–91; see p. 71.

44. Khuri, *From Village to Suburb*, p. 217.

45. Ibid., p. 101.

46. Samuel P. Huntington and Joan M. Nelson, *No Easy Choice: Political Participation in Developing Countries*, p. 113.

47. Harik, "The Political Elite as a Strategic Minority," p. 71.

48. On the preservation of sectarian identity in Beirut, see Fuad I. Khuri, "The Social Dynamics of the 1975–1977 War in Lebanon," *Armed Forces and Society* 7 (Spring 1981): 383–408; and Khuri, "A Comparative Study of Migration Patterns in Two Lebanese Villages," *Human Organization* 26, no. 4 (1967): 206–213: see also Smock and Smock, *Politics of Pluralism*, p. 93.

49. Hudson, *Precarious Republic*, p. 61.

50. Johnson, "Popular Movements," p. 181.

51. Suad Joseph, "Politicization of Religious Sects in Borj Hammoud" (Ph.D dissertation, Columbia University, 1975), p. 210.

52. A unique and valuable study of Sunni *zuʿama* and *qabadayat* in Beirut is found in Michael Johnson, "Political Bosses and Their Gangs: *Zuʿama* and *Qabadayat* in the Sunni Muslim Quarters of Beirut," in *Patrons and Clients*, ed. Ernest Gellner and John Waterbury, pp. 207–224. In the same volume, also consult Samir Khalaf, "Changing Forms of Political Patronage," pp. 185–206.

53. Johnson, "Popular Movements," p. 192.

54. Joseph, "Politicization of Religious Sects," p. 109.

55. Khuri, "Social Dynamics of the War," p. 392.

56. Touma al-Khouri, "The Election Bus," in *Modern Arabic Short Stories*, trans. Denys Johnson-Davies, pp. 173–181; quotation at p. 173.

57. For an instructive (and controversial) fictional treatment of a young Shiʿi woman's attempt to "escape" from her village and her sect, see Tawfik Yusuf Awwad, *Death in Beirut*, trans. Leslie McLoughlin.

58. An important exception is Richard Antoun and Iliya Harik, eds., *Rural Politics and Social Change in the Middle East*. In their introduction, Antoun and Harik observe: "In terms of participation in political organizations and elections, holding opinions on national affairs, and involvement in the local community for the solution of community problems, villagers may be more highly 'politicized' than urbanites" (p. 11).

59. Daniel Lerner, *The Passing of Traditional Society: Modernizing the Middle East*, p. 61.

60. Ibid., p. 50.

61. Deutsch, "Social Mobilization," pp. 497–498.

62. Ibid., p. 499.

63. Samuel P. Huntington, *Political Order in Changing Societies*, p. 47.

64. While the urban-rural distinction may have lost much of its meaning in the context of political development, there is no denying that the individual Lebanese finds the distinction very important, since the rural village is a place of relaxation, refuge, retreat, and retirement.

65. Iliya Harik, *The Political Mobilization of Peasants: A Study of an Egyptian Community*, p. 212.

66. Antoun and Harik, *Rural Politics and Social Change*, p. 7.

67. Eric Hooglund, "Rural Participation in the Revolution," *MERIP Reports* 87 (May 1980): 3–6; quotation at p. 5.

68. Cf. Khuri's claim, note 55 above, that 83 percent of the Lebanese population is urban.

69. Fouad Ajami's work in progress will focus on the reality of village life in contemporary Lebanon.

70. Iliya Harik, "Voting Behavior: Lebanon," in *Electoral Politics in the Middle East: Issues, Voters and Elites,* ed. Jacob Landau, Ergun Özbudun, and Frank Tachau, p. 156.

71. Khuri, *From Village to Suburb,* p. 8.

72. Joe Stork, "Report from Lebanon," *MERIP Reports* 118 (October 1983): 3–13, 22; see p. 13.

73. Of course, speaking of the periphery as if it were a unified whole can be deceiving. A less concise, but more revealing, description would note that the center has been unable to dominate a highly segmented political system. For an interesting discussion of center and periphery in the developing world, see Gerald A. Heeger, *The Politics of Underdevelopment,* pp. 47–74.

74. Antoun and Harik, *Rural Politics and Social Change,* p. 10.

75. I follow the distinction between autonomous and mobilized participation made by Ergun Özbudun in *Social Change and Political Participation in Turkey.* In its narrowest form, the concept of political participation has often been restricted to voting. In fact, Daniel Lerner, in his influential book *The Passing of Traditional Society,* quite explicitly identifies participation with voting, and much of the extant participation literature, while often denoting a wide range of participatory activities, seldom moves beyond electoral studies for the practical reason that research on participation that is not centered on the ballot box is simply very difficult to do.

In contrast, a wider construction of the participation concept has the merit of capturing the interesting, if violent, range of political activities— what Louis Cantori has called "AK-47 participation"—that has characterized what has passed for a political system in Lebanon since 1975. For our purposes, a useful definition is offered by Myron Weiner, who uses "participation" to refer to "any voluntary action, successful or unsuccessful, organized or unorganized, episodic or continuous, employing legitimate or illegitimate methods intended to influence the choices of public policies, the administration of public affairs, or the choice of political leaders at any level of government, local or national" (Myron Weiner, "Political Participation: Crisis of the Political Process," in *Crises and Sequences in Political Development,* by Leonard Binder, James S. Coleman, Joseph LaPalombara, Lucian W. Pye, Sidney Verba, and Myron Weiner, pp. 159–204; quotation at p. 164).

While the range of activities subsumed in the broader definition is much more difficult to measure, incidents of protest, demonstration, violence, and intimidation are certainly measures—albeit imprecise—of the extent to which given communities or individuals seek to affect the direction of politics. Given the keen difficulties of distinguishing legality and legitimacy in an environment where the legal authorities have been in steady retreat, it is especially important that we not confuse the inquiry by attempting to discern only "lawful" or legitimate participation.

For a relatively broad construction of participation, see Sidney Verba and Norman H. Nie, *Participation in America.*

76. Arnold Hottinger, "*Zu'ama'* in Historical Perspective," in *Politics in Lebanon*, ed. Binder, pp. 85–105.

77. Samir Khalaf, "Adaptive Modernization: The Case for Lebanon," in *Economic Development and Population Growth in the Middle East*, ed. Charles A. Cooper and Sidney S. Alexander, pp. 567–598. Khalaf notes the role that the family associations have played in the process of social change among all of Lebanon's major communities: "These major religious communities followed generally the same order in undergoing the process of absorbing some of the secular tendencies inherent in modernization. In this sense family associations can be viewed as both symptoms of and reactions to social change" (p. 584). The Smocks note in *Politics of Pluralism* that most of the family associations operating in the early 1970s were probably those of the Shi'a (p. 87).

78. Leonard Binder, while avoiding explicit prescription, has provided one of the more thoughtful critiques of the literature on political participation in the developmental process, and in particular on the widely variant interpretations of the meaning of participation for the political process ("Review Essay: Political Participation and Political Development," *American Journal of Sociology* 83 [November 1977]: 751–760).

79. "Pseudoparticipation" is from Green, *Revolution in Iran*, p. 5. Cf. David E. Apter, *The Politics of Modernization*; Huntington and Nelson, *No Easy Choice*; and Huntington, *Political Order in Changing Societies*. As Binder notes, referring to Huntington's work, "Participation and institutionalization are conceived of as contradictories during the developmental stage" ("Review Essay," p. 754).

80. Weiner, "Political Participation," p. 187.

81. Cameron, "Toward a Theory," p. 145.

82. Ibid., p. 147.

83. Norman H. Nie, G. Bingham Powell, and Kenneth Prewitt, "Social Structure and Political Participation," *American Political Science Review* 63 (June 1969): 361–378; (September 1969): 808–832.

84. Cameron, "Toward a Theory," p. 140.

85. Walid Khalidi, *Conflict and Violence in Lebanon: Confrontation in the Middle East*, p. 42.

86. The differences over the role of religion and religious (i.e., personal status) law are plainly reflected in the following comment by Mufti Muhammad Mahdi Shams al-Din, since 1978 the senior Shi'i cleric in Lebanon: "I belong to the current which considers the abolition of political confessionalism and its ramifications in the administration and in representation in the Chamber a guarantee of correcting most of what we complain of in the Lebanese system. I would also add that there is need for changes in the liberal economic system. *The other current with the National Movement aiming at what is called complete secularization is, in my opinion, an erroneous current*" (Center for the Study of the Modern Arab World, "Islamic Law and Change in Arab Society," *CEMAN Reports*, vol. 4 [1976]: 105; emphasis added).

3. The Political Mobilization of the Shiʿa

1. Michael C. Hudson, *The Precarious Republic: Political Moderniza-tion in Lebanon*, see pp. 31–32.

2. The incipient political organization was verified by a senior associate of Musa al-Sadr in a private interview, February 1984.

3. A useful discussion of family associations and their role in the politi-cal and socioeconomic development of Lebanese communal groups may be found in Samir Khalaf, "Adaptive Modernization: The Case for Lebanon," in *Economic Development and Population Growth in the Middle East*, ed. Charles A. Cooper and Sidney S. Alexander, pp. 567–598.

4. This observation is borrowed from Fouad Ajami, who expounded it in a private interview, April 1984.

5. The regional variations between the South and Biqaʿ are discussed by Raymond Adams in "Paradoxes of Religious Leadership among the Shiʿites of Lebanon," *MERA Forum* 6 (Winter 1983): 9–12

6. Quoted in *al-Sadr!?*, p. 27.

7. Karim Pakradouni, *La paix manquée*, see pp. 105–107; quotation at p. 106. Much of the material in the next few paragraphs was gleaned from this publication.

8. Quoted in Thom Sicking and Shereen Khairallah, "The Shiʿa Awaken-ing in Lebanon: A Search for Radical Change in a Traditional Way," *Vision and Revision in Arab Society, 1974*, CEMAM Reports 2 (1975): 97–130; quotation at pp. 115–116.

9. Quoted in Raphael Calis, "The Shiite Pimpernel," *Middle East* (No-vember 1978), 52–54, quotation at p. 54.

10. Shahpur Bakhtiar, "The Catastrophe" (excerpts from his book, *Ma fidelité*), *al Watan al-ʿArabi*, October 8–14, 1982.

11. Pakradouni, *La paix*, p. 106.

12. Sicking and Khairallah, "The Shiʿa Awakening," p. 111.

13. See *al-Musawwar* (Cairo), May 27, 1977.

14. Pakradouni, *La paix*, p. 106.

15. *al-Dustur* (London), June 26–July 2, 1978.

16. For representative comments by Imam Musa about the *fidaʾi* presence in Lebanon, see *al-Musawwar*, May 27, 1977; *al-Hawadith*, December 24, 1976; and *al-Dustur*, June 26–July 2, 1978.

17. *al-Dustur*, June 26–July 2, 1978.

18. Pakradouni, *La paix*, p. 107.

19. Based on discussions between the author and al-Fatah officials, in south Lebanon, 1980–1981.

20. *al-Hawadith*, March 1, 1975.

21. The May 24, 1970, manifesto of the Supreme Shiʿi Council, quoted in Sicking and Khairallah, "The Shiʿa Awakening," p. 109.

22. David R. Smock and Audrey C. Smock, *The Politics of Pluralism: A Comparative Study of Lebanon and Ghana*, p. 141.

23. Many Lebanese refer to the council as the *Majlis al-Juyub* (Council of the Pockets) in recognition of its reputation for bribery and illegal diversions

of funds. The council became an important target of Amal activism in 1980, when it occupied council offices in Sidon to dramatize its demands that the council be more honestly and efficiently operated.

In 1982, Husain Kan'an, an early associate of Imam Musa, became the chairman of the council. He was subsequently replaced by Muhammad Baidun, who has assumed a leading role in Amal. Under the chairmanships of Kan'an and Baidun, the council seems to have been operated with much greater integrity, although that may be a function of the council's irrelevance in the continuing malaise, rather than more honest management.

24. Sicking and Khairallah, "The Shi'a Awakening," p. 110.

25. Ibid., p. 99. The extent to which al-Sadr's opponents saw him as a usurper of power that was rightly theirs is illustrated by the following comment by Hamid Dakrub, a deputy in al-As'ad's bloc: "Neither Imam [Musa al-] Sadr nor the Higher Shia Council is responsible for the affairs of the Shia community. The only responsible person is Kamel Assad alone" (quoted in *Arab World Weekly*, February 16, 1974).

26. *Arab World Weekly*, February 16, 1974.

27. Quoted in Sicking and Khairallah, "The Shi'a Awakening," pp. 117–118. See *al-Nahar*, February 18, 1974; and *al-Hayat*, same date.

28. Quoted in *al-Nahar*, March 18, 1974.

29. Ibid.

30. Kamal S. Salibi, *Crossroads to Civil War: Lebanon 1958–1976*, p. 78.

31. Ibid., p. 119.

32. The British correspondent John Bulloch argues that the August 6, 1976, fall of Nab'a was facilitated by al-Sadr's defection (in league with Kamil al-As'ad!) to the Syrians, who were at the time allied with the Kata'ib (see his *Death of a Country: The Civil War in Lebanon*, pp. 172–173).

Cf. Magida Salman's account, which does not contradict Bulloch's claim, but puts the matter in a very different light ("The Lebanese Communities and Their Little Wars," *Khamsin* 10 [1983]: 13–20; quotation at p. 17):

> At the beginning of the civil war, the inhabitants of Naba'a supported the various organizations of the Palestinian movement or of the Lebanese left, which had located their central headquarters in this geographically strategic neighbourhood. But the longer the war dragged on, as the bombing and shelling took their mounting toll of lives and a stifling blockade strangled the neighbourhood, the more the enthusiasm of the inhabitants of Naba'a gave way to rancour. The organizations of the "Islamo-Palestinian left" [sic] cared little about the problems faced by the local population in their daily civilian life (housing, food, and so on), and acted exclusively in the military domain. Shi'i communal sentiments were inflamed again, and flared higher when Musa Sadr established a small hospital in the neighbourhood, in sharp contrast to the politico-military organizations, which spent money only on arms.
>
> Soon afterwards, when Naba'a fell to Phalangist assault, the Shi'i population did not resist; in a battle between rival "occupation forces," the neighbourhood's inhabitants felt themselves unconcerned.

33. Quoted in the *Jerusalem Post*, March 25, 1981.

34. *Monday Morning* (Beirut), December 22–28, 1980.

35. See Smock and Smock, *Politics of Pluralism*, p. 142; and Salibi, *Crossroads to Civil War*, pp. 63–64.

36. For a noteworthy recounting, see David K. Shipler, "Lebanese Tell of Anguish of Living under the P.L.O." *New York Times*, July 25, 1982.

37. See Walid Khalidi, *Conflict and Violence in Lebanon: Confrontation in the Middle East*, pp. 115–116.

38. Based on my observations during a thirteen-month stay in south Lebanon, 1980–1981.

39. See Augustus R. Norton, "Political Violence and Shi'a Factionalism in Lebanon," *Middle East Insight* 3, no. 2 (1983): 9–16; or *New Outlook: Middle East Monthly* (Israel) (January 1984): 19–21, for an abbreviated version.

40. Letter from a member of the Command Council, May 1982.

41. *al-Sadr!?*, pp. 61–62. The documentation produced in this book substantiates the claims of al-Sadr's followers.

42. Private interview with a former senior official, June 1983.

43. A report of September 9, 1980, indicated that al-Sadr was being held in a Libyan military camp near the Algerian border (*New York Times*, September 10, 1980).

44. Letter from a member of the Command Council, May 1982.

45. *Christian Science Monitor*, April 17, 1978.

46. Sadiq Tabataba'i, quoted in *L'Orient–Le Jour*, September 16, 1980.

47. Bakhtiar, "The Catastrophe," see esp. p. 56.

48. Some influential Shi'is, who were also close associates of Musa al-Sadr, have privately expressed the possibility of Iranian involvement in the imam's disappearance; however, their claims may simply be attempts to provide an American observer with evidence of the independence of Amal from Iranian control, thereby rendering the movement more palatable to an American audience.

49. *al-Watan al-'Arabi*, September 30–October 6, 1983; and AFP (Paris), 1422 GMT, July 18, 1983, reproduced in Foreign Broadcast Information Service, *Middle East and Africa*, no. 139, July 19, 1983, p. A1 (Foreign Broadcast Information Service is hereafter referred to as "FBIS").

50. In the movement's publications, the imam is said to be in "concealment" (*ikhfa'*).

51. Michel M. Mazzaoui, "Shi'ism and Ashura in South Lebanon," in *Ta'ziyah: Ritual and Drama in Iran*, ed. Peter J. Chelkowski, pp. 228–237; quotation at pp. 229–230.

52. For a brief discussion of the relationship between Jabal 'Amil and Iran, see also Tarif Khalidi, "Shaykh Ahmad 'Arif al-Zayn and al-'Irfan," in *Intellectual Life in the Arab East, 1890–1939*, ed. Marwan R. Buheiry, pp. 110–124.

53. Others included 'Abbas Qafuri-Fard, minister of energy, and Muhammad Biravi, Iranian ambassador to Nicaragua (*al-Majallah* [London], November 5–11, 1983).

54. Donald E. Smith, *Religion and Political Development*, p. 124.

55. Augustus R. Norton, "Militant Protest and Political Violence under the Banner of Islam," *Armed Forces and Society* 9 (Fall 1982): 3–19; quotation at p. 17.

4. The End of a "Natural Alliance"

1. Lydia George, interview with Nabih Berri, *Monday Morning*, February 1–7, 1982, trans. by FBIS, *Daily Report—Middle East and Africa*, February 10, 1982, pp. G1–G6; quotation at p. G4.

2. For example, see John Yemma, "Lebanon's Shiite Muslims Flex Their Military Muscles," *Christian Science Monitor*, January 12, 1982; Thomas L. Friedman, "One Civil War Is Over, Others Fast Multiply," *New York Times*, May 23, 1982; "The Rise of Yet Another Enemy for the Palestinians," *Economist*, May 1, 1972; and Scheherazade Faramarzi, "Shiites Get Some Hope: New Force Arises in Lebanon," *Sunday Record* (Middletown, N.Y.), February 28, 1982. Cf. Augustus R. Norton, "Lebanon's Shiites," *New York Times*, April 16, 1982.

3. Nabih Berri interview, February 1–7, 1982, p. G2.

4. For descriptions of the situation in Lebanon circa 1981 and 1982, see Augustus R. Norton, "Lebanon's Shifting Political Landscape," *New Leader* (March 8, 1982): 8–9; idem, "The Violent Work of Politics in Lebanon," *Wall Street Journal*, March 18, 1982; and William Haddad, "Divided Lebanon," *Current History* (January 1982): 30–35.

5. Lest the reader be left with the wrong impression, it should be noted that members of the movement were not reluctant to take offensive action when possible. Nor was the movement shy about taking action against its opponents. For example, on February 18, 1981, an attempt was made to kidnap a cleric, Shaikh Ahmad Shawki al-Amin of the southern village of Majdal Silm, who opposed Amal. In Beirut, Amal was thought to have initiated hostilities on a number of occasions.

6. Private interview with a member of the Command Council, 1981.

7. *Le Matin* (Paris), May 28, 1982.

8. For the positions of various groups and factions prior to June 1982, see *Monday Morning* issues of December 22–28, 1980; December 29–January 4, 1981; January 12–18, 1981; January 19–25, 1981; and January 26–February 1, 1981.

9. For a personal account stressing this dimension of the civil war, especially in Beirut, see Lina Mikdadi Tabbara, *Survival in Beirut: A Diary of Civil War*, trans. Nadia Hijab.

10. *N.B.*—it was only in early 1982 that the public statements of Amal officials began to match their private assessments.

11. Figures on the confessional profile of the Lebanese Armed Forces are closely held, and even authoritative estimates are hard to find. It seems that officer recruitment is being carried out along strict confessional lines, with a fifty-fifty split between Muslims and Christians and proportionate allocations within each major category for the respective seventeen sects. Some estimates hold that there is a sixty-forty split among the enlisted ranks in

favor of the Muslims, and a sixty-forty split in the officer corps favoring the Christians (reflecting Maronite overrepresentation in the grades of major and above). For a rare detailed discussion by the armed forces commander, see interview with Ibrahim Tannus, *al-Watan al-ʿArabi,* June 17–23, 1983. Tannus concedes that in 1983 there were three Muslim recruits for every two Christians.

12. *al-Nahar,* September 18, 1980.

13. Nabih Berri interview, February 1–7, 1982, p.G2.

14. Ibid.

15. See Abu Iyad [Salah Khalaf] with Eric Rouleau, *My Home, My Land: A Narrative of the Palestinian Struggle,* trans. Linda Butler Koseoglu.

16. Private communication from an Amal official who was present.

17. *Economist,* May 1, 1982.

18. *al-Watan* (Kuwait), November 25, 1981.

19. From a speech by Salah Khalaf, broadcast by the Voice of Palestine, trans. by FBIS, February 4, 1982, p. G3.

20. Interview with Mufti Muhammad Mahdi Shams al-Din, *al-Nahar al-ʿArabi wa al-Duwali,* May 24–30, 1982, trans. by FBIS, June 3, 1982, p. G2.

21. A number of Amal officials, among them some key moderates, were critical of Berri's penchant for equivocation.

22. Interview with Nabih Berri, *Monday Morning,* May 10–16, 1982, reprinted by FBIS, May 25, 1982, p. G3.

5. Contradiction versus Consistency in Amal's Politics

1. Cf. Marius K. Deeb, "Lebanon: Prospects for National Reconciliation in the Mid-1980s," *Middle East Journal* 38 (Spring 1984): 267–283; see especially p. 271, where Deeb asserts that Amal and its splinter groups are "first and foremost, armed militias." In my view, this perspective misunderstands the sociopolitical meaning of Amal and implicitly reifies the old political guard.

2. Useful summaries of the pre–civil war perspectives of various communal groupings on such matters as the independence of Lebanon, the meaning of Lebanese nationalism, and sectarianism in politics may be found in Abdo I. Baaklini, *Legislative and Political Development: Lebanon, 1842–1972,* pp. 103–139.

3. See Fouad Ajami, "The End of Pan-Arabism," *Foreign Affairs* 57 (Winter 1978/1979): 355–373.

4. Referring to the factions that fought the civil war, Iliya Harik notes that "none of the warring factions demanded the establishment of a different political system or an overthrow of the constitutional order; only changes in the existing system" (*Lebanon: Anatomy of Conflict,* American University Field Staff Reports, no. 49 [1981], p. 3).

5. *Mithaq Harakat Amal,* n.d. My copy was given to me in 1982, but I presume it to be a revised copy of the version published in November 1974. The 1974 version was endorsed by 190 public figures from most of Lebanon's

sects. Unless noted, or otherwise indicated, all subsequent quotations in the chapter are drawn from the *Mithaq*.

6. Nabih Berri, quoted in *al-Hawadith*, May 9, 1980.

7. Interview with Nabih Berri, *Monday Morning*, May 10–16, 1982, reprinted by FBIS, May 25, 1982, p. G4; see especially p. G4.

8. See Lydia Georgi, "Inside the Amal Movement (A Discussion with Nabih Berri)," *Monday Morning*, February 1–7, 1982. Berri notes that he wanted the army in the South "even if it was 100 percent Maronite [in order] to extend the authority of the State to the international borders and put an end to the mini-state of Saʿad Haddad."

In another interview, Berri exclaimed: "When the homeland's borders are exposed to aggression, when parts of its territories are faced with the threat of occupation while other areas are actually occupied, and when the residents of the South are divided into the displaced and the tormented, then there is no room for a discussion about the gender of the angels. Protecting the homeland, whose gate is the South, deserves greater attention than the sect of this or that officer and whether this position should belong to that officer and that position to this officer" (*al-Watan* [Kuwait], June 20, 1980).

9. This was one of many points made by Berri in an important speech delivered in Baʿalbak on August 31, 1985, the seventh anniversary of Musa al-Sadr's disappearance. The speech is translated by FBIS, September 3, 1985, pp. G2–G5; see esp. p. G4.

10. Ibid.

11. Ibid., p. G3.

12. *Monday Morning*, February 1–7, 1982.

13. "The Arabs are treating the South as if it were not part of the Arab world, as if it were a province of China or India" (Nabih Berri, quoted in *Monday Morning*, May 10–16, 1982).

14. The working paper was translated and reprinted by *An-Nahar Report & Memo* (February 20, 1984): 4–7; quotation at p. 4.

15. The demands may be found in *al-Hayat* (Beirut), February 12, 1974.

16. Quoted in Baaklini, *Legislative and Political Development*, pp. 109–110.

17. For a representative non-Shiʿi view, see the article by ex–prime minister Salim al-Huss in *al-Mustaqbal*, July 30, 1983.

18. Berri, quoted in Lydia Georgi, "The 'New Lebanon' File—Part 6: The Amal Movement: The Myth of Pluralism," *Monday Morning*, January 26–February 1, 1981.

Berri's analysis is certainly shared by a number of longtime observers, including Michael Hudson: "The confessional system itself—as the embodiment of a consociational model—was the root of the problem" ("The Lebanese Crisis: The Limits of Consociational Democracy," *Journal of Palestine Studies* 5, nos. 3–4 [Spring/Summer 1976]: 114).

19. Berri, quoted in Georgi, "The 'New Lebanon' File."

20. Ibid.

21. Berri, quoted in Georgi, "Inside the Amal Movement."

22. Berri's Baʿalbak speech, August 31, 1985, p. G4.

23. Interview with Hasan Hashim, *Amal*, April 17, 1981.

24. See, for example, an interesting commentary by a movement writer on an article that appeared in the *Kataʾib* organ, *al-ʿAmal*, on the subject of Harakat Amal: *Amal*, April 17, 1981.

25. See Berri's comments in *al-Nahar al-ʿArabi wa al-Duwali*, April 20–25, 1981.

26. Ibid.

27. Quoted in Georgi, "The 'New Lebanon' File."

6. The Israeli Invasion and Its Aftermath

1. Israel's ambitions with respect to south Lebanon are treated in Augustus R. Norton, "Israel and South Lebanon," *American-Arab Affairs* 4 (Spring 1983): 23–31; and idem, "Lebanon for the Lebanese," *New York Times*, February 22, 1983.

2. See Bob Woodward, Richard Harwood, and Christian Williams, "Beirut Bombing: Political Warriors Used Men Who Crave Death," *Washington Post*, February 1, 1984. Unfortunately, this article is rife with errors and should only be used with caution. See also Augustus R. Norton, "Political Violence and Shiʿa Factionalism in Lebanon," *Middle East Insight* 3, no. 2 (1983): 9–16 (an abbreviated version may be found in *New Outlook*, January 1984).

3. After a number of unconfirmed news reports indicating that Syria had significantly restricted the activities of pro-Iranian and Iranian forces in and around Baʿalbak, it seems that by August 1984 they had actually begun to do so. (Subsequently, Syria further tightened the screws.) See G. G. LaBelle, "Syrian Army Takes Control of Baalbek in Lebanon," *Washington Post*, August 17, 1984.

4. The information on the 1983 convention was provided by a western diplomat posted to Beirut. For description and analysis of earlier Amal conventions, see the following articles: Marc Kravetz, "The Shiʿite Resurgence," *Le Matin* (Paris), May 28, 1982; *al-Safir*, April 5, 1980; and ʿAli Hamada, "Harakat Amal," *al-Nahar al-ʿArabi wa al-Duwali*, April 6–12, 1981.

5. The best account of the Maronite Lebanese Forces, and one that offers several parallels with contemporaneous developments among the Shiʿa, is Lewis W. Snider, "The Lebanese Forces: Their Origins and Role in Lebanon's Politics," *Middle East Journal* 38, no. 1 (Winter 1984): 1–33.

6. I met Shaikh Qabalan in the southern village of Burj Rahal in October 1982 when we were both guests at an Amal gathering. I was struck by his easy manner and his very effective technique of driving home his points, which he did by using homely examples and a fast wit. Of great interest is the fact that he was urging the Amal members in attendance to be patient with the government. At the time, the government was demolishing the homes of a number of Shiʿi squatters living near the airport. Instead of taking a stridently antigovernment position, he explained that the homes erected by the squatters jeopardized the safe operation of the airport (some of the structures risked impeding the flight path), "and who," he asked,

"works at the airport?" The point was that, if the airport could not operate, Shiʿi employees would not have a job. In the next breath, he added that, of course, the government would have to see to adequate housing for those who had been evicted.

7. For press reports on the competition, see Kravetz, "Shiʿite Resurgence," and Jim Muir, "A Strike That United Beirut," *Arabia: The Islamic World Review* (June 1982): 26–27.

8. Quoted in an interview with Qabalan, *al-Mustaqbal*, October 8, 1983.

9. Interview with Muhammad Mahdi Shams al-Din, *al-Mustaqbal*, March 5, 1983.

10. My copy of the document was given to me by Husain al-Husaini in November 1984. At the time, attempts were being made by those associated with Shams al-Din to give the "Islamic Position" wide circulation in the West. The document was promulgated on September 21, 1983, at the Dar al-Fatwa al-Islamiya in Beirut.

11. A seemingly reliable press account indicates that the price of Shams al-Din, for a reconciliation with Amal, is the reinstatement of the sixteen men appointed to the Amal political bureau by Musa al-Sadr. Of the sixteen, only three—Berri, Haidar, and Husain al-Yatim—remain in controlling positions in Amal. The status of the other thirteen is as follows: Husain al-Husaini, currently Speaker of the National Assembly after his victory over Kamil al-Asʿad in October 1984; Husain Kanʿan, chairman of the Council of the South from 1982 to 1984 after an extended period of residence in the United States; ʿAbbas Makki, colonel in the army; ʿAli al-Hasan, physician; Malik Badr al-Din, physician and hospital owner; Ahmad Ismaʿil, status unknown; Jamal Mansur, physician; Jaʿfar Sharaf al-Din, member of a prominent southern family and a former cabinet minister; Rafiq Shara, painter; Muhammad Saʿad, status unknown; Muhammad Yaʿqub, cleric, and ʿAbbas Badr al-Din, journalist—both disappeared with Musa al-Sadr in 1978; and Mustafa Chamran, the first Iranian defense minister in the first cabinet formed after Khomeini's return from exile in 1979 under Mahdi Bazargan, later killed—in an airplane crash—on the Iraqi front. Obviously, the reinstatement of the ten living political bureau members would significantly dilute Berri's political authority and, even more, his legitimacy (see *al-Tadamun* [London], November 3, 1984).

12. I base this information on numerous discussions that I held with Amal leaders in October 1982.

13. As Jim Muir notes, the Israelis were playing several different cards in the fighting: "Also, from the early days, they pursued a classic divide-and-rule policy in the Shuf and Aley districts, allowing the entry of Phalangist forces but permitting the Druze to receive large quantities of heavy arms and supplies which passed through Syrian and Israeli lines. Having lost Beirut's cooperation, the Israelis appeared to fall back on a policy of encouraging Lebanon's fragmentation into vying sectarian entities" ("Lebanon: Arena of Conflict, Crucible of Peace," *Middle East Journal* 38, no. 2 [Spring 1984]: 204–227; quotation at p. 211, fn. 6.

14. See Hirsh Goodman, "A Pragmatic Ideologue," *Atlantic* (September

1983): 22ff. Samuel Lewis, who was U.S. ambassador to Israel during the 1982 invasion and who was a participant in the diplomatic process that produced the May 17 agreement, has also stressed the significance of the agreement as a means of healing the strained U.S.-Israeli relationship. As Lewis notes: "It was a gamble, but it was much better to complete it and have it rejected than not to be able to complete it at all. *It wasn't a failure, either, because it was an important achievement in beginning to heal the U.S.-Israeli split, and not to have completed it would have been ridiculous"* (quoted in Tammi Gutner, "Sam Lewis and His Middle East Mission," *SAISPHERE* [Winter 1986]: 12–13; emphasis added).

15. See Augustus R. Norton, "Lebanon for the Lebanese," *New York Times*, February 22, 1983; idem, "Lebanese Quagmire," *New York Times*, July 11, 1984; and idem, "Occupational Risks and Planned Retirement," *Middle East Insight* 4, no. 1 (March/April 1985): 14–18.

16. The point is well made by Jim Muir, who notes: "Associated with a Beirut government which many Muslims regarded as Phalangist-dominated, the U.S. Marine contingent in the Multinational Force (MNF) became a party in what was now indisputably again, on one level, a civil war" ("Lebanon: Arena of Conflict," p. 213).

17. Nabih Berri, for instance, spoke of "U.S. support and participation with the aim of perpetrating a massacre against West Beirut, the suburb, and its inhabitants" (quoted in a clandestine Voice of Arab Lebanon Arabic broadcast, on August 31, 1983, cited in FBIS, *Daily Report* [*Middle East and Africa*], September 1, 1983, p. G5.

18. For an informed analysis of U.S. policy in Lebanon during this period, see Roy Gutman, "Battle over Lebanon," *Foreign Service Journal* (June 1984): 28–33.

19. *Le Matin* (Paris), July 26, 1983. Berri's views are mirrored by ʿAkif Haidar, who noted that he thought the NSF was "too closely tied to the Syrians" (quoted in *Le Monde*, September 20, 1983).

20. Berri discussed his concerns with me a year later, on October 1, 1984: "for the time-being I can keep the river flowing and free of debris, but at some point I will no longer be able to do so." If anything, Berri understated the challenge he was facing. Also see *Le Monde*, September 20, 1983.

21. The *Christian Science Monitor*, April 29, 1985, reports that Syria has reduced Pasdaran presence from 1,000 to 400. This is consistent with G. G. LaBelle's earlier report, "Syrian Army Takes Control."

For an informed and unusually pithy account of Syria's use of the radical Shiʿa as a tool with which to control other population groups in Lebanon, see William Harris, "The View from Zahle: Security and Economic Concerns in the Central Bekaa 1980–1985," *Middle East Journal* 39, no. 3 (Summer 1985): 270–286.

22. Although definitive information is unavailable, some apparently accurate information has been published on the links between Iran and some of the radical and extremist groups in Lebanon. In particular, Robin Wright's book *Sacred Rage: The Wrath of Militant Islam* is an interesting reference.

See also Augustus R. Norton, *Political and Religious Extremism in the Middle East.*

23. Sharif al-Husaini, "Hizb Allah: Harakat ʿAskariya am Siyasiya am Diniya?" (Hizb Allah: Military, Political, or Religious Movement?), *al-Shiraʿ*, March 15, 1986.

24. "Details about 'Hizbullah' and Its Leaders," *Middle East Reporter*, March 22, 1986.

The London-based *al-Dustur*, October 14, 1985, reports that one-third (one billion riyals) of Iran's budget for supporting the "international *jihad*" is earmarked for Lebanon.

25. See *al-Nahar al-ʿArabi wa al-Duwali*, June 10–16, 1985.

26. al-Husaini, "Hizb Allah," p. 19.

27. A competent concise political biography has been written by Martin Kramer, "Muhammad Husayn Fadlallah," *Orient: German Journal for Politics and Economics of the Middle East* 26, no. 2 (June 1985): 147–149.

A detailed interview with Fadl Allah may be found in *al-Harakat al-Islamiya fi Lubnan*, pp. 246–277.

28. Robin Wright notes that Fadl Allah owes much of his prominence to reports linking him with the bombing of the contingents of the Multinational Force in October 1983: "After the bombings, Fadl Allah overnight became one of the best known and most feared men in the region. In calculated leaks, the Christian 'Lebanese Forces' militia alleged that he had possibly provided but definitely blessed the two 'smiling' kamikaze drivers in a special ceremony on the eve of their attacks on the Marines and French forces. Israeli and U.S. sources gave strong credence to the report, while admitting they had nothing first-hand" (*Sacred Rage*, p. 91).

The article that was most important in bringing Fadl Allah to the world's attention was Woodward, Harwood, and Williams, "Beirut Bombing." The latter article is widely believed to have been very heavily dependent upon Israeli sources, who were purportedly very cooperative in their dealings with the authors. Cf. Thomas L. Friedman, "State-Sponsored Terror Called a Threat to U.S.," *New York Times*, December 30, 1985, where Friedman does not link Fadl Allah to the bombings.

29. Quoted in an interview in *Monday Morning*, October 15–21, 1984.

30. Quoted in an interview in *Middle East Insight* 4, no. 2 (June/July 1985): 12–19; quotation at p. 15.

31. See the interview with Fadl Allah in *Monday Morning*, October 15–21, 1984.

32. *Nass al-risala al-maftuha allati wajjaha hizb allah ila al-mustadʿafin fi lubnan wa al-ʿalam* (Text of Open Letter Addressed by Hizb Allah to the Downtrodden in Lebanon and in the World), February 16, 1985, p. 6.

33. Ibid.

34. Ibid., p. 11.

35. Ibid., pp. 12–13.

36. One veteran Lebanon watcher notes in a private correspondence that Hizb Allah "has emerged as a real organization, with flags, uniforms, and

offices. Recently [during the early summer of 1985], they have been roaming around with M-113s [armored personnel carriers] marked with Hizb Allah symbols, Sagger anti-tank weapons, GRAD rockets [improved version of the Katyusha] mounted on armored personnel carriers, and towed artillery pieces. It is becoming a potent—by Lebanese standards—military force."

7. Making Enemies in South Lebanon

1. See Augustus R. Norton, "Israel and South Lebanon," *American-Arab Affairs* 4 (Spring 1983): 23–31.

2. The two most notable Arabists who served in south Lebanon were Clinton Bailey and Moshe Sharon.

3. Moshe Sharon, "Storing Up Troubles with the Shiʿites," *Jerusalem Post*, February 15, 1985.

4. Clinton Bailey, "A Change of Partners," *Jerusalem Post*, December 14, 1982.

5. Ibid.

6. Fouad Ajami, "Lebanon and Its Inheritors," *Foreign Affairs* 63 (Spring 1985): 778–799; quotation at p. 787.

7. Major James C. Judkins, Jr., "The Expanding Role of the Shiʿa in Lebanon" (Master of Military Art and Science thesis, U.S. Army Command and General Staff College, 1983), p. 95.

8. Based on private interviews with Amal officials in south Lebanon, October 1982.

9. Based on a superb piece of reporting by Robin Wright in *Christian Science Monitor*, September 8, 1983.

10. David Hirst, "Israel's Strange Partners in the Occupied Zone," *Guardian*, August 14, 1985.

11. Ibid.

12. The new name appeared in a Voice of Hope broadcast, May 13, 1983, trans. by the Joint Publications Research Service (JPRS), *Near East/South Asia Report*, no. 2759, May 26, 1983, p. 133.

13. For an interview with a leader of the Lebanese National Resistance Front, see *al-Hurriya*, May 22, 1983, translated in JPRS 83900, *Near East/South Asia Report*, no. 2784, July 15, 1983, pp. 45–51.

Hisham Melhem gives the date of the formation of the National Resistance Front as September 16, 1982 ("The Case for the Lebanese Resistance," *AAUG [Association of Arab-American University Graduates] Mideast Monitor* no. 3 [May 1985]; 2–4, 6).

14. *Jerusalem Post*, February 15, 1985.

15. For the text of the *fatwa*, see *al-Nahar*, October 18, 1983. For comments by various Muslim ʿ*ulama* at Friday prayer, October 21, 1983, see *al-Safir*, October 22, 1983.

16. *al-Safir*, October 22, 1983.

17. Information provided by a UN official. The Beirut weekly *al-Masaa*, September 17, 1984, reports about seventy attacks per month in June, July, and August 1984.

18. *al-Safir*, December 1, 1983.

19. *New York Times*, October 7, 1983.

20. Lubrani was previously in Tehran as the Israeli liaison with the Peacock Throne. The association has not gone unnoticed in the South. In fact, given Lubrani's previous position, one could almost say that a relationship with the Shi'a was never seriously pursued. One seasoned observer in the South makes the latter assertion.

21. Robin Mannock, "Hit and Myth of the Occupation Forces' Policy of Terror in South Lebanon," *Daily Star* (Beirut), June 21, 1984. See also Scott MacLeod, "A Dangerous Occupation," *New York Review of Books*, August 16, 1984.

22. Robin Wright, *Christian Science Monitor*, August 4, 1983.

23. *New York Times*, July 29, 1983.

24. Yisre'el Zamir, "The Bluff Called Security Arrangements," *'al Hamishmar*, February 23, 1984.

25. See *al-Hawadith*, March 4, 1983; *al-Mustaqbal*, October 23, 1982; and *al-Majallah*, June 23–29, 1984.

26. Clinton Bailey, "Facing a Wounded Tiger," *Jerusalem Post Magazine*, March 15, 1985.

27. Israeli military sources claim that Nahas was killed while trying to escape from custody (Jerusalem Television Service, August 15, 1984, trans. by FBIS, August 16, 1984, p. 15); however, press accounts and reports by impartial United Nations observers raise doubts about the Israeli version. See Colin Smith, "Death in Lebanon: Israel Admits Guilt," *Observer*, August 19, 1984; and John Kifner, "Southern Lebanon: A Trauma for Both Sides," *New York Times*, July 22, 1984.

28. *New York Times*, November 12, 1984.

29. For an analysis of the Israeli decision of January 18, 1985, see Augustus R. Norton, "Occupational Risks and Planned Retirement: The Israeli Withdrawal from South Lebanon," *Middle East Insight* 4, no. 1 (March/April 1985): 14–18.

Perhaps the most notorious incident that occurred during the spring of 1985—when the "iron fist" policy was in full force—was the bombing of the Husainiya in the village of Maraka on March 4. No conclusive evidence has been produced that categorically connects the blast to Israel, but many Lebanese and United Nations personnel believe the circumstantial evidence is persuasive.

In the incident, an explosive device, widely described as a remote-controlled bomb, exploded twenty-four hours after a large Israeli raiding party had withdrawn from the village. The explosion killed fifteen and wounded fifty. According to persons who were in the village, the source of the explosion was a bomb that had been concealed on the upper floor of the building, where Israeli personnel spent a period of time free from the villagers' observation. Among the dead were Muhammad Sa'ad and Khalil Jaradi, veteran leaders in the southern Amal organization. Sa'ad was a quiet and committed man who was revered in the South. Unlike many of his compatriots in the leadership of Amal, Sa'ad had a meek and diffident demeanor, and to the casual observer he seemed to lack the dynamism of a leader, but such appearances were deceiving. He had earlier been a student of Mustafa Chamran at the Jabal ʿAmil Technical Institute in Burj al-Shimali; since the late 1970s, he had played an important role in Amal. I knew Saʿad reasonably well, and I was consistently impressed with his fearlessness and his candor. He was a riveting public speaker and one of the three or four most effective Amal leaders in the South. His followers will not soon forget him.

In response to the incident in Maraka—a village noteworthy for being Muse al-Sadr's ancestral home and a hard rock for both the Israelis and the PLO—Mufti Muhammad Mahdi Shams al-Din called for a holy war against Israel (*al-jihad al-difaʿi,* defensive *jihad;* see *al-Safir,* March 5, 1985).

It was incidents like that in Maraka—whatever the level, if any, of Israel's actual culpability—that helped to make it impossible for Amal even to seem to be cooperating with Israel. As an Israeli writer notes, "there is probably not a single Shiʿa in Southern Lebanon who believes Israel's categorical denial of any involvement in the blast" (David Bernstein, "Repercussions from the Blast," *Jerusalem Post,* March 6, 1985).

30. Interview with Rabin by Eytan Haber, *Yediʿot Aharonot* (Weekend Supplement), March 15, 1985.

31. Uri Lubrani, "Peace Is Up to the Shiites," *New York Times,* April 9, 1985. Even some of Lubrani's closest colleagues were surprised by his decision to call for secret negotiations from the pulpit of a newspaper.

32. Quoted in *New York Times,* May 9, 1985. Even Shaikh Muhammad Husain Fadl Allah candidly noted that the Lebanese did not have the resources to liberate Palestine, and therefore they should not attempt to do so. For example, see Beirut Domestic Service (radio) trans. by FBIS, v. 5, no. 62, April 1, 1985.

33. Associated Press dispatch published in *Daily-News Record* (Harrisonburg, Va.), July 5, 1985.

34. Interview with ʿAkif Haidar, *L'Unité,* March 1, 1985.

35. Quoted in *New York Times,* May 26, 1985.

36. One Amal commander in the South, Abdul Majid Salih (involved as early as 1980 in anti-PLO activities), was quoted in the *New York Times,* June 26, 1985, as follows: "On the day we entered Tyre [following the exit of the IDF], we announced that no Palestinian fighters would be allowed to enter the area. The Israeli security belt has attracted all kinds of groups to the area. If there were no security belt, no other groups would come. Amal does not want to undertake operations inside Israel. We are against rocket attacks. We only want this area to be peaceful."

37. For instance, the commander of the IDF Northern Command, General Ori Orr, noted that Amal had assumed control in Sidon and Nabatiya and was not permitting "terrorists" to operate in those areas. Jerusalem Domestic Service (radio), May 13, 1985, trans. by FBIS, v. 5, no. 94, May 15, 1985.

Along the same lines, an IDF Radio broadcast of May 9, 1985, noted that Amal was preventing hostile Palestinian activity toward Israel, trans. by FBIS, v. 5, no. 91, May 10, 1985.

38. For descriptions of the residual Israeli forces in south Lebanon, see

Christopher Walker, "Incognito Israeli Troops Join SLA Militia as Withdrawal Hopes Fade," *Times*, June 6, 1985; and William Claiborne, "U.N. Officers in South Lebanon Complain of Israeli Encroachment," *Washington Post*, September 27, 1985.

39. Ze'ev Schiff notes in a *Ha'aretz* article, March 7, 1985, that both Moshe Arens and Ariel Sharon were still urging that Israel maintain control over parts of Lebanon.

40. *Jerusalem Post*, May 17, 1985.

8. Sectarian Estrangement and Social Fragmentation

1. Interview with Mufti Hasan Khalid, *al-Watan al-ʿArabi*, July 19–25, 1985.

2. A clear expression of such rejection is found in an interview with Walid Jumblatt, *al-Safir*, August 5, 1985.

3. *al-Tadamun*, April 6, 1985.

4. See Lewis W. Snider, "The Lebanese Forces: Their Origins and Role in Lebanon's Politics," *Middle East Journal* 38 (Winter 1984): 1–33.

5. *An-Nahar Arab Report & Memo* (May 6, 1985): 2–3.

6. The intricacies of Lebanon are sometimes Byzantine to the extreme. It is widely rumored that the man who sold the shells to the Lebanese army that were used to bombard the suburbs was a Shiʿi who brokered the sale with Israel.

7. Jim Muir, "Assad Tightens His Grip on Lebanon," *Middle East International* 249 (May 3, 1985): 3–5.

8. Jim Muir, "In the Lap of the Syrians," *Middle East International* 258 (September 13, 1985): 8–9.

9. Ibid., p. 9.

10. A report on the presidents' meeting in Smar Jubail on September 18, 1985, was broadcast by Beirut Domestic Service, September 18, 1985, trans. by FBIS, *Middle East and Africa* v. 5, no. 182, September 19, 1985.

11. Asʿad AbuKhalil, "Druze, Sunni and Shiite Political Leadership in Present-day Lebanon," *Arab Studies Quarterly* 7, no. 4 (Fall 1985): 33. AbuKhalil's excellent article is pithy, well argued, and full of insights.

12. Kamal Joumblatt, *I Speak for Lebanon*, trans. Michael Pallis and recorded by Phillippe Lapousterle. The enmity between the Druze and the Maronites is unmistakable in Jomblatt's rendition of Lebanese politics from a distinctively Druze point of view.

13. The key paragraph of the program, paragraph IV-D, follows:

> The establishment of a proper balance between the legislative and procedural authorities; the guarantee of judiciary independence under the canopy of a parliamentary, democratic, nonsectarian presidential system. The procedural power shall be vested in the cabinet, which will exercise the executive and administrative powers and formulate the state's general policy. The cabinet will be answerable to the Chamber of Deputies and to the people. The Chamber of Deputies will select the prime minister and declare confidence in or withdraw confidence from the government.

A supreme constitutional court will be established. A higher council will be formed to try presidents and ministers. The basic rules for implementing this will be formulated.

14. *al-Safir,* April 5, 1985.

15. AbuKhalil, "Druze, Sunni and Shiite Political Leadership," pp. 40–41.

16. (Clandestine) Radio Free Lebanon in English, August 7, 1985, transcribed by FBIS, v. 5, no. 152, August 8, 1985, p. G4.

17. Interview with Shaikh Sha'ban, *al-Nahar al-'Arabi wa al-Duwali,* July 21, 1985.

18. *Daily Star* (Beirut), November 14, 1984.

19. AbuKhalil, "Druze, Sunni and Shiite Political Leadership," p. 42.

20. Augustus R. Norton, "Changing Actors and Leadership among the Shiites of Lebanon," *Annals of the American Academy of Political and Social Science,* no. 482 (November 1985): 109–121.

21. Iran's funding for Hizb Allah is no secret. For instance, when Shaikh 'Abbas Musawi, a key figure in the party, was asked how the party was financed, he replied, "The money comes from Iran" (Paris AFP in English, July 10, 1985, transcribed by FBIS, v. 5, no. 133, pp. G2–G3).

22. Similarly pessimistic conclusions are reached in Ronald D. McLaurin, "Peace in Lebanon" (unpublished paper read at the University of Southern California, April 9, 1985).

Selected Bibliography

Newspapers and Magazines

Daily Star (Beirut) (1983–1985).
Guardian (1978–1986).
Jerusalem Post (1978–1986).
Monday Morning (Beirut) (1980–1986).
al-Nahar (1974–1986).
al-Nahar al-ʿArabi wa al-Duwali (1980–1986).
New York Times (1943–1986).
al-Safir (1980–1986).
Times (London) (1980–1986).
Wall Street Journal (1982–1986).
Washington Post (1978–1986).

Sources of Translated Materials

Foreign Broadcast Information Service.
Joint Publications Research Service.

Books and Articles

Abu Iyad [Salah Khalaf] and Eric Rouleau. *My Home, My Land: A Narrative of the Palestinian Struggle.* Translated by Linda Butler Koseoglu. New York: Times Books, 1981.
AbuKhalil, Asʿad. "Druze, Sunni, and Shiite Political Leadership in Present-day Lebanon." *Arab Studies Quarterly* 7, no. 4 (Fall 1985): 28–58.
Adams, Raymond. "Paradoxes of Religious Leadership among the Shiʿites of Lebanon." *MERA Forum* 6 (Winter 1983): 9–12.
Ajami, Fouad. *The Arab Predicament: Arab Political Thought and Practice since 1967.* New York: Cambridge University Press, 1981.
———. "The End of Pan-Arabism." *Foreign Affairs* 57 (Winter 1978/1979): 355–373.
———. "Lebanon and Its Inheritors." *Foreign Affairs* 63 (Spring 1985): 778–799.

———. *The Vanished Imam: Musa Al Sadr and the Shia of Lebanon.* Ithaca, N.Y.: Cornell University Press, 1986.

Almond, Gabriel A. "Approaches to Developmental Causation." In *Crisis, Choice and Change: Historical Studies of Political Development,* ed. Gabriel A. Almond, Scott C. Flanagan, and Robert J. Mundt. Boston: Little, Brown, 1973, pp. 1–41.

Almond, Gabriel A., and James S. Coleman, eds. *The Politics of the Developing Areas.* Princeton: Princeton University Press, 1960.

Almond, Gabriel A., and G. Bingham Powell, Jr. *Comparative Politics: A Developmental Approach.* Boston: Little, Brown, 1966.

Alpher, Joseph, ed. *Israel's Lebanon Policy: Where To?* Tel Aviv: Jaffee Center for Strategic Studies, Tel Aviv University, August 1984.

Antoun, Richard, and Iliya Harik, eds. *Rural Politics and Social Change in the Middle East.* Bloomington: Indiana University Press, 1972.

Apter, David E. *The Politics of Modernization.* Chicago: University of Chicago Press, 1965.

Arjomand, Said Amir, ed. *From Nationalism to Revolutionary Islam.* Albany: State University of New York Press, 1984.

Awwad, Tawfik Yusuf. *Death in Beirut,* trans. Leslie McLoughlin. London: Heinemann Educational Books, 1976.

Ayubi, Nazih N. M. "The Political Revival of Islam: The Case of Egypt." *International Journal of Middle East Studies* 12 (December 1980): 481–499.

Azar, Edward E., Paul Jureidini, Ronald D. McLaurin, Augustus R. Norton, Robert J. Pranger, Kate Shnayerson, Lewis W. Snider, and Joyce R. Starr. *The Emergence of a New Lebanon: Fantasy or Reality?* New York: Praeger Publishers, 1984.

Baaklini, Abdo I. *Legislative and Political Development: Lebanon, 1842–1972.* Raleigh, N.C.: Duke University Press, 1976.

Bailey, Clinton. "Facing a Wounded Tiger." *Jerusalem Post Magazine,* March 15, 1985.

Ball, George W. *Error and Betrayal in Lebanon: An Analysis of Israel's Invasion of Lebanon and the Implications for U.S.-Israeli Relations.* Washington, D.C.: Foundation for Middle East Peace, 1984.

Bill, James A. *Politics in the Middle East.* 2d ed. Boston: Little, Brown, 1984.

———. "Resurgent Islam in the Persian Gulf." *Foreign Affairs* 63 (Fall 1984): 108–127.

Binder, Leonard. *The Ideological Revolution in the Middle East.* New York: John Wiley and Sons, 1964.

———. *In a Moment of Enthusiasm: Political Power and the Second Stratum in Egypt.* Chicago: University of Chicago Press, 1978.

———. "National Integration and Political Development." *American Political Science Review* 58 (September 1964): 622–631.

———, ed. *Politics in Lebanon.* New York: John Wiley and Sons, 1966.

———. "Review Essay: Political Participation and Political Development." *American Journal of Sociology* 83 (November 1977): 751–760.

Binder, Leonard, James S. Coleman, Joseph LaPalombara, Lucian W. Pye,

Sidney Verba, and Myron Weiner. *Crises and Sequences in Political Development.* Princeton: Princeton University Press, 1971.

Bulloch, John. *Death of a Country: The Civil War in Lebanon.* London: Weidenfeld and Nicolson, 1977.

————. *Final Conflict: The War in Lebanon.* London: Century Publishing, 1983.

Calis, Raphael. "The Shiite Pimpernel." *Middle East* (November 1978): 52–54.

Cameron, David R. "Toward a Theory of Political Mobilization." *Journal of Politics* 36 (February 1974): 138–171.

Center for the Study of the Modern Arab World. "Islamic Law and Change in Arab Society." *CEMAN Reports,* vol. 4 [1976] [Beirut: Dar al-Mashreq Publishers, 1978].

Chamie, Joseph. "The Lebanese Civil War: An Investigation into the Causes." *World Affairs* 139 (Winter 1976/1977): 171–188.

————. *Religion and Fertility: Arab Christian-Muslim Differentials.* Cambridge, Eng.: Cambridge University Press, 1981.

Chrara, Waddah. *Transformations d'une manifestation religieuse dans un village du Liban sud.* Beirut: Publications du Centre de Recherches, Université Libanaise, 1968.

Cobban, Helena. *The Making of Modern Lebanon.* Boulder: Westview Press, 1985.

Cole, Juan R. I., and Nikki R. Keddie, eds. *Shi'ism and Social Protest.* New Haven: Yale University Press, 1986.

Connor, Walker. "Nation-Building or Nation-Destroying?" *World Politics* 24 (April 1972): 319–355.

Crow, Ralph E. "Electoral Issues: Lebanon." In *Electoral Issues in the Middle East: Issues, Voters and Elites,* ed. Jacob M. Landau, Ergun Özbudun, and Frank Tachau. Stanford: Hoover Institution Press, 1980, pp. 39–68.

Deeb, Marius K. *The Lebanese Civil War.* New York: Praeger, 1980.

————. "Lebanon: Prospects for National Reconciliation in the Mid-1980s." *Middle East Journal* 38 (Spring 1984): 267–283.

————. "Lebanon's Continuing Conflict." *Current History* (January 1985): 13–15, 34.

Dekmejian, Richard H. "The Anatomy of Islamic Revival: Legitimacy Crisis, Ethnic Conflict and the Search for Islamic Alternatives." *Middle East Journal* 34 (Winter 1980): 1–12.

————. "Consociational Democracy in Crisis: The Case of Lebanon." *Comparative Politics* 10 (January 1978): 251–266.

————. *Patterns of Political Leadership: Egypt, Israel, Lebanon.* Albany: State University of New York Press, 1975.

Dessouki, Ali E. Hillal, ed. *Islamic Resurgence in the Arab World.* New York: Praeger Publishers, 1982.

"Details about 'Hizbullah' and Its Leaders." *Middle East Reporter,* March 22, 1986.

Deutsch, Karl W. *Nationalism and Social Communication: An Inquiry into the Foundations of Nationality.* Cambridge: MIT Press, 1966.

————. *Politics and Government: How People Decide Their Fate.* 2d ed. Boston: Houghton Mifflin, 1974.

————. "Social Mobilization and Political Development." *American Political Science Review* 55 (September 1961): 493–514.

Dominguez, Jorge. "Political Participation and the Social Mobilization Hypothesis: Chile, Mexico, and Cuba, 1800–1825." *Journal of Interdisciplinary History* 5 (Autumn 1974): 237–266.

Early, Evelyn A. "The Emergence of an Urban Zaʿim: A Social Network Analysis." *Journal of the Social Sciences* (Kuwait) 5 (April 1977): 1–25.

Eickelman, Dale F. "The Study of Islam in Local Contexts." *Contributions to Asian Studies* 17 (1982): 1–16.

Enayat, Hamid. *Modern Islamic Political Thought.* Austin: University of Texas Press, 1982.

Entelis, John P. "Ethnic Conflict and the Reemergence of Radical Christian Nationalism in Lebanon." *Journal of South Asia and Middle Eastern Studies* (Spring 1979). Reprinted in *Religion and Politics in the Middle East,* ed. Michael Curtis. Boulder: Westview Press, 1981, pp. 227–245.

————. *Pluralism and Party Transformation in Lebanon: al-Kataʾib 1936–1970.* Leiden, The Netherlands: E. J. Brill, 1974.

Fadl Allah, Muhammad Husain. *al-Islam wa Mantaq al-Quwa.* 2d ed. Beirut: Dar al-Islamiya, 1981.

————. *al-Maqawama al-Islamiya: Afaq wa Tatalluʿat.* 2d ed. Bir al-ʿAbd, Lebanon: Lajnat Masjid al-Imam al-Rida, 1986.

Farah, Tawfic. *Aspects of Consociationism and Modernization: Lebanon as an Exploratory Test Case.* Lincoln, Neb.: Middle East Research Group, 1975.

Faris, Hani A. *Beyond the Lebanese Civil War: Historical Issues and the Challenges of Reconstruction.* Washington, D.C.: Center for Contemporary Arab Studies, Georgetown University, April 1982.

Fawaz, Leila Tarazi. *Merchants and Migrants in Nineteenth Century Beirut.* Cambridge: Harvard University Press, 1983.

————. "Understanding Lebanon." *American Scholar* 54 (Summer 1985): 377–384.

Fischer, Michael M. J. "Islam and the Revolt of the Petit Bourgeoisie." *Daedalus* 111 (Winter 1982): 101–125.

Foltz, William J. "Modernization and Nation-Building: The Social Mobilization Model Reconsidered." In *From National Development to Global Community: Essays in Honor of Karl W. Deutsch,* ed. Richard L. Merritt and Bruce M. Russett. London: George Allen and Unwin, 1981, pp. 25–45.

Fuller, Anne H. *Buarij: Portrait of a Lebanese Muslim Village.* Cambridge: Harvard University, Center for Middle Eastern Studies, 1969.

Geertz, Clifford. *Old Societies and New States: The Quest for Modernity in Asia and Africa.* New York: Free Press, 1963.

Gellner, Ernest. "Post-Traditional Forms in Islam: The Turf and Trade and Votes and Peasants." *Daedalus* 102 (Winter 1973): 191–206.

Gilmour, David. *Lebanon: The Fractured Country.* New York: St. Martin's Press, 1983.

Gilsenan, Michael. *Recognizing Islam: Religion and Society in the Modern Arab World.* New York: Pantheon Books, 1982.

Goodman, Hirsh. "A Pragmatic Ideologue." *Atlantic* (September 1983): 22ff.

Green, Jerrold. "Countermobilization as a Revolutionary Form." *Comparative Politics* 16 (January 1984): 153–169.

———. "Islam, Religiopolitics, and Social Change: A Review Article." *Comparative Studies in Society and History* 27 (April 1985): 312–322.

———. "Islam and Politics: Politics and Islam." *Middle East Insight* 3, no. 5 (1984): 3–7.

———. *Revolution in Iran: The Politics of Countermobilization.* New York: Praeger, 1982.

Gutman, Roy. "Battle over Lebanon." *Foreign Service Journal* (June 1984): 28–33.

Gutner, Tammi. "Sam Lewis and His Middle East Mission." *SAISPHERE* [John Hopkins University School of Advanced International Studies] (Winter 1986): 12–13.

Haddad, Wadi D. *Lebanon: The Politics of Revolving Doors.* Washington Papers, no. 114. New York and Washington, D.C.: Praeger Publishers, and the Center for Strategic and International Studies, Georgetown University, 1985.

Haddad, William. "Divided Lebanon." *Current History* (January 1982): 30–35.

———. "Lebanon in Despair." *Current History* (January 1983): 15–18ff.

Hagopian, Elaine, and Samih Farsoun, eds. *South Lebanon.* Detroit: Association of Arab-American University Graduates, August 1978.

Haley, Edward P., and Lewis W. Snider, eds. *Lebanon in Crisis: Participants and Issues.* Syracuse: Syracuse University Press, 1979.

Hamada, ʿAli. "Harakat Amal." *al-Nahar al-ʿArabi wa al-Duwali,* April 6–12, 1981.

Harik, Iliya. *Lebanon: Anatomy of Conflict.* Hanover, N.H.: American Universities Field Staff Reports, no. 49, 1981.

———. "The Political Elite as a Strategic Minority." In *Leadership and Development in Arab Society,* ed. Fuad I. Khuri. Beirut: American University of Beirut, Center for Arab and Middle East Studies, 1981, pp. 62–91.

———. *The Political Mobilization of Peasants: A Study of an Egyptian Community.* Bloomington: Indiana University Press, 1974.

———. "Voting Behavior: Lebanon." In *Electoral Politics in the Middle East: Issues, Voters and Elites,* ed. Jacob Landau, Ergun Özbudun, and Frank Tachau. Stanford: Hoover Institution Press, 1980.

Harris, William. "The View from Zahle: Security and Economic Concerns in the Central Bekaa: 1980–1985." *Middle East Journal* 39, no. 3 (Summer 1985): 270–286.

Heeger, Gerald A. *The Politics of Underdevelopment.* New York: St. Martin's Press, 1974.

Hegland, Mary. "Two Images of Husain: Accommodation and Revolution in an Iranian Village." In *Religion and Politics in Iran: Shi'ism from Quietism to Revolution,* ed. Nikki R. Keddie. New Haven: Yale University Press, 1983, pp. 218–235.

Hof, Frederic C. *Galilee Divided: The Israel-Lebanon Frontier.* Boulder: Westview Press, 1985.

Hooglund, Eric. "Rural Participation in the Revolution." *MERIP Reports* 87 (May 1980): 3–6.

Horowitz, Dan. "Dual Authority Politics." *Comparative Politics* 14 (April 1982): 329–349.

Hourani, Albert H. *Syria and Lebanon: A Political Essay.* London: Oxford University Press, 1946.

Hudson, Michael C. *Arab Politics: The Search for Legitimacy.* New Haven: Yale University Press, 1977.

———. "Democracy and Social Mobilization in Lebanese Politics." *Comparative Politics* 1 (January 1969). Reprinted with a postscript in *Analyzing the Third World,* ed. Norman W. Provizer. Boston: G. K. Hall, 1978, pp. 271–391.

———. "Islam and Political Development." In *Islam and Development: Religion and Sociopolitical Change,* ed. John L. Esposito. Syracuse: Syracuse University Press, 1980, pp. 1–24.

———. "The Islamic Factor in Syrian and Iraqi Politics." In *Islam in the Political Process,* ed. James P. Piscatori. Cambridge, Eng.: Cambridge University Press, 1983, pp. 73–97.

———. "The Lebanese Crisis: The Limits of Consociational Democracy." *Journal of Palestine Studies* 5, nos. 3–4 (Spring/Summer 1976): 104–122.

———. "The Palestinian Factor in the Lebanese Civil War." *Middle East Journal* 32 (Summer 1978): 261–278.

———. *The Precarious Republic: Political Modernization in Lebanon.* New York: Random House, 1968.

———. *The Precarious Republic Revisited: Reflections on the Collapse of Pluralist Politics in Lebanon.* Washington, D.C.: Georgetown University, Center for Contemporary Arab Studies, Institute of Arab Development, February 1977.

Humphreys, R. Steven. "Islam and Political Values in Saudi Arabia, Egypt and Syria." *Middle East Journal* 33 (Winter 1979): 1–19.

Huntington, Samuel P. "The Change to Change: Modernization, Development, and Politics." *Comparative Politics* 3 (April 1971): 283–322.

———. *Political Order in Changing Societies.* New Haven: Yale University Press, 1968.

Huntington, Samuel P., and Joan M. Nelson. *No Easy Choice: Political Participation in Developing Countries.* Cambridge: Harvard University Press, 1976.

al-Husaini, Sharif. "Hizb Allah: Harakat ʿAskariya am Siyasiya am Diniya?" *al-Shiraʿ,* March 15, 1986.

Jaber, Talal. "Le discours Shi'ite sur le pouvoir." *Peuples Mediterranéens– Mediterranean Peoples* 20 (July–September 1982): 75–92.

Jafri, S. H. M. *The Origins and Development of Shi'a Islam.* London: Longman, Librairie du Liban, 1979.

Johnson, Michael. "Factional Politics in Lebanon: The Case of the 'Islamic Society of Benevolent Intentions' (al-Maqasid) in Beirut." *Middle Eastern Studies* 14 (January 1978)" 56–75.

———. "Political Bosses and Their Gangs: *Zu'ama* and *Qabadayat* in the Sunni Muslim Quarters of Beirut." In *Patrons and Clients,* ed. Ernest Gellner and John Waterbury. London: Duckworth, in association with the Center for Mediterranean Studies of the American University Field Staff, 1977.

———. "Popular Movements and Primordial Loyalties in Beirut." In *Sociology of "Developing Societies": The Middle East,* ed. Talal Asad and Roger Owen. New York: Monthly Review Press, 1983, pp. 178–194.

Joseph, Suad. "Politicization of Religious Sects in Borj Hammoud." Ph.D. dissertation, Columbia University, 1975.

Joumblatt, Kamal. *I Speak for Lebanon.* Translated by Michael Pallis and recorded by Phillippe Lapousterle. London: Zed Press, 1982.

Judkins, (Major) James C., Jr. "The Expanding Role of the Shi'a in Lebanon." Master of Military Art and Science thesis, U.S. Army Command and General Staff College, Fort Leavenworth, Ks., 1983.

Jureidini, Paul A., and Ronald D. McLaurin. "The Impact of Social and Generational Change on Lebanese Politics." Unpublished paper, March 1984.

Kazemi, Farhad. *Poverty and Revolution in Iran: The Urban Poor, Urban Marginality and Politics.* New York: New York University Press, 1980.

Keddie, Nikki R. "Iran: Change in Islam; Islam and Change." *International Journal of Middle East Studies* 11 (July 1980): 527–542.

Khalaf, Samir. "Adaptive Modernization: The Case for Lebanon." In *Economic Development and Population Growth in the Middle East,* ed. Charles A. Cooper and Sidney S. Alexander. New York: American Elsevier Press, 1972, pp. 567–598.

———. "Changing Forms of Political Patronage in Lebanon." In *Patrons and Clients in Mediterranean Societies,* ed. Ernest Gellner and John Waterbury. London: Gerald Duckworth, 1977, pp. 185–205.

———. "On the Demoralization of Public Life in Lebanon: Some Impassioned Reflections." *Studies in Comparative International Development* 17 (Spring 1982): 49–72.

———. "Parliamentary Elites: Lebanon." In *Electoral Issues in the Middle East: Issues, Voters and Elites,* ed. Jacob M. Landau, Ergun Özbudun, and Frank Tachau. Stanford: Hoover Institution Press, 1980, pp. 243–271.

———. *Persistence and Change in 19th Century Islam: A Sociological Essay.* Beirut: American University of Beirut, 1979.

Khalid, Hasan. *al-Muslimin fi Lubnan wa al-Harb al-Ahliya.* Beirut: Dar al-Kindi, 1978.

Khalidi, Tarif. "Shaykh Ahmad 'Arif al-Zayn and al-'Irfan." In *Intellectual Life in the Arab East, 1890–1939,* ed. Marwan R. Buheiry. Beirut: American University of Beirut, Center for Arab and Middle East Studies, 1981, pp. 110–124.

Khalidi, Walid. *Conflict and Violence in Lebanon: Confrontation in the Middle East.* Cambridge: Harvard University, Center for International Affairs, 1979.

al-Khouri, Touma. "The Election Bus." In *Modern Arabic Short Stories,* ed. Denys Johnson-Davies. London: Heinemann, 1976, pp. 173–181.

Khoury, Elias, and Nubar Hovsepian. "Israel's Future in Lebanon." *MERIP Reports* 108–109 (September–October 1982): 28–32.

Khuri, Fuad I. "The Changing Class Structure in Lebanon." *Middle East Journal* 23 (Winter 1969): 29–44.

———. "A Comparative Study of Migration Patterns in Two Lebanese Villages." *Human Organization* 26, no. 4 (1967): 206–213.

———. *From Village to Suburb: Order and Change in Greater Beirut.* Chicago: University of Chicago Press, 1975.

———, ed. *Leadership and Development in Arab Society.* Beirut: American University of Beirut, Center for Arab and Middle East Studies, 1981.

———. "The Social Dynamics of the 1975–1977 War in Lebanon." *Armed Forces and Society* 7 (Spring 1981): 383–408.

Kifner, John. "Life among the Ruins in Beirut." *New York Times Magazine,* December 6, 1981.

Koury, Enver M. *The Crisis in the Lebanese System: Confessionalism and Chaos.* Washington, D.C.: American Enterprise Institute, Institute for Public Policy Research, June 1976.

Kramer, Martin. "Muhammad Husayn Fadlallah." *Orient: German Journal for Politics and Economics of the Middle East* 26, no. 2 (June 1985): 147–149.

———, ed. *Shiʿism, Resistance and Revolution.* Boulder: Westview Press, forthcoming 1987.

Kravetz, Marc. "Le Shi'ite resurgence." *Le Matin* (Paris), May 28, 1982.

Lavran, Aharon. "UN Forces and Israel's Security." *Jerusalem Quarterly* 37 (1986): 57–76.

Lerner, Daniel. *The Passing of Traditional Society: Modernizing the Middle East.* New York: Free Press, 1958.

Lijphart, Arend. "Consociational Democracy." *World Politics* 21 (January 1969): 207–255.

———. *Democracy in Plural Societies.* New Haven: Yale University Press, 1977.

Lipset, Seymour Martin, ed. *Politics and the Social Sciences.* New York: Oxford University Press, 1969.

Lustick, Ian. "Stability in Deeply Divided Societies: Consociationism versus Control." *World Politics* 31 (April 1979): 325–344.

McLaurin, Ronald D. "Peace in Lebanon." Unpublished paper read at the University of Southern California, April 9, 1985.

MacLeod, Scott. "A Dangerous Occupation." *New York Review of Books,* August 16, 1984.

McRae, Kenneth. *Consociational Democracy: Political Accommodation in Segmented Societies.* Ottowa: McClelland and Steward, 1974.

Mannock, Robin. "Hit and Myth of the Occupation Forces' Policy of Terror in South Lebanon." *Daily Star* (Beirut), June 21, 1984.

Mazzaoui, Michel M. "Shiʿism and Ashura in South Lebanon." In *Taʿziyah: Ritual and Drama in Iran,* ed. Peter J. Chelkowski. New York: New York University Press and Soroush Press, 1979, pp. 228–237.

Melhem, Hisham. "The Case for the Lebanese Resistance." *AAUG [Association of Arab-American University Graduates] Mideast Monitor* 2, no. 3 (May 1985): 2–4, 6.

Melson, Robert, and Howard Wolpe. "Modernization and the Politics of Communalism: A Theoretical Perspective." *American Political Science Review* 64 (December 1970): 1112–1130.

————. *Nigeria: Modernization and the Politics of Communalism.* East Lansing: Michigan State University Press, 1971.

Meo, Leila M. T. *Lebanon: Improbable Nation: A Study in Political Development.* Bloomington: Indiana University Press, 1965.

Migdal, Joel S. *Peasants, Politics and Revolution: Pressures toward Political and Social Change in the Third World.* Princeton: Princeton University Press, 1974.

Mortimer, Edward. *Faith and Power: The Politics of Islam.* New York: Vintage Books, 1982.

Mountjoy, Alan B. "Migrant Workers in the Arab Middle East." *Third World Quarterly* 4 (July 1982): 530–531.

Muir, Jim. "Assad Tightens His Grip on Lebanon." *Middle East International* 249 (May 3, 1985): 3–5.

————. "In the Lap of the Syrians." *Middle East International* 258 (September 13, 1985): 8–9.

————. "Lebanon: Arena of Conflict, Crucible of Peace." *Middle East Journal* 38, no. 2 (Spring 1984): 204–227.

————. "A Strike That United Beirut." *Arabia: The Islamic World Review* (June 1982): 26–27.

al-Muqawama al-Wataniya fi al-Janub al-Lubnani. Beirut: Dar Iqraʾ, 1984.

Nasr, Salim. "Backdrop to Civil War: The Crisis of Lebanese Capitalism." *MERIP Reports* 73 (December 1978): 3–13.

Nie, Norman H., G. Bingham Powell, and Kenneth Prewitt. "Social Structure and Political Participation." *American Political Science Review* 63 (June 1969): 361–378.

Norton, Augustus R. "Changing Actors and Leadership among the Shiites of Lebanon." *Annals of the American Academy of Political and Social Science,* no. 482 (November 1985): 109–121.

————. *External Intervention and the Politics of Lebanon.* Washington, D.C.: Washington Institute for Values in Public Policy, 1984.

————. "Harakat Amal (The Movement of Hope)." Paper presented at the annual meeting of the American Political Science Association, Denver, Colorado, September 2–5, 1982. Revised edition in *Religion and Politics* (Political Anthropology, 3), ed. Myron J. Aronoff. New Brunswick, N.J.: Transaction Books, 1984, pp. 105–131.

———. "Israel and South Lebanon." *American-Arab Affairs* 4 (Spring 1983): 23–31.

———. "Lebanese Quagmire." *New York Times*, July 11, 1984.

———. "Lebanon for the Lebanese." *New York Times*, February 22, 1983.

———. "Lebanon's Old Politics Must Yield to the New." *New York Times*, January 3, 1984.

———. "Lebanon's Shifting Political Landscape." *New Leader* (March 8, 1982): 8–9.

———. "Lebanon's Shiites." *New York Times*, April 16, 1982.

———. "Making Enemies in South Lebanon: Harakat Amal, the IDF, and South Lebanon." *Middle East Insight* 3, no. 3 (1984): 13–20.

———. "Militant Protest and Political Violence under the Banner of Islam." *Armed Forces and Society* 9 (Fall 1982): 3–19.

———. "Occupational Risks and Planned Retirement: The Israeli Withdrawal from South Lebanon." *Middle East Insight* 4, no. 1 (March/April 1985): 14–18.

———. *Political and Religious Extremism in the Middle East.* Washington, D.C.: Middle East Institute, Executive Report No. 7, March 7, 1985.

———. "The Political Mood in Lebanon." *Middle East Insight* 2, no. 5 (January–February 1983): 9–13.

———. "Political Violence and Shi'a Factionalism in Lebanon." *Middle East Insight* 3, no. 2 (1983): 9–16. A shorter version appears in *New Outlook: Middle East Monthly* (Israel) (January 1984): 19–21.

———. "The Violent Work of Politics in Lebanon." *Wall Street Journal*, March 18, 1982.

Owen, Roger, ed. *Essays on the Crisis in Lebanon.* London: Ithaca Press, 1976.

Özbudun, Ergun. *Social Change and Political Participation in Turkey.* Princeton: Princeton University Press, 1977.

Pakradouni, Karim. *La paix manquée.* Beirut: Editions FMA, 1983.

Pearse, Richard. *Three Years in the Levant.* London: Macmillan, 1949.

Peters, Emrys L. "Aspects of Rank and Status among Muslims in a Lebanese Village." In *Mediterranean Countrymen: Essays in the Social Anthropology of the Mediterranean*, ed. Julian Pitt-Rivers. Paris: Mouton, 1963, pp. 159–200.

———. "Shifts of Power in a Lebanese Village." In *Rural Politics and Social Change in the Middle East*, ed. Richard Antoun and Iliya Harik. Bloomington: Indiana University Press, 1972, pp. 165–197.

Picard, Elizabeth. "De la 'Communauté-Classe' à la Résistance 'Nationale.'" *Revue Française de Science Politique* 35 (December 1985): 999–1028.

Polk, William R. *The Opening of South Lebanon, 1788–1840: A Study of the Impact of the West on the Middle East.* Cambridge: Harvard University Press, 1963.

Ramazani, R. K. "Iran's Islamic Revolution and the Persian Gulf." *Current History* (January 1985): 5–8, 40–41.

Randal, Jonathan C. *Going All the Way: Christian Warlords, Israeli Adventurers, and the War in Lebanon.* New York: Viking Press, 1983.

al-Sadr!? Beirut: Dar al-Khalud, 1979.

Safa, Muhammad Jabir Al. *Tarikh Jabal ʿAmil.* Beirut: Dar al-Nahar, 1981.

Salem, Elie Adib. "Lebanon's Political Maze: The Search for Peace in a Turbulent Land." *Middle East Journal* 33 (Autumn 1979): 444–463.

————. *Modernization without Revolution: Lebanon's Experience.* Bloomington: Indiana University Press, 1973.

Salibi, Kamal S. *Crossroads to Civil War: Lebanon 1958–1976.* Delmar, N.Y.: Caravan Books, 1976.

————. *The Modern History of Lebanon.* New York: Frederick A. Praeger Publishers, 1965.

Salman, Magida. "The Lebanese Communities and Their Little Wars." *Khamsin* 10 (1983): 13–20.

Schahgaldian, Nikola B. "Prospects for a Unified Lebanon." *Current History* (January 1984): 5–8, 41–42, 48.

Schiff, Ze'ev, and Ehud Ya'ari. *Israel's Lebanon War.* New York: Simon and Schuster, 1984.

al-Shiraʿ. al-Harakat al-Islamiya fi Lubnan. Beirut: Dar al-Sanin, n.d. [1984].

Sicking, Thom, and Shereen Khairallah. "The Shiʿa Awakening in Lebanon: A Search for Radical Change in a Traditional Way." *Vision and Revision in Arab Society, 1974,* CEMAM Reports 2 (1975): 97–130. Beirut: Dar al-Mashreq, 1975.

Skoçpol, Theda. "What Makes Peasants Revolutionary?" *Comparative Politics* 14 (April 1982): 351–375.

Smith, Donald E. *Religion and Political Development.* Boston: Little, Brown, 1970.

Smock, David R., and Audrey C. Smock. *The Politics of Pluralism: A Comparative Study of Lebanon and Ghana.* New York: Elsevier, 1975.

Snider, Lewis W. "The Lebanese Forces: Their Origins and Role in Lebanon's Politics." *Middle East Journal* 38 (Winter 1984): 1–33.

————. "Political Instability and Social Change in Lebanon." Unpublished paper, January 1984.

Stork, Joe. "Report from Lebanon." *MERIP Reports* 118 (October 1983): 3–13.

Suleiman, Michael W. *Political Parties in Lebanon: The Challenge of a Fragmented Political Culture.* Ithaca, N.Y.: Cornell University Press, 1967.

Tabbara, Lina Mikdadi. *Survival in Beirut: A Diary of Civil War.* Translated by Nadia Hijab. London: Onyx Press, 1979.

Tabbarah, Riad B. "Background to the Lebanese Conflict." *International Journal of Comparative Sociology* 20, nos. 1–2 (March 1979): 101–121.

————. "Rural Development and Urbanization in Lebanon." *Population Bulletin of the U.N. Economic Commission for Western Asia* 4 (1977): 3–25.

Tueni, Ghassan. "Lebanon: A New Republic." *Foreign Affairs* 61 (Fall 1982): 84–89.

————. *Une guerre pour les autres.* Paris: Editions Lettes, 1985.

U.S. Congress, House. Subcommittee on Europe and the Middle East of the Committee on Foreign Affairs. *Islamic Fundamentalism and Islamic Radicalism,* 99th Cong., 1st sess., 1985.

Urquhart, David. *The Lebanon: Mt. Souria, A History and a Diary.* London: Thomas Cautley Newby, 1860.

Verba, Sidney, and Norman H. Nie. *Participation in America.* New York: Harper and Row, 1972.

World Bank. *World Development Report.* New York: Oxford University Press, 1982.

Wright, Robin. *Sacred Rage: The Wrath of Militant Islam.* New York: Simon and Schuster, 1985.

Zabih, Sepehr. "Aspects of Terrorism in Iran." *Annals of the American Academy of Political and Social Science* 463 (September 1982): 84–94.

al-Zain, Muhammad Hussain. *al-Shiʿa fi al-Tarikh.* Beirut: Dar al-Athar, 1979.

Zonis, Marvin. "Iran: A Theory of Revolution from Accounts of the Revolution." *World Politics* 35 (July 1983): 586–606.

———. "Self-Objects, Self-Representation, and Sense Making Crises: Political Instability in the 1980s." Unpublished paper, 1983.

Index